Force Benedict

Force Benedict

Churchill's Secret Mission to Save Stalin

Eric Carter with Antony Loveless

HODDER &
STOUGHTON

First published in Great Britain in 2014 by Hodder & Stoughton
An Hachette UK company

1

Copyright © Eric Carter 2014

Maps © Rodney Paull

A CIP catalogue record for this title is available from the British Library

Hardback ISBN 978 1 444 78513 5
Trade paperback ISBN 978 1 444 78512 8
Ebook ISBN 978 1 444 78511 1

Printed and bound by Clays Ltd, St Ives plc
Typeset by Hewer Text UK Ltd, Edinburgh

Hodder & Stoughton policy is to use papers that are natural, renewable
and recyclable products and made from wood grown in sustainable
forests. The logging and manufacturing processes are expected to
conform to the environmental regulations of the country of origin.

Hodder & Stoughton Ltd
338 Euston Road
London NW1 3BH

www.hodder.co.uk

To the band of brothers that comprised 151 Wing of the Royal Air Force; all those who exist now only in memory, and the ever-smaller group who survive still.

It is of the Air Force I'm going to sing,
Not of their exploits but a different thing,
Of 81 Squadron and 151 Wing,
And 134 Squadron to finish the string.
They're bound for a place the name I don't know,
From what I have heard it is covered in snow,
They'll keep the flag flying I bet you'll agree,
Where the Northlands of Russia jut out to the sea.

Taken from *Fourteen Letters*, the diary of
Polish war artist Feliks Topolski

Contents

Contents

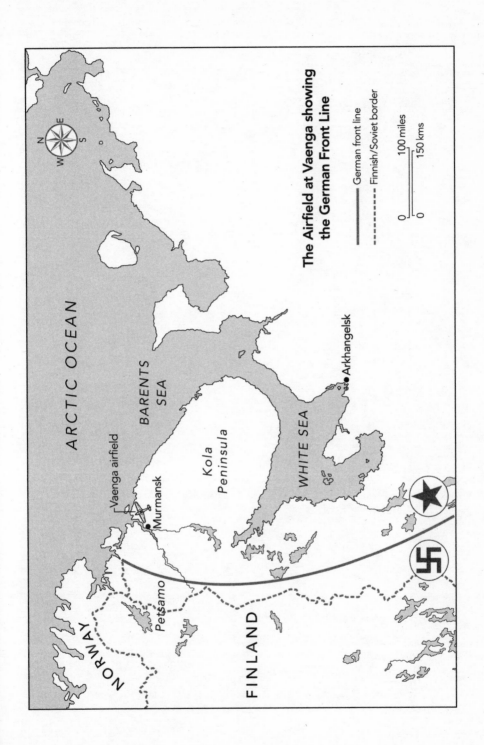

The Airfield at Vaenga showing
the German Front Line

ARCTIC OCEAN

BARENTS
SEA

Vaenga airfield

Murmansk

Kola
Peninsula

WHITE SEA

Arkhangelsk

NORWAY

Petsamo

FINLAND

German front line
Finnish/Soviet border

100 miles
150 kms

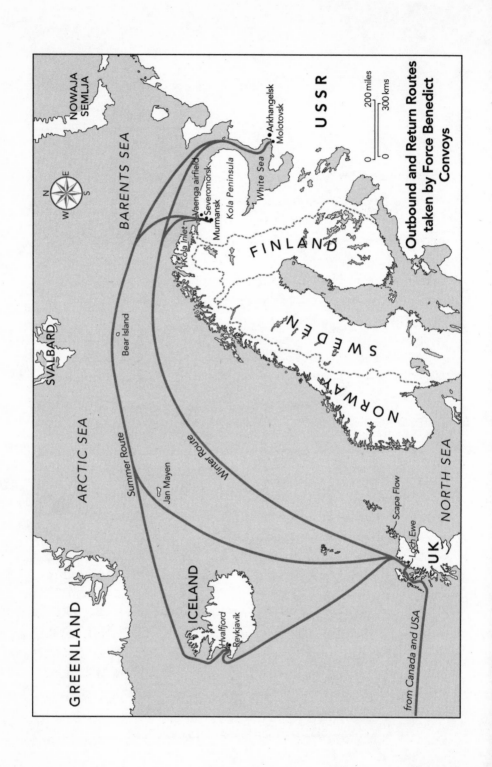

GREENLAND

SVALBARD

NOWAJA
SEMLJA

ARCTIC SEA

BARENTS SEA

Bear Island

USSR

Arkhangelsk
Molotovsk

White Sea

Kola Peninsula

Vaenga airfield
Severomorsk
Murmansk

Kola Inlet

FINLAND

SWEDEN

Summer Route

Jan Mayen

Winter Route

NORWAY

ICELAND

Hvalfjord
Reykjavik

Scapa Flow

Loch Ewe

UK

NORTH SEA

from Canada and USA

Outbound and Return Routes
taken by Force Benedict
Convoys

200 miles

300 kms

Foreword

I first met Eric Carter at a fund-raising dinner in the spring of 2013 at the RAF Club. At first, the eleven-year-old boy inside me was very excited to know I was sitting next to a Spitfire pilot from the Second World War but, to be honest, the evening was a surreal and humbling experience. Eric kept asking why he had been chosen to be seated with us 'nice people', leaving my friends and me to look at each other and our guest of honour in bafflement. This, for me, is typical of the man, and so many of that generation. What we see as extraordinary sacrifice for the freedom of Europe and the world, they see as simply their duty.

We are only two generations from that time, and many of my friends had grandparents who served in the war. I was brought up with the classic boys'-own tales of Douglas Bader and Guy Gibson, and I was addicted to the Airfix models of the Spitfire, Hurricane and Messerschmitt 109.

As you get older, you realise the true sacrifice that that generation gave and how war was anything but an adventure. The bloodshed, fear and loss that they experienced must have been horrific, and you can understand why so many of them never wanted to talk about their experiences. Instead they wanted to put it all behind them, and live a life in peace.

With this in mind, and as the evening wore on, I had to resist the temptation to pepper Eric with questions about his time in the war. Sure, he was candid and honest about Force Benedict, but he did make a point of saying that he didn't really want to talk about it too much, as it brought back sad memories. Simply put, he missed the friends he'd left behind.

The keynote speaker that night was Geoffrey Wellum, DFC, who wrote the book *First Light*, which is seen by most as the definitive account of being a Spitfire pilot in the Battle of Britain. As he spoke you could have heard a pin drop. Later, I asked Eric whether he had ever thought of putting down his experiences in writing. He said that he had, but didn't think anyone would be that interested in what he had done . . . cue more baffled looks from me. I told my publisher about him the very next day.

Eric was part of something that was truly a turning point in history. In 1941 Stalin was desperate for help to stop the Germans conquering the Soviet Union and asked Churchill for assistance. If Murmansk fell to the Nazis, the Russians would have no port to bring in essential supplies, so Force Benedict was hastily put together and dispatched to defend that city 'at all costs'. Eric told me that, as the mission neared its end, he and his RAF companions became convinced that they'd been abandoned. They thought Force Benedict was a suicide mission. Among many fascinating things the research for this book has revealed is that Churchill – in spite of all the other things he had to deal with in the autumn of 1941 – had a personal interest in the mission and was very keen to know what was going on and how Eric and his fellow fighters were going to be repatriated.

The more I've learned about Force Benedict, the more I admire the men who were part of it. There are so many amazing things about Force Benedict. They could easily have been torpedoed on the way there. The Luftwaffe could have bombed the planes on the ground before they'd been assembled. The Germans could have captured the airfield. They could have been torpedoed on the voyage back to Britain. All in all, it was a miracle they survived.

I'm very pleased to have played a small part in getting the story of Force Benedict to a wider audience through this book, because it's a story that certainly deserves to be told. Many of the top-secret documents that were discovered in the research for this book were released only in the past few years – so now the truth can be revealed at last.

When I first met Eric, he had a glint in his eye that made me think he'd tell a good story, plus the notion of someone that can still fly a Spitfire at ninety-three is extraordinary. As you read this book you'll see how men like Eric and his comrades made Force Benedict a triumph of skill and guts over logic and strategy. I believe it's vital we document that generation's experiences, and salute their sacrifice. If they had not done what they did, we'd be living in a very different country now.

When I left Eric that night, I went for a walk to digest my dinner, and my meeting with this extraordinary man. I found myself by the Bomber Command memorial in Green Park. I know Eric was (is) a fighter pilot, but it was the same war, the same sacrifice, the same horror. As the years go by it's so important to preserve these first-hand memories. Please God, our children, and our children's children, will never have to endure what Eric and his generation did. But they should know, learn and be grateful for the sacrifice that was made by so many for so much.

Dermot O'Leary

Author's Note

Following Dermot's chance encounter with Eric Carter, I travelled up to meet Eric on a sunny afternoon in May 2013. Over an enjoyable lunch at a pub near his house in the Worcestershire village of Chaddesley Corbett, Eric recounted his tale as I listened intently. The story he told heralded the start of what has proved a fascinating journey for me, a journey that in August 2013 saw me spending time with Eric, before driving around the southern half of England to meet with two other UK-based survivors. Along with Eric, Tim Elkington and Peter Knapton had been members of 151 Wing in a secret RAF mission to Russia in the Second World War.

I sat with Tim at his delightful Cotswold family home in the picturesque village of Little Rissington on one of the summer's hottest days. I listened as he talked at length about his memories as one of 'The Few' flying in the Battle of Britain, and then his recollections of that secret mission to save Stalin over seventy years ago. He showed me his beautifully bound logbook, which recorded the flights he'd made, each flight telling its own story.

The following day, I headed into central London to meet with Peter, another pilot from that mission who'd led a fascinating life even after the war, which saw him return to Russia as Assistant Air Attaché, and then join MI5 on his retirement from the RAF. England was taking on Australia in the fifth Ashes Test at the Oval when I met Peter at his nearby apartment in Camberwell, and I was touched to discover he'd gone to the trouble of making lunch, which we shared with a bottle of wine. I listened intently as he told me his story and showed me some of the mementoes of his truly fascinating career.

All three men are now well into their tenth decade of life, and while their bones may be weary, their minds were pin-sharp in bringing to life the story of the time they spent in Russia dogfighting the Luftwaffe.

I then spent three days being generously hosted as the guest of retired RAF Air Commodore Phil Wilkinson and his wife Angie. Phil had first met the survivors of 151 Wing in 1993 when he coordinated their first return visit to Russia in his role as Defence Attaché at the British Embassy in Moscow. He has been involved with them ever since.

Just as vital as the time I spent with Phil, and the three surviving pilots left in the UK, was the time I spent at the National Archives, and in the Sound and Vision department of the Imperial War Museum. The official records of the mission held at the National Archives have been key in filling in the gaps. We are unquestionably lucky here in the UK that such a generous resource exists. It's difficult to convey how it feels to find a single paper in a file that brings additional colour, or confirms something you've suspected but couldn't prove. And finding within the then Chief of the Air Staff's personal file on the mission a private memo, written and signed by Winston Churchill himself – holding that was like holding history itself in my hand. That memo – and the other documents I found – helped to shine a light on what follows.

Antony Loveless, Belfast, March 2014

1

The Gathering Storm

War had already been declared when I joined the RAF in late 1939, aged nineteen. I'd always been interested in flying; I grew up in Birmingham and used to go to Elmdon Aerodrome [which is now more commonly known as Birmingham International Airport] to look at the aircraft there. It was only a little field in those days, and I would stand at a small wooden fence and watch the aircraft landing. They were pretty primitive, even by the standards of the day, but they awoke within me a love of aviation that persists to this day.

I was dating a young lady at the time, and her father was the recruiting officer for the Royal Air Force in Dale End, which was local to me. She knew all about my love of flying and she told me, 'Eric, you go along and see my dad; tell him that I sent you and tell him you want to be a pilot.' So that's what I did. I went to the recruiting office. I met her father and explained how I felt and how I'd arrived at his desk. 'Do you want to be a pilot?' he asked me, and I of course said yes. It was that simple.

I was so focused on my immediate future – the fact I was in the RAF – that I gave little thought to the fact that I – and all of my contemporaries – had had our futures hijacked by the actions of Adolf Hitler, Führer and dictator of Nazi Germany. Circumstance would eventually bring me together with a number of other fledgling pilots, in one of the war's most secretive missions. That mission remains little known, even today. It was forged in the crucible of Hitler's actions on 15 March 1939, as he cast aside the Munich Agreement he'd signed with Neville Chamberlain the previous year and moved to finally occupy all of Czechoslovakia.

I was eighteen by the time Hitler invaded Poland. I remember that his actions forced the Conservative prime minister Neville Chamberlain to recognise that his long-held foreign policy of appeasement lay in tatters; he was backed into a corner politically and left with no option but to declare war on Germany, which he did reluctantly on Sunday, 3 September. Was Britain ready for war? As I recall, it's difficult to say we were; no nation is ever fully prepared but then the evidence speaks for itself; despite all our deficiencies, against all the odds, we defeated Germany in the air, and later, with our allies, on the ground too.

One of our biggest advantages over Germany at the outbreak of war was radar. Even now, it's a technology that fascinates me, but back then, it seemed just so advanced; it was like something out of science fiction! I remember that in the earliest stages of the war, it had been fitted to a number of Blenheim bombers, greatly increasing the chances of aircraft finding their targets as well as giving early warning of enemy attacks.

On the ground, we had two systems of radar detection: Chain Home and Chain Home Low, two networks of radar stations that had been built along England's south coast in the 1930s. Chain Home could detect formations of aircraft flying over the coast of France. This enabled the RAF to scramble fighter squadrons to intercept bomber formations, allowing them to counter the Luftwaffe's movements in the event of an attack on northern France, the Low Countries or Britain. Chain Home Low provided radar coverage against low-flying aircraft. The development of this system of radar (there were twenty-one Chain Home stations and thirty Chain Home Low stations operational in 1940) meant that defensive sorties against the Luftwaffe could be easily co-ordinated. This was to become of paramount importance during the Battle of Britain.[1]

Although I'd signed up with the recently formed RAF Volunteer Reserve [RAFVR] in autumn 1939, it wasn't until June 1940 that I began training. The RAF had created the Volunteer Reserve

[VR] in 1936. Pilots under instruction signed on for five years, with an up-front requirement to attend a ten-week-long intensive course covering theory of flight and some hands-on flying experience. They were given the rank of sergeant pilot and continuation flying training would be conducted at weekends on airfields close to their homes. Travelling expenses were reimbursed, and they were paid £25 (roughly £1,500 in today's money) annually. For most of us who joined, it was a dream come true – we could continue to work or attend further education, but were being paid to learn to fly by the RAF at our leisure. The only downside was that enlistment in the VR meant immediate and automatic mobilisation to the regular RAF in event of war. That seemed unlikely at the time; we were young and carefree and thought only of flying.

I made a good friend in training in Johnny Mulroy. We did our basic training down in Paignton, near Torquay. The RAF had commandeered a hotel there to accommodate us and it was sheer bloody luxury, so we felt really blessed. By the time we moved to Meir near Stoke-on-Trent and started our flying training, we were inseparable. We learned to fly in Miles Magisters, which were known affectionately as 'Maggies' – they were simple two-seat monoplanes but they were easy to fly, the first aircraft specifically designed and built as trainers for the RAF. We were encouraged to form friendships and stick together with our fellow pilots – the Air Force thought we'd fight better in a scrap if we had our pals with us rather than complete strangers.

It was by no means certain that I'd end up as a fighter pilot, of course; the RAF needed pilots right across the service, but I wasn't interested in anything other than being a fighter pilot, so, from the off, I set out to do the very best I could at every level of my training. It was never going to be good enough for me to simply succeed; I had to be the best and throw everything I had into achieving that. I spent more hours than I needed to, studying every aspect of flight: navigation; Morse – I could get out twelve words a minute; flying – I did lots of that in my own time. It must have impressed the instructors because they stamped my logbook with the words 'above average'.

Following our elementary flying training on the Magister, we then moved to Hullavington, near Bristol, for more advanced training on Harts and Audaxes. These were old First World War fighter aircraft – biplanes, with just two machine guns. We acquired about fifty or sixty hours on these learning evasive action manoeuvres and other flying techniques.

Early on in our flying training, Winston Churchill replaced Neville Chamberlain as prime minister. Chamberlain had lost the support of both the Labour and Liberal parties, which were bitterly resentful of his eight years of appeasement of Hitler, and eight months of insipid wartime leadership. Both Parliament and the people wanted a warrior to lead the country through its darkest days, a lion with the heart for a fight and the will to dig deep after so many years adrift. Churchill was that man and, with the support of the Labour Party, he seized the reins of power and formed a coalition government.

The challenge confronting him was immense – for starters, I well remember how Britain was in the doldrums after a decade of depression, mass unemployment, strikes and poor leadership. Our economy wasn't set up on a war footing then. As A. J. P. Taylor put it, 'The war machine resembled an expensive motor car beautifully polished, complete in every detail, except that there was no petrol in the tank.'[2]

In addition to sorting out the economic strategy, Churchill had other issues to deal with, foremost of which was dealing with the debacle of the Battle for [fall of] France. From its start on 10 May, it took little more than six weeks for German forces to achieve their goal, with Allied forces routed and neutral Luxembourg, Belgium and Holland, plus France, all under Nazi occupation. By 16 June, while I was in the first few weeks of training, it was effectively all over. Back in Britain, those men of the BEF (British

Expeditionary Force) who had been evacuated from the beaches at Dunkirk were licking their wounds. Britain, at that point, truly stood alone.

With France defeated, Hitler was now free to turn his attentions towards Great Britain. He made a number of overtures to Churchill, offering what he misguidedly believed to be favourable terms, but Churchill was having none of it, rejecting them all out of hand.

So on 16 July 1940, Hitler's growing impatience led to him issuing Führer Directive No. 16, setting in motion the preparations for an invasion of Britain. He gave these plans the code name Operation Sea Lion (*Unternehmen Seelöwe*). He prefaced the order by stating: 'As England, in spite of her hopeless military situation, still shows no signs of willingness to come to terms, I have decided to prepare, and if necessary to carry out, a landing operation against her. The aim of this operation is to eliminate the English Motherland as a base from which the war against Germany can be continued, and, if necessary, to occupy the country completely.'

For the invasion to take place, Hitler needed to ensure that the RAF was thoroughly annihilated, giving his forces unfettered control of the skies over Britain. This placed responsibility for Sea Lion's success squarely on the rather large shoulders of his corpulent, effete and rather vain head of the Luftwaffe, Reichsmarschall Hermann Göring. Previously, the plan had been inconceivable, but with the fall of France enabling the German Air Force to base itself on French soil, suddenly the distances weren't so huge; England, at least geographically, was within easy reach.

Churchill realised that, to keep the country with him and maintain morale, he would have to tie himself inextricably to what was, for Britain, a fight for its very survival. His rhetoric was purposeful, defiant, upbeat and resolute. It was our good fortune that Hitler chose to attack us from the air by launching what became known as the Battle of Britain because it was the only arena in which we could match him on terms anywhere near parity. The Army, and the British people, would have had a bitter fight on their hands had Hitler sent the Wehrmacht, and his feared Waffen SS, to land on our shores – and it's highly unlikely that we would have emerged from that particular battle covered in glory. But by sending the Luftwaffe to attack us in the air, Hitler made perhaps his first great strategic error.

Single-seat fighter aircraft were the one class of weapon with which we could match Hitler's forces in capability. We weren't quite there in terms of quantity – but we weren't far off. On 1 June 1940, Fighter Command had just 331 Spitfires and Hurricanes, but by the last day of the month, there were 587 ready and serviceable with plenty more on their way.[3] Our edge was our sophisticated radar network, our application of science and technology, and our greatest asset – our *people*. We would prove much stronger in defence than the Luftwaffe was in attack. The whole defence of our country, our very way of life, was not to be decided by hundreds of thousands of soldiers, tanks and heavy armament – no, just a few hundred young and inexperienced pilots in the RAF.

The Luftwaffe's opening salvo in the Battle of Britain came on 10 July 1940, when it began to attack maritime targets, such as coastal shipping convoys, and shipping hubs such as Portsmouth. On 12 August, it shifted its focus to destroying infrastructure such as our radar installations with limited success; in that raid, four radar stations were attacked. They were briefly taken off the air but were back working within six hours.[4] Had Göring persisted with this strategy, it's highly likely the outcome would have been different. However, the Luftwaffe's attention to our radar stations was brief and ineffective; assuming our radar infrastructure was difficult to knock out, it then sent its bombers to target RAF airfields. With our radar functioning as normal, it gave those fighter squadrons on stand-by ample time to scramble, intercept and engage the Luftwaffe in the air.

As the battles over the skies of southern England intensified through the hot summer months of 1940, those of us still in training could do little more than vent our frustration at being so close, yet so far. Those fellows farther ahead in the system found themselves in the midst of battles that were watched daily from the ground by the British people looking up at the skies overhead, while we could only read about their antics and listen to first-hand accounts from those who were involved. It was painful being so close yet being unable to join in. We were all eager to do our bit, get stuck in and fight the Luftwaffe, which was doing its best to bomb us back into the Stone Age, but we were stuck in flying training and unable to do a thing about it.

2

The Battle of Britain

While Johnny and I were stuck in training during the Battle of Britain, a significant number of the pilots whose futures were soon to be intertwined with ours were getting involved. John Francis Durham Elkington (known to all as 'Tim') was one such pilot. Born in Warwickshire in 1920, Tim entered Cranwell as a flight cadet around the time I was just about to sign up. He was commissioned on 14 July 1940 and posted to No. 1 Squadron at Northolt, where he proved to be quite a talented fighter pilot with no small amount of luck on his side – something that all of us needed.

Says Tim,

My first encounter with the enemy came on 15 August.
Everything happened at once, but I did manage to get my
guns on one unfortunate Me109, which I then watched
disappear seawards through the clouds near Harwich,
smoke billowing from it.

But something changed on the 16th. We'd been scrambled
to intercept a raid on Tangmere and I made the fatal error
of failing to look behind me. You can't afford to do that in
a dogfight and I paid the price. I am now fairly sure that I
was the eighteenth victim of the Luftwaffe's leading fighter
ace Helmut Wick, who had me in his sights and put a few
rounds into my aircraft; they hit the fuel tank and suddenly
my Hurricane was on fire. He was quite an experienced
chap, so I'm not too put out!

Leaving a burning aircraft is easy; you simply pull back
the canopy and just throw yourself over the side. But first,

make sure that you disconnect your radio and oxygen connections. On the second attempt, I was out and floating down. It was a lovely sunny day, and I could see Portsmouth, which was just visible through the haze. I couldn't feel any pain, although there was a fair amount of blood. But of more immediate concern was the fact that I was over the sea and I had not thought to inflate my Mae West.

Then out of the blue appeared my flight leader, Flight Sergeant Fred Berry. Somehow, and I've no idea how, he identified me, realised what was happening and he came to my rescue using the slipstream from his aircraft to drift me on to West Wittering. That's something I've never heard of before or since but there's no question in my mind that without his aid, I would have died. I was exceptionally lucky; few pilots who baled out offshore were recovered for the simple fact that a man in the sea looked pathetically small to rescue-launch crews scouring the choppy waters of the Channel, and that's assuming one didn't drown first. I don't remember anything else after Fred came to my aid until I woke up on the ground with a freckle-faced ambulance girl cutting my trousers off. That was a strange homecoming!

My mother was in the habit of watching the dogfights from her balcony on Hayling Island and this day was no exception. As usual, she was out there with my stepfather's naval glasses, watching it all happen. She was unsurprised when the phone rang from the hospital thirty minutes later, and she arrived there not long after I did!

I had shrapnel holes in both legs and some tiny fragments across the right side of my face, including one in the eye. It took months for that to work itself out – it would periodically surface after a hot bath and catch on the towel as I dried my face! That said, I was incredibly lucky really – my injuries put me out of action right through deadly September, so by the time I was operational again, it was at the tail end of the Battle of Britain.

We were schoolboys really, stupid idiots – what does anyone know at that age?

Tim was nineteen, I was nineteen, so was Johnny, and I don't think any of our peers were much older than twenty. Some of them were even younger than us. Perhaps if we'd been older, we wouldn't have been so eager to throw ourselves into harm's way, but then that's part of the naivety of youth – you feel invincible even in the face of overwhelming danger. We were young, optimistic and unstoppable, enjoying the camaraderie flying allowed us, so the possibility of death never entered our minds. Little did we know . . .

In his book *All Hell Let Loose*, Max Hastings says that 'Allied aircrew, once deployed on operational fighter or bomber squadrons, until the last 18 months of the war confronted a statistical probability of their own extinction'.[1] The upshot of that was that our lives on the ground were immeasurably better than those of the rank-and-file soldiers; American journalist Ernie Pyle put it rather succinctly, saying, 'A man approached death rather decently in the Air Force. He died well-fed and clean-shaven.'[2]

Ironically, it was our very youth which made us uniquely qualified for the job. Air combat was, and remains, a form of warfare reserved for very young men. Who else has reflexes sharp enough to cope with closing speeds of more than 600 mph?

In the earliest stages of the war, when the RAF had been engaged in the Battle for France, many of its commanders were over forty; a considerable number were even in their early fifties. By August 1940, though, it wasn't unusual for squadron commanders to be in their early twenties. The vast majority of those in their thirties couldn't cope with air combat because the speed at which dogfighting occurred, and the demands it placed on both the mind and body, were beyond them.[3]

Even for those of us young enough to engage in air combat with any degree of success, it wasn't an easy pursuit by any stretch of the imagination – far from it, in fact. For all the mayhem and the free-for-all nature of aerial combat, it was a surprise to me when I realised just how few aircraft either side destroyed. Over a Channel convoy on 25 July, for instance, scores of British and German planes exchanged fire but only two Spitfires were shot down, and one Messerschmitt Me109. Exceptional eyesight, marksmanship and the nerve to get close were the decisive factors.[4]

Enemy action wasn't all we had to worry about. We and the Germans alike suffered heavily from non-combat mishaps, born in the crucible of momentary carelessness or recklessness. Add in our ages, being perpetually tired and vastly lacking experience, and you can start to see just how easily mistakes were made: between 10 July, when the Battle of Britain started, and 31 October, 463 Hurricanes suffered damage in this way, and many men died as a result of their own mistakes. As many as one third of the RAF's and the Luftwaffe's overall losses were accidental.

Tim wasn't the only young pilot I would become friends with who was earning his combat spurs in the Battle of Britain. A short distance away from him, Charlton 'Wag' Haw was cutting his teeth with 504 Squadron, based at Hendon in North London. Wag was a Yorkshireman, strong and compact in build, with an agile mind and an aggressive spirit – both good qualities for a budding fighter pilot. His passion for aviation started when he was really young – at the age of ten – following a joyride with Sir Alan Cobham's Flying Circus. Wag worked as an apprentice lithographer in Leeds until shortly before the Second World War. He had joined the RAF in February 1939 after being passed by the RAF Selection Board in Leeds and kitted out as a sergeant in the RAF Volunteer Reserve.

It'd been his lifelong dream to become a pilot and, as he soon discovered, he was very good at it. Going solo is, for almost all trainee pilots, one of the biggest moments in their lives. And for

Wag, that moment came far sooner than he could have imagined. Eleven or twelve hours of dual instruction was generally considered the average for most pilots before they were considered to be capable of making that first flight alone. Nine hours was reckoned to be the mark for those of above-average ability. Wag was invited to fly his first solo after just four hours and twenty minutes of dual instruction. It was to be a seminal moment in his career, putting him way ahead of his contemporaries.

He got his call-up papers on 1 September, just two days before the then PM Neville Chamberlain made his now famous radio broadcast advising listeners that Great Britain was at war with Germany. Wag hadn't thought there was the remotest chance of him becoming a fighter pilot with the regular Air Force and considered himself lucky to have even made the RAFVR. But war changes everything, and here he was being handed his life's dream on a plate as a result. He was posted to 504 Squadron, at that time based at Wick in Scotland, to do his operational training on the Hurricane. The squadron had been pulled out of the line in France on 20 May with just four serviceable Hurricanes to its name, after a period of savage fighting over France and Belgium as the RAF sought to delay the advance of Hitler's ground forces through the Low Countries.

There's no substitute for experience, however, and the remaining pilots in 504 Squadron had it in spades. Aerial warfare was a relatively new concept and Wag was fortunate indeed to join a squadron that had played such a major part. Consequently, he and his fellow replacements learned the strategy and tactics that the RAF's pilots had employed during the blitzkrieg onslaught waged by Hitler's forces in Europe.

The few weeks between 504's return from France and the start of the Battle of Britain gave Wag a chance to settle down in the squadron, but there was some action and he had a lucky escape early on. At the time, 504 was carrying out convoy patrols and defending Scapa Flow against Luftwaffe Heinkel 111s and Ju88s.

Wag had been scrambled early one morning after radar had picked up an unidentified aircraft. He was part of 'A' Flight, which was on readiness. They climbed up to intercept it and soon spotted a Heinkel 111 silhouetted below them against a grey blanket of mist. The pilot saw them and dived for cover as the Hurricanes engaged, but Wag's was the last aircraft to attack and he noticed tracer coming up at him. He fired back but he was out of range, so he dived in closer to press home the attack, firing again before breaking away. By this time, the Heinkel was lost in the heavy mist, so 'A' Flight returned home. It was only after he'd landed that his ground crew pointed out two holes in the cockpit of Wag's aircraft where a shell had gone clean through, missing him by no more than a couple of inches.

He was quickly accepted by the other boys in the tight-knit squadron – not only had he had a close shave, but it was quickly becoming clear that he was an above-average fighter pilot. 'A' Flight commander Tony Rook had noticed that many of the experienced pilots had been unable to shake Wag off in mock dogfights. Additionally, Wag was the only member of the squadron able to play the piano, and this made him popular whenever there was a piss-up. RAF squadrons are naturally competitive, so Wag's musical abilities impressed the officers there and singled him out among the sergeant pilots.

Early September saw 504 Squadron arrive at Hendon when the Battle of Britain was at its height. Fighter Command's resources were stretched as tight as piano wire – after eight weeks of continuous combat, its pilots were utterly drained and exhausted and 504 represented one of Air Chief Marshal Sir Hugh Dowding's last reserves of fresh pilots. Saturday, 7 September saw the Luftwaffe change tactics, directing its bomber force exclusively on London, and it was into this cauldron of activity that Wag and his associates were propelled. Talk about in at the deep end – thirty-one British fighters went down that day, while the Luftwaffe lost thirty-nine. Wag had to wait until late afternoon before he and his section were scrambled to intercept a huge wave of bombers. Wag engaged a Dornier at close quarters in an attack that lasted some ninety seconds. On landing, he was debriefed by the squadron intelligence officer and a short time later found himself scrambled yet again. Fighter Command's pilots saw a frenzy of activity that day that continued without respite until dusk.

After tea, Wag and a few of the pilots made their way to a local pub, where they were warmly welcomed by the locals, who sent a steady stream of beer over to them all evening. The next day saw more of the same, which set the pattern for the next three weeks. A frenzy of non-stop aerial combat by day, and parties into the dark hours, against the backdrop of night-time air raids by the Luftwaffe. There were overcast days when the pilots were stood down owing to the weather, so they would adjourn to the bar only to find themselves scrambled when the sky cleared. Sometimes, as one pilot of the time said, 'Fighter Command's pilots frequently took to the air so soaked in alcohol, they were a fire hazard.'[5] It didn't seem to hamper them in any noticeable way, though – it's not like there's anything to hit in the sky.

In the last week of September, 504 Squadron moved to Filton, near Bristol, which had seen heavy bombing. On the 27th, they were scrambled to intercept a wave of more than forty bombers, which they broke up, shooting down five Me110s. Wag got one of them, but in the ensuing melee his aircraft started to overheat, leading him to deduce he'd taken rounds in the fight. He broke away and shut down his engine, belly-landing in a cornfield. Emerging from his stricken aircraft without injury, he caught a lift from a passing car and, after stopping at a pub, where once again the customers insisted on buying the drinks for Wag, he caught a train back to Bristol Temple Meads.

I think he must have spent a lot of time on the journey back ruminating on his feelings when he'd engaged the Me110 earlier. Fragments of the dogfight must have came back to him, and with them, the emotions he'd felt at the time. Was he scared in the midst of it all? I'm pretty sure he was, but then, given his experience, he was no stranger to paroxysms of terror in the most frenzied moments of aerial combat. That said, despite the fear he may have felt in the moment, adrenalin will have surged like never before, and I know from my own experiences how addictive that is, so I imagine that, after a few drinks in the pub, he would have looked forward to getting back up there and doing it all over again.

Undoubtedly useful though introspection can sometimes be, it was almost Wag's undoing as his train pulled into the station. There'd been a raid on Bristol a short time earlier and the blackout was in force. With his mind elsewhere, he struggled to get up, still carrying his parachute pack over his shoulder. It was as he approached the carriage door on the wrong side and went to turn the handle that a kindly fellow passenger saved him. 'I wouldn't get out that side, mate, if I were you,' he shouted.[6]

One of Wag's contemporaries at 504 Squadron was Raymond Towers Holmes, another sergeant pilot. A journalist and writer in civilian life, known by all and sundry as 'Artie' (from his initials 'R. T.'), Ray had joined the RAFVR in 1937, although the pace of training was slow until the outbreak of the war when Ray, like all those who'd joined the VR, was automatically mobilised in the regular armed forces. After completing his flying training, he was posted to 504 at Wick.

Ray had, shall we say, an 'interesting' start to his career as a pilot. He'd been posted for flying training to Sealand, an old First World War training school in North Wales. Low flying is a vital skill for fighter pilots, but it's a contentious issue even now for local residents, who take exception to the noise and disruption to everyday life. On one particular authorised low-flying sortie, Ray's wingman asked to see where he lived, so they flew a course at the regulation 250 feet and circled his home on Grange Hill. As he describes, 'Unfortunately, we hadn't allowed for the hill being 200 feet high, and when we landed back at Sealand, two military policemen met us as we climbed out of our cockpits and informed us we were under open arrest.'[7]

Ray and his wingman were grounded and confined to quarters while their 'bumptious, bombastic, dyed-in-the-wool' CFI [a squadron leader], who regarded pilots from the RAFVR as a 'necessary wartime evil', laid plans for their court martial. Several days later, Training Command started to enquire why two pilots were no longer clocking up flying hours. When the CFI signalled that they'd been grounded and were awaiting court martial for low flying,

> *a snorting reply rebounded from the Air Ministry demanding to know if 5 FTS [Sealand Flying Training School] had not heard there was a war on, and that Britain was desperately short of fighter pilots. The signal concluded by ordering our immediate return to flying duties, and demanded that our daily flying time be doubled until we were level with the rest of the course. As an afterthought, the signal added that the Squadron Leader who had grounded us was posted forthwith to a desk job at the Air Ministry.*[8]

They never saw him again.

Ray soon put the incident behind him, and once he'd finished his training, and was subsequently posted to 504, he went from strength to strength. Following 504 Squadron's transfer to Hendon in September 1940, he was soon showing just what a capable pilot he was with an astonishing feat of aerial combat that saw him claim three Dornier 215s which he shot down over central London, bale out of his stricken Hurricane, and then receive an invitation to an audience with Her Majesty the Queen at Buckingham Palace. His Hurricane buried itself 15 feet down in Ebury Bridge Road, Chelsea, bursting a water main, and the jerk of his parachute on opening caused both boots to fly off his feet and fall somewhere near Victoria Station. He never saw those, or his aircraft, again.[9] The story of Artie's extraordinary afternoon in battle over central London is well worth expanding on, and I can do no better in detailing what happened than quote the *Sunday Express*, which published a piece about his amazing feat on the occasion of the fortieth anniversary of the Battle of Britain:[10]

'The hottest tip', cabled London correspondent H. R. Knickerbocker to his New York newspaper, 'is that the German invasion of England is coming tomorrow, Friday.'

Friday the 13th. Friday 13th September 1940. He added that there was no place on earth where he would rather be.

He was not alone in that. Almost every Londoner wanted to be at the centre of the excitement.

One homesick evacuee child wrote this imaginative appeal: 'Dear Mum, we had an air raid yesterday and the village is wiped out. I am the only evacuee still living. Will you let me come home?'

Also drawn toward London were the men of the fighter squadrons and the pilots whose task it was to defend it. One such Merseysider was Ray Holmes, Sergeant R. T. Holmes. With his Hurricane squadron, No 504, he had been moved south from Scotland to Hendon as a replacement for one of the tired and depleted squadrons that were being withdrawn.

'Arty' Holmes, as he was nicknamed because of his initials, had joined the RAF Volunteer Reserve – the VR – when it was first formed in 1936. He was entrant number 55. Fair-headed and blue eyed, and 5ft 7in tall, he had a strong athletic frame which disguised his lack of inches. At weekends, when not playing cricket or tinkering with his three-wheeler sports car he was learning to fly. Mobilised at the outbreak of war, he was eventually posted to 504 Squadron. Operating from Hendon their task was to back

up the forward squadrons who were intercepting the raiders nearer the coast. They were to challenge any bombers that got through. They made their first interception when London's dockland was set ablaze.

After helping to break up several large bomber formations Holmes's squadron was released at dusk on Saturday September 14th and that evening he visited London's West End. Londoners took little notice of the sirens during the day, work continuing in office and factory until roof spotters sounded an urgent warning. Buses continued to run until bombs actually fell. But at night it was different. Arriving by Underground on the Northern Line, Holmes and his companions found women and children sprawled on the platforms, selecting pitches for the night. Children were doing their homework on tables fashioned from luggage, men played cards and acrobats entertained.

On Sunday September 15, Holmes's flight was brought to readiness at dawn. The cloud of the previous day had dispersed and it promised to be a fine late-summer day. Yet the radar stations were reporting no activity and the squadron was stood down. Feeling scruffy after the early call and the long wait at dispersal, Holmes took a bath. He was luxuriating in it when someone banged on the door.

'Quick, Arty, there's a flap on – we're on readiness!'

There was no question of saying, 'I'll be down in a minute'; he leapt out the bath, and with no time to towel himself properly, slipped into a blue open-necked sports shirt with no badges or rank, pulled on his blue RAF trousers, and ran out to the transport, socks in hand. Someone pulled up the tailboard after him and the truck moved off. Pulling his socks over wet feet was a struggle as the Humber brake bumped and swerved round the perimeter track, at the northern end of the field. As they piled out, the loudspeakers were already ordering them to scramble. Holmes ran shoeless to his locker in the dispersal hut, grabbed his flying boots and his Mae West lifejacket, and chased out to the plane, where the ground crew were waiting. They had already started the Merlin engine and put his parachute harness in position in the cockpit and they helped him on with his safety straps as he climbed in.

His helmet, already connected to the oxygen supply and the radio, was hanging on the reflector sight, and he grabbed and rammed it over his head, covering his bedraggled unkempt hair. It had been a breathtaking flurry of activity, and he was still wringing wet.

Ahead of him he saw the Squadron Leader, John Sample, taxiing towards the far end of the field for the take-off into wind. He waved 'chocks away' and tucked in behind the other Hurricanes as they flattened the grass with their slipstream. Hendon was a small airfield with no runways and they would be taking off over houses. They needed a good take-off run. There were twelve Hurricanes altogether, six from 'A' Flight and six from 'B' Flight, and once airborne they would form up into two parallel lines, each line in three sections of two. This was the formation they had found gave them most room to manoeuvre. Holmes was leading Green section in 'B' Flight – the weavers – keeping a look-out astern.

The take-off itself was a shambles, each pilot ramming his throttle fully open to keep up, but as they climbed over the airfield they settled into formation. The orders were to orbit the airfield at 12,000 feet and await instructions. Soon they were climbing in tight formation through banks of cumulus cloud.

At 8,000 feet they emerged from the cloud into a clear sunlit sky. Orbiting at 12,000 Holmes, drying out rapidly, shivered with cold. The airfield itself, camouflaged and partly obscured by cloud, was impossible to keep in view, but Holmes picked out the silvery expanse of the Welsh Harp. Then they were ordered to climb to 17,000 feet and given a course to steer to the south-east to intercept a raid of thirty-plus Dornier bombers heading for London.

'Tally-ho!'

From the rear of the formation, flying straight into the sun, Holmes could see very little ahead. High above the Dorniers would be their fighter escort of Messerschmitt 109s. But the tactical plan was to leave the enemy fighters to the Spitfire squadrons, which were much better equipped in terms of speed, ceiling and rate of climb to deal with them. The Hurricanes would go for the bombers. For the moment it was still Holmes's job to guard the squadron from the rear. Ahead and slightly to the right, crossing their track diagonally, he saw what might have been a flock of seagulls, until they loomed incredibly quickly into focus and he felt the familiar leap of the heart that was not exactly fear yet was horribly near it. He recognised all too readily the bulbous nose, like a festering blister, the pencil-like fuselage, tapering to the delicate, toy-like twin tail.

As predicted, they were Dornier 215s and there were thirty-plus all right. They formed a disciplined, symmetrical horde heading for Central London that it was the job of the Hurricane pilots to break up. It was at moments like this that Holmes looked to the leader. John Sample, the squadron commander, was an auxiliary. He had already won a DFC as a flight commander in France before Dunkirk, and he inspired confidence.

On this wing of the bombers there were twelve Dorniers in close formation in four sections of three. Sample turned so that he appeared to be approaching at right angles, but he allowed the bombers to pass ahead of him so that he led

*the squadron into a quarter attack, with the Hurricanes
nicely placed at an oblique angle slightly astern.*

*The swarm of Dorniers occupied a sizable area of sky.
As the Hurricanes wheeled in, skidding and sliding as they
jostled for position, the pilots in the leading sections picked
their targets. One after another they said to themselves
'That one's mine'.*

*The Dorniers became ragged, but they put down a fierce
barrage for the Hurricanes to fly through. By the time
Holmes, the last one to attack, had fired his first burst, the
scene ahead of him was kaleidoscopic and he was
uncomfortably aware of a blistering return fire. Now to
break away without exposing the Hurricane's belly to the
Dornier's guns. As the Dornier disappeared from his sights
to the right, he did a vertical bank to the left and used
bottom rudder to skid away before closing the throttle and
diving steeply to complete his escape. So far as he knew he
had not been hit. He eased the Hurricane out of the dive,
then climbed steeply, intent on rejoining his squadron for
another attack. As he looked round, the sky was
bewilderingly empty. The squadron it seemed, had
disappeared. So had the Dorniers.*

*Breathing deeply to settle his diaphragm, he scanned the
sky above him, then glanced westwards, wondering how
many of the Dorniers had got through. All he could see was
a tightly-formed section of three, probably the original
leaders, still on course for London.*

*There was no one about to intercept them but him.
These, he said to himself, are mine. He hoped there were no
'109s to interfere.*

*A last searching look round and he opened the throttle,
aiming to overtake the Dorniers on the port side, keeping
for the moment out of range of their guns. A lone attack
from astern was out – he would be exposed to the guns of*

all three bombers. Instead he picked the wingman on the port side and angled his approach so that as he came within range, the other two Dorniers could not fire at him without hitting their own man.

He started firing at 400 yards range and was closing in steadily when a cloud of smoke from the Dornier blackened his windscreen. He was so nonplussed that for a moment he just sat there not knowing what to do next, but instinctively he shut the throttle. It wasn't smoke on his windscreen it was oil, a treacly deposit that must have gushed from the Dornier. As the airstream dispersed it he was aware of a monstrous shape right in front of him, filling his windscreen, blotting out the sky. It was the Dornier, slowing down rapidly, and he was about to collide with its tail.

He rammed the stick forward and felt the shoulder straps of his safety harness cutting into his collarbone. Without them he would have gone straight through the cockpit hood. As he grazed under the Dornier's belly he thought he would hit the propellers. Then he realised with a shock that they were stationary. For the moment at least, he had put both its engines out of action, which was why the Dornier had slowed down so suddenly. When he looked back the Dornier was gliding earthwards. But the other two were still sticking close together, holding grimly to their course.

He would try the same attack on the other wingman. Crossing over to the starboard side, he opened the throttle to draw level. Judging the angle as before, he crabbed in for a quarter attack. His first burst was right on target, and a tongue of flame licked back from the Dornier.

Someone was trying to get out of the back of the plane, presumably the gunner. Holmes was aware of a white flicker of silk in front of him, but then he almost lost control. Correcting hurriedly, he realised that the German

*gunner's parachute canopy had draped itself over his
starboard wing, leaving the gunner trailing helplessly
behind.*

*He had not stopped to think, before this moment, of the
men in the Dorniers. His attitude was entirely impersonal,
and he was concentrating on avoiding their gunfire and
preventing them from getting through to central London.
Now, he thought only of the poor devil suspended under
his wing.*

*He jerked the stick from side to side, but nothing
happened. The chap was still there. Using hard right rudder
he yawed the Hurricane in a skidding movement to
starboard. He saw the canopy billow slightly, then it
flattened briefly, slid along the leading edge to the wingtip
and was gone.*

*The third Dornier – the leader – was still pressing on
towards central London, apparently undeterred, height
17,000 feet, speed unchanged. A flash of involuntary
admiration turned quickly to anger. The pilot must be
hell-bent on some suicidal mission, like bombing St Paul's
or even Buckingham Palace. Both had been hit in the last
few days.*

*He felt as though he was facing some resolute wing
three-quarter on the rugger field, legging it for the line, with
himself the last hope for the defence. He might be
concussed himself in the tackle but he had to bring his man
down.*

*Oil was seeping over his windscreen now but it was not
outside. It was coming up inside from his own engine.
Someone in the previous attacks must have hit him. That,
with no one else about to help him, made the destruction
of the Dornier all the more urgent. His engine was running
rough and the rev-counter was starting to surge. His
ammunition too, must be almost exhausted. He would*

have to bring the Dornier down with no more than a two- or three-second burst.

He could not avoid the Dornier's return fire, but he could minimise it by making a head-on attack. That would give him a point-blank shot into the pilot's glass-fronted cockpit. Overtaking the lone Dornier, he turned to make his frontal attack, not quite from head-on, but slightly to port, offset about twenty degrees. That would give him a chance to break away before there was any risk of collision. The closing speed must be something like 500 miles an hour. He had only seconds left, and his thumb felt for the firing button. As the bomber came fully into focus he pressed it. He had reached lethal range when his guns sputtered to a stop.

He was hurtling straight for the Dornier. In a moment he must break away. But the German pilot had not deviated one inch from his course. There was only one way to stop him now. Hit him for six.

It was something he had never so much as dreamt of before, a split second revelation, quite unpremeditated. But in the heat of battle, with his own machine crippled, and in a desperate bid to smash this inexorable invader before it broke through to his target – he was more than ever convinced now that some deadly precision attack was intended – he shunned the instinct which bawled him to turn away before it was too late and held his course.

How flimsy the tailplane looked as it filled his windscreen, as fragile as glass; the tough little Hurricane would splinter like balsa wood. He no longer felt cold. As he aimed his port wing at the nearside fin of the Dornier's twin tail, he was sweating.

He felt only the slightest jar as the wing of the Hurricane sliced through. Incredibly, he was getting away with it. The Hurricane was turning slightly to the left, and diving a little. He applied a gentle correction. Nothing happened. The dive steepened, and he shut the throttle. He jerked the stick violently now, forwards and sideways, but he still had no control. The angle increased to the vertical.

Suddenly he was conscious as the cloud tops rushed to meet him, of his speed in the dive, four to five hundred miles an hour, 8,000 feet; already he was halfway down.

He unlocked and slid back the hood. The cloud thickened around him, blindingly white, hurting his eyes and the screech of the dive was deafening. He undid his safety harness and tried to climb out.

The buffeting was so violent that for a moment he thought his head was caught in the propeller. Yet something in the cockpit was holding him back. He had forgotten to unplug the radio lead to his helmet. He climbed back in to release it, and this time, as he struggled blindly out, eyelids clenched against the blast, the airstream caught him with renewed savagery and draped him with arched back over the hump of the Hurricane fuselage. In doing so it snagged his seat type parachute somewhere inside the cockpit.

The Hurricane was diving vertically now. He could still see nothing, but time must be short. Kicking frantically, he thudded his boots against the control column. As the Hurricane lurched into a spin, he was catapulted out by centrifugal force.

Immediately behind him was the tail fin of the Hurricane and as he was blown backwards it struck his right shoulder. He was scarcely aware of it at first, but the shoulder went dead. The sudden cessation of sound and the curious hush told him he was out. He felt for the D-ring of his parachute, but he sought it in vain.

'Where is it? Where is it?'

At last his fingers closed around it. But when he tried to pull it, he could exert no pressure. His right arm, paralysed by the bruised shoulder, was useless. He was talking to himself now, desperately urging himself to act. He was still clutching the rip-cord ring in his right hand, unable to move it, and the ground must be terrifyingly close. What could he do?

He grabbed his wrist with his left hand and tried to tug his arm across his body. There was a sudden explosion above him. For a moment he thought that with the speed of his fall his chute had collapsed. Then he found himself spinning like a top and swinging like a pendulum, all in one motion.

He reached up and grabbed the rigging lines, and that stopped the spin. He was still swinging as if on a trapeze. Gyrating above him, in lazy slow-motion, but uncomfortably close, was the Dornier. Twisting and turning like a falling leaf, it was exuding a bright jet of flame. Its wingtips were severed, and its tailplane had snapped where it joined the fuselage and was falling separately. Below him, nose-down and diving vertically, was the Hurricane.

He did not know it, but his scrap with the stricken Dornier had been witnessed by hundreds of Londoners through a break in the cloud, smack over Hyde Park Corner. Knots of people were pointing excitedly upwards as a Dornier, parachute and Hurricane, in reverse order, came tumbling out of the sky.

Holmes had seen nothing of the ground since the start of the scrap. Now, as he looked down, he saw that he was swinging back and forth across a vast expanse of railway lines. They were less than 300 feet below him. Each set of parallel lines had a third line beside it. The tracks were electrified.

He was drifting over the junction approaches to Victoria Station.

To the right of his lateral swing was a three-storey block. They were flats, facing Ebury Bridge Road, and their roofs were steeply raked. If he could only control his drift he might just manage to clear those flats on his next sideways swing and drop down in the road.

Within a few seconds he could see that he was not going to make it. He hit the roof, and he looked for some handhold or foothold. It was better than being electrocuted.

For a moment, as he slid down the roof, the parachute supported his weight and he tip-toed on the slates in his stockinged feet like a marionette, for his flying boots had both jerked off when the parachute opened. The air began to spill out of the canopy.

Clawing desperately with nothing to grip, he started to slide and roll down the slates. Snatching in vain at the gutter, he recoiled from the dizzy drop below. After all he had gone through he was going to break his neck falling off a roof.

A terrific jolt jerked him to a halt. He had both legs inside an empty dustbin and his toes puppet-like again were just touching the bottom. His parachute had wrapped itself round the top of the drainpipe and arrested his fall.

He freed himself from his harness and stepped out of the dustbin. Around him the silent stillness of London on a Sunday seemed undisturbed. He was in a garden at the back of the flats. Two girls appeared in a garden next door and he vaulted the fence to greet them. Elated at his succession of escapes, from the plane, from electrocution and from falling off the roof, he embraced and kissed them both. 'I hope you don't mind,' he said, 'I'm so pleased to see you.' They seemed equally pleased to see him.

Inside the flats he telephoned his squadron to say where he was, then turned to see a Home Guard Sergeant, middle-aged but almost twice his size approaching with an iron bar.

'Hold it,' Holmes called. 'I'm on your side!'

'Would you like to see your aeroplane?'

'Yes, where is it?'

'Just up the road.'

The Hurricane had come down at a crossroads and missed all the buildings. It had plunged fifteen feet into the ground and was scarcely visible. He collected a souvenir of his Hurricane by scrambling down the crater – a piece of the Merlin's valve cover bearing the S of Rolls and the R of Royce. Bits of the Dornier had meanwhile landed in the forecourt of Victoria Station. Two of its bombs had fallen on Buckingham Palace, one on the Queen's apartments and one in the grounds, more than justifying Holmes's anger and his readiness for personal sacrifice.

The Dornier was the first German aircraft brought down over central London. The crew, baling out at a much greater height, drifted down on Kennington Oval. A crowd gathered where the Hurricane had gone in, and they gave Holmes a spontaneous cheer, patting him on the back and pumping his hand. Then the Home Guard Sergeant, seeing that he had hurt his shoulder and strained his side, walked him to Chelsea Barracks to see a doctor. It was his second excursion that day in his socks.

After he had seen the doctor they opened the bar in the Sergeants' Mess and it was drinks all round. 'Do you always fly dressed like that?' the CO asked. Someone came in with a message: 'There's a lady outside wants to see you.'

They found him a pair of brown Army plimsolls, and he walked across the parade ground to the gate. A frail woman in her thirties was waiting for him.

'Was that you that came down in that plane?'

'Yes.'

She held out a flat-fifty tin of cigarettes. 'Will you take these as a present?'

*'No really – I couldn't possibly.' She did not look as if
she could afford them.*

*'Please do. My baby was outside in his pram. They're for
making your plane miss my baby.'*

*He could not tell her that at 17,000 feet and all the way
down the last thing in his thoughts had been missing her
baby.*

Nor had he the heart to tell her he was a non-smoker . . .

Although Ray parachuted to safety after crashing into the Dornier,
the aircraft's pilot wasn't so lucky. He had the misfortune to come
down in Kennington, an area that had received more than its fair
share of German bombs over the past week. The residents were
understandably angry, and smelled blood when they saw that one
of the pilots who had been dealing such misery to them had
landed in their midst. A crowd of civilians suddenly surrounded
him, and they showed him no mercy as they attacked him with
fists and feet and whatever they could lay their hands on; people
ran out of their houses with pokers and kitchen knives to join the
screaming melee around the dying pilot, all caught up in the same
avenging frenzy that was being played out thousands of feet above
their heads.[11]

Ray was dispatched back to Hendon from Chelsea Barracks
courtesy of a taxi, the Army kindly footing the bill. He immediately asked for another aircraft so that he could resume readiness
to scramble, but an eagle-eyed medical orderly spotted that his
shoulder appeared to be stiffening. A quick X-ray diagnosed a
chipped shoulder bone, occasioned by Ray's bump with the tailplane. Despite his protestations, he was grounded for seven days
to allow it to heal. It was probably for the best, as it enabled him
to deal with the rapidly expanding press interest in the story,
which was widely covered by Fleet Street, and the BBC. He was
given a week's sick leave by the CO, who then cancelled it almost
immediately as he received a signal from Group HQ which said,

'Her Majesty the Queen has graciously commanded an audience at Buckingham Palace with Sergeant Pilot R. T. Holmes.'

Artie was promptly whisked off to the stores and issued with a new uniform, which the camp's tailor altered on the spot so that it fitted like a bespoke suit. He was bought new shoes, which he polished to a mirror shine, and finished off with a visit to the camp's barber for a trim. Sadly, it was all in vain, though; that night, London was bombed in one of the heaviest blitzes so far and the Royal Family was moved to Windsor for safety. Ultimately, his visit to the Palace never happened, although it was never ascertained whether this was due to 504 moving en masse to Bristol, the Royal Family moving en masse to Windsor, Group HQ being heavily bombed, his court martial catching up with him or some other happening.[12] For his courage and determination in that legendary and much-reported battle over Chelsea, he was later awarded a Mention in Dispatches.

Another contemporary of ours whom we would all meet in 1941 was Neil Cameron, a tall, rangy Scot who hailed from Perth. Like Wag, Ray and myself, he had also applied for the RAFVR. His application was submitted in early 1939, and his call-up for training came in May, just as the clouds of war were beginning to gather. And like the rest of us in the VR, he too was called up for regular service on 1 September. Although he came from the humblest of beginnings – he was raised by his mother, his father having passed away when Neil was just three weeks old, and times were hard, money short – he was destined for greatness and high office.

His RAF career didn't get off to the best of starts – succumbing to overconfidence while low flying in the Tay Valley in March 1940, an area he knew well, he flew through some telephone wires, hit some trees and barely managed to remain airborne. Some of the wires ended up hanging off the tail of his aircraft, the radiator was full of leaves, and the pitot head – a vital component responsible for measuring airspeed – was facing the wrong way. The result was an engine temperature that was off the clock and an airspeed indicator that didn't register airspeed! How he managed to get back to the airfield at Montrose before the engine blew up is anybody's guess yet, somehow, he did. He may have escaped with his life, but he didn't escape the wrath of the CFI. He'd been recommended for a commission following flight training and, although this was withdrawn, he got off lightly. Had the war not been on, he'd more than likely have been court-martialled and thrown out of the service in disgrace. There but for the grace of God and all that.

To those who knew him, his display of overconfidence wasn't perhaps a great surprise. The Neil I came to know was someone who often sailed close to the edge, was always pushing at boundaries, looking for an advantage. He was driven, confident and somewhat charismatic – more of a leader than a follower. That much was obvious, even at the beginning.

He sailed through the rest of his training, and on its completion on 26 September, was posted briefly to 1 Squadron at Wittering and a month or so later to 17 Squadron at Debden on the edge of Saffron Walden, in Essex. While the Battle of Britain was well past its climax, the Luftwaffe still sent bombers over to attack targets in southern England, so the squadron was frequently called on to scramble and intercept them. By the time things started to quieten down, Neil was no longer the young, inexperienced fighter pilot he'd been when he arrived. Like most of his peers, he'd accumulated a bit of experience and some memorable operational sorties to write up in his logbook.

3

Ad Astra

While it's widely acknowledged that the Battle of Britain began on 10 July 1940, there is no official date for its end, although it's generally considered that, by the end of October, the immediate threat of a German invasion had been averted. Göring's strategic plan to bomb Britain into submission and neutralise the Air Force to clear the way for Wehrmacht and Waffen SS troops to land on UK soil lay in tatters. That said, though, there was still a feeling that we were living on borrowed time as a nation and that all we'd succeeded in doing was delaying the inevitable. The defeat of the Luftwaffe really struck a chord with the British public, however, and Churchill wasted no time in promoting the RAF's achievement to a grateful public.

Although we failed to destroy the Luftwaffe outright, we denied it Göring's ultimate aim – dominance of the skies over the Channel and southern England – while imposing on it unacceptable and unsustainable losses. In total, Fighter Command lost 544 men in the Battle of Britain, roughly 20 per cent of all its pilots who'd taken part. Sir Hugh 'Stuffy' Dowding, the head of Fighter Command during the battle, said that every death was like losing a son. That figure of 544 dead, though, is dwarfed by the Luftwaffe's disastrous loss of 2,698 highly skilled airmen and some 1,900 of its 2,800 aircraft.[1]

Churchill's gratitude and inspirational rhetoric were again in evidence in a speech he made to Parliament on 20 August 1940, midway through the war over Britain's skies. That speech gave rise to the widely used phrase 'The Few' to refer to the aircrew of Fighter Command, some of whom I would soon be proud to fly

alongside, who risked all and showed immense courage in fighting the Luftwaffe. He said,

> *The gratitude of every home in our Island, in our Empire,*
> *and indeed throughout the world, except in the abodes of*
> *the guilty, goes out to the British airmen who, undaunted*
> *by odds, unwearied in their constant challenge and mortal*
> *danger, are turning the tide of the World War by their*
> *prowess and by their devotion. Never in the field of human*
> *conflict was so much owed by so many to so few.*[2]

Although the country was riding the crest of a wave in the aftermath of the Battle of Britain, Churchill knew that, if the public
only realised just how precarious our position was, if they
succumbed to inertia through an understanding of Britain's impo-
tence in the face of Germany's overall might, then their doggedness,
determination and spirit would evaporate. Morale had to be
maintained, and Churchill went about that job with aplomb. Had
Hitler managed to invade, or had he found a way to do so prior to
sending the Luftwaffe with the objective of achieving air superiority, we couldn't have hoped to meet his ground forces on equal
terms – that much was painfully evident in the Battle for France.
To keep the public pliable, Churchill maintained the fiction of the
threat of invasion long after the danger had passed.[3]

The aftermath of the Battle of Britain left a dangerously
depleted Fighter Command but again, in comparison with the
Luftwaffe, the RAF had got off lightly. The Luftwaffe had suffered
heavy losses during the battle for France, which, coupled with its
defeat in the Battle of Britain, left it reeling. One upside for the
RAF was that victory gave it a massive boost; countless young
men both at home and across the Empire had been captivated by
the exploits of 'The Few' and set their sights on becoming fighter
pilots. Meanwhile, those of us still in training would provide a
constant stream of new recruits to squadrons desperate for

numbers to bring them up to full strength. More important than the headline figures, though, was the fact that our victory in the Battle of Britain not only saved the United Kingdom from invasion but, in the long term, it saved Europe too. The battle over the skies of England represented a turning point for Nazi Germany because, for the first time, it had been unable to impose its will on the rest of Europe through threat or military aggression. Göring's much-vaunted Luftwaffe had tasted defeat in battle for the first time and was immeasurably weaker as a result.

For me personally, things changed rapidly once I arrived at my first posting – 615 Squadron – on 23 April 1941; after the joy of learning to fly, something I'd found that I was rather good at, it was a bit of a culture shock to arrive at an operational squadron. After the high of completing flying training and gaining our wings, it was something of a comedown to realise that we were far from the finished article. Johnny and I set off early on the morning of the 23rd, leaving Ouston, near Newcastle, where we were based while doing our flying training. I drove us in my Morris 12, and it was late afternoon before we arrived at RAF Valley in North Wales and made our way to the squadron headquarters. We found the adjutant's office a lot more easily than we found the base itself, and Johnny knocked on the adjutant's door. A disembodied voice reached us from behind it and told us to enter.

An amiable-looking flight lieutenant greeted us. He wore the same blue tunic as us, save for the rings at the bottom of his sleeve denoting his rank and status. Both Johnny and I snapped to attention and threw him a salute. I introduced us both. He looked us over and smiled.

'At ease, boys. I'm Ron Sawyer. Straight from training, are you?'

'Yes, sir,' I replied.

'Great, and how many hours flying have you got?'

'Er, one hundred and seventy-two. Johnny here has one hundred and sixty-five.'

He rolled his eyes at this. 'How many of those on the Hurricane?'

'Er, not many, sir. Neither of us,' said Johnny.

I passed him our logbooks. 'Come on, then,' he said with raised eyebrows and a sigh. 'I'll introduce you to the CO.'

If the number of flying hours in our logbooks seems low, that's because it was. We were boys, all of us, and we weren't just inexperienced, we were positively green when it came to flying. Even today, it takes an average of fifty hours just to qualify as a private pilot. With just three times that, we were now at a front-line fighter squadron equipped with a proven modern fighter. To put that into perspective, it takes almost five years of training and costs almost £13 million to get a newly qualified RAF Typhoon pilot to the same stage today. When he or she arrives at their squadron direct from flight training, they'll have more than double the flying hours we had and they're still more than a year away from being combat ready. To keep us flying, we had us, and the aeroplane – that was it. No bells or whistles, no air conditioning, no fly-by-wire. I really believe that the flying we did then was so much purer, closer to man's first dream of flight.

I was quite chuffed that we'd been posted to 615 and regarded it as something of a prestige posting as 615 was known as Winston Churchill's 'own' squadron, but when Johnny and I arrived, things were rather in disarray as they'd lost a lot of pilots in the Battle of Britain. The squadron had moved to RAF Valley on Anglesey to restock, as it were, and for those boys who'd survived the Battle of Britain to lick their wounds. Unsurprisingly, Johnny and I were regarded as somewhat 'green', being the new boys, so the old guard – who had mostly arrived from university air squadrons – kept us at arm's length until we 'proved ourselves'. The CO was great, though, and he gave us a lot of help in the early days. He'd let us practise aerial combat on a regular basis.

Although Johnny and I were now at an operational squadron, we were far from useful at that point with just our basic flying training behind us. Neither of us had a great many hours of experience on the mighty Hurricane. What we lacked in experience, we more than made up for in enthusiasm, but we knew nothing of high-frequency radio, of being moved around in a three-dimensional sky by a ground controller. We'd never had to wear an oxygen mask or a Mae West inflatable jacket. To cap all that, we'd done almost no dogfighting at all.

Ron soon sorted that.

'Right, you fellows, weather's set fair in the morning. We'll get you up then.'

Even now, some seventy years on, if I close my eyes, I can still remember that flight in a Hurricane as if it was yesterday . . .

I can hardly wait and spend that night re-reading the Hawker Hurricane's handling notes, memorising all the data about the aircraft that will be my airborne chariot and constant companion for the foreseeable future.

The following morning dawns like it's been made for getting airborne. It's a perfect early-spring day for flying; balmy, sunny, and the deep blue sky above me is peppered with bright white cumulus drifting languorously across the North Wales countryside. No April showers today.

'It's just like riding a bike, Eric,' I tell myself.

I'd wanted to fly a Hurricane ever since I'd first heard about them. Visually, they were like the biplane Harts I'd flown in training – take the top wing off, and the fuselage, tail and front end share more than just the essence of that earlier aircraft. The design was never quite as iconic as R. J. Mitchell's Spitfire – whichever angle you view a Spitfire from, she's all sleek curves and promise. Where the Spitfire is graceful and sleek, though, the Hurricane is more forgiving and workmanlike, but its supercharged 27-litre, V12 Rolls-Royce Merlin power plant promises great power and the sort of speed we could only dream of in the Magister.

My feet leave tracks in the early morning dew as I walk across the grass dispersal to the aircraft. I look around me as I walk to see what the weather is doing – what are the clouds like, where are they, and most importantly, a quick glance at the windsock to see what direction the wind is coming from. My head is full of remembered commands and instruction from my flying instructor. 'Come on, Eric!' I chide myself. 'This should be seared into your brain now. Relax, it'll all come to you.' I pull on my leather flying helmet; I can feel my parachute pack, which dangles just below my derrière, banging into the back of my thighs as I walk. As I get closer, the scent of high-octane aviation fuel reaches my nose. I gulp it down; its unique aroma heralds the excitement to come.

I take time to drink in the Hurricane's lines and take in its familiar-looking fuselage. As I walk towards the cockpit, I reach my arm out and my fingers trace a line along the leading edge of the wing. Four patches of canvas protect the barrels of the aircraft's eight Browning machine guns from the elements. With my finger on the trigger, they could spit out 160 .303 bullets each second – enough to tear a 13-foot diameter hole in a wall from 250 yards. Just imagine what they could do to a Nazi Messerschmitt Me109.

The suspension is provided by 'oleo' legs, which are telescopically sprung on oil and air; after take-off, the wheels swing inward to retract flush into wing cavities. A tail wheel completes the technical arrangements for take-off and landing.

Before take-off, all pilots inspect their aircraft visually. During the Battle of Britain, when 615 was the duty squadron on stand-by to scramble, the pilots would do it ahead of time; every second counts. Pre-flight checks done, the Hurricanes would sit there, poised, ready to spring into action and intercept the Luftwaffe's fighters and the bombers they escorted the second that circumstances dictated.

Today, however, I'm just taking her up for a familiarisation flight, so I do a quick walk around the aircraft to do the pre-flight checks. The tyres are fully inflated with no obvious cuts or defects. I look at the three-bladed propeller; no nicks or fluid leaks there. I check the position of the elevators carefully; any distortion there is going to make the aircraft difficult to control. I check the rudder – it has full and unrestricted movement. The trim tab is neutral, the hinge satisfactory. I walk around the rear of the aircraft to the port side and along the fuselage; the radio hatch there is closed and secure. OK, then, looks like we're good to go; I give her a quick kiss and tell her silently to look after me.

I step up on to the wing root via a pull-down footstep (it's reminiscent of a stirrup on a horse and I momentarily wonder whether it's a throwback to the days of cavalry) and climb into the cockpit via the footstep in the side of the fuselage. As I ease myself in a member of the aircraft's ground crew – the fitter – helps me to strap in. The parachute pack that was hanging down beneath me as I walked now forms the cushion on which I will sit while flying. I adjust the seat so that it affords me maximum visibility, but still keeps the top of my head beneath the topmost part of the canopy. If I need to get out in a hurry, I need to be able to jettison the canopy without obstruction, as quickly as possible. I secure the parachute harness to the quick-release box on the front of the harness. I clip the Hurricane's radio leads to my helmet; I'm now fused to the aircraft, an integral part, with it, in turn, an extension of me.

I breathe in the distinctive, intoxicating smell that is exclusive to every Hurricane; a unique combination of oil, metal, sweat, hydraulic fluid, aviation fuel and rubber. It's a potent aroma, both reassuring and evocative. If they could bottle this, it'd walk off the shelves.

I pull on my calf-leather flying gloves; these will afford me a degree of protection in the event of a fire or should I otherwise need to bale out but, for now, they provide a more secure grip on the controls. The Hurricane's cockpit is familiar yet different; it's far more advanced than that of the Magister, much more ordered. I place my feet on the rudder pedals and begin to run through the cockpit checks: indicator switch on, undercarriage selector down, fuel gauge shows 37 gallons in the lower tank – all good so far. I grab the stick and pull it towards me, then away. Move it left, then right – free movement of the control surfaces. Then I apply the brakes by pulling a lever that is attached to the spade grip on the 'stick' and move a small metal mechanism to hold the brake lever in place. I smile; the brake lever looks just like the one on my first bicycle. I set the elevator trim, and wind the rudder bias fully right; this will counteract the Hurricane's swing to the left on take-off caused by the immense torque from the mighty Merlin engine. Flaps up – check. Landing lamps – up. Artificial horizon – set. I check outside the cockpit to confirm that the lead from the accumulator trolley alongside us is plugged into the cowling; that'll supply sufficient power for me to start the engine.

Air pressure's good; brakes are on. I move my left hand, settle it on the throttle control and push it forward to the start position. With my right hand I switch the radio on, then shift it to the engine start isolation switch and move it to the 'on' position. I do the same for the fuel cock, then flip down the covers to the starter and booster coil buttons. The magneto switches are off. I push the propeller control lever fully forward to select 'fine pitch' for take-off.

I pull the control stick back and grip it between my knees – it's tricky, this next bit, as I need both hands at once to start the engine. I unscrew the priming plunger locknut and pump it three times until I feel the 'wall' – a stiffening of the pump action that indicates there's fuel in the cylinders. With my left hand, I switch the magnetos on, and then finally simultaneously press the engine start and booster coil buttons. 'Contact!' I think, as I work the priming pump.

I hear the engine start to turn; the propeller begins spinning ahead of me and the Merlin engine roars into life with a stab of flame from the exhaust cowls. Clouds of black smoke envelop the cockpit, then quickly clear away. The Hurricane feels alive, the mighty Merlin engine its beating heart. The fuselage shakes and strains against the brakes like a thoroughbred racehorse waiting to be let loose.

Magnetos both live; oil pressure and temperatures are rising; fuel pressure warning light is off. I maintain the backward pressure on the control stick with its spade handle; if I relax my grip at this stage, the torque generated by the Merlin's 1,100 horses could cause the aircraft to pitch forward on to its nose. Temperatures, pressures and controls are all good, the engine's firing nicely; I replace the priming plunger and hold it in place with its locknut.

Can't hang around; I remember the words of my flying instructor: 'Have to be delicate on the brakes – over-heavy application and the Hurricane will be nose down in the mud! Don't you dare break it!'

I nod to the ground crew and they pull the wheel chocks clear. A glance outside and I see them unplug the lead from the accumulator trolley and pull it free from the cowl. A final look around and I pull the sliding canopy forward and secure it. I'm clear to roll.

My forward vision is all but wiped out by the cowling, which dominates my field of view. It's a symptom of all 'tail draggers' – the aircraft sit nose up on the ground, a result of the undercarriage's two main wheels being forward of the centre of gravity, with a small wheel to support the tail. The Hurricane's cowling points imperiously at the sky, a visual reminder perhaps of where it wants to be. I know how it feels. I check the engine temperature again. Come on, Eric, what are you waiting for? I push the throttle lever slowly through the gate to the rated boost position and the engine note increases as I release the brakes. I can feel it as much as hear it, a resounding roar that resonates through me. The fuselage vibrates to its rhythm.

I zigzag slowly to gain some degree of forward vision and I feel the power coming on as a huge surge, deep and throaty, but smooth and seemingly endless. The acceleration is out of this world; it's nothing like the Magister or the Hart, the power from that Merlin is unimaginable. As the aircraft rolls forward, the port wing dips groundward, an effect of the astonishing torque produced by that engine. I hold it in check with the rudder and a touch of aileron. Steady as she goes, Eric.

As the power continues to build, I ease the stick forward gently. The rear of the aircraft rises and the cowling lowers, affording me a view of the grass runway ahead. I check the speed; 95 mph already? If I'm not careful, this aircraft is going to run away with me and I'll be struggling to catch up. I ease back on the stick and feel the Hurricane slip the chains of gravity and lift seamlessly into the air. Come on, Eric, get a grip, I tell myself. Positive climb; we're hurtling skywards, into the blue. I check the temperatures and pressures; all good. I give a quick squeeze on the brake lever to stop the wheels turning and then change hands so that I can select the undercarriage up. I feel the wheels settle into their wing wells and see the lights on the dash that tell me that they are fully retracted. Push the airscrew speed control fully forward to adjust the propeller to coarse pitch and move the rpm lever to 2,400 rpm for climbing. The aircraft's 'clean' now; I'm beginning to feel I've got the hang of this.

I look back and see the airfield falling away as we race into the sky; there's no stopping this wonderful aeroplane, she's an absolute joy to fly, benign and forgiving in nature. The Magister, with its similar wide, fixed undercarriage, was a gift to take off and land in, but it's a donkey compared to the thoroughbred stallion that I'm flying now. Without question, this is the best day of my life so far.

4

Transition

Our progression to readiness as fully trained and combat-ready fighter pilots continued apace. Formation flying, oxygen climbs to altitudes of 25,000 ft and beyond, R/T procedure, aerial gunnery and basic combat manoeuvres were all part of the syllabus we worked through in April and the beginning of May 1941. Combat manoeuvring or 'dogfighting' is all about getting above or behind your opponent. Achieving this allows you to get 'guns on' first, hopefully shooting down the enemy's aircraft.

Before we could be of any use to the squadron, we needed to be effective in the 3D space of the sky, and get comfortable with the operation of the Hurricane's eight machine guns. To do that, we'd head out to sea (it was never far away from RAF Valley, whichever direction you flew in!) and, after carefully checking to make sure there were no fishing boats or other vessels within range – then checking again – we'd fly in at about 100 ft above the water and hit the firing button.

Having switched on the reflector sight, you'd take aim on a white wave crest and blast away. Even with a helmet on, and the noise of that supercharged V12 Merlin, the noise was deafening, and you felt it as much as heard it. You smelt it too; the most amazing whiff of cordite would envelop the cockpit as the guns fired, assaulting the senses and hitting you full on and lifting one's spirits just as I imagine a drug would. The guns worked in much the same way as conventional firearms – every action has a reaction, so when you shoot a rifle, you feel the recoil as the round leaves the barrel and the butt jerks back into your shoulder.

The recoil has a purpose – the explosion from each round forces the breech block back to eject the spent cartridge case and, as it slides forward, it catches a new round and rams it into the barrel. In a machine gun, such as the eight we had on the Hurricane, that process was repeated twenty times a second for as long as you held the firing button or until you ran out of rounds. In the Hurricane's case it only took thirteen seconds. Not a lot. The recoil from those eight machine guns the first time I fired them was amazing and, although the gun itself absorbed some of it, it still had a marked effect on the Hurricane, slowing it down noticeably and making the nose sink. That really focuses the mind when you're flying at just 100 ft!

Johnny and I would get airborne and practise together; it made sense because we always flew in pairs, with one aircraft behind the other rather than side by side. The job of the lead aircraft was to inflict the damage on the enemy aircraft; the wingman's job was to make sure you weren't jumped from behind – a favourite manoeuvre of the Luftwaffe. You'd think you had one in your sights and before you knew it, there'd be a 109 on your tail trying to take you out.

My first mission with 615 came about a month after I joined the squadron. I may have been considered 'combat ready' and signed off, but I felt far from prepared. We were ordered to escort a convoy of ships out of Liverpool, providing aerial support to them as far as South Wales. The Luftwaffe regularly sent Blohm & Voss BV 138 maritime reconnaissance aircraft, flying boats that carried an effective armament of machine guns and bombs or depth charges which they'd drop on the convoys.

That was a dangerous job even without the enemy because the ships had their own barrage balloons, which they'd fly from the decks to stop dive bombers getting in close, but they caused us the same problems as their land-based counterparts – barrage balloons were as much a problem for us as they were for German bombers. The Navy used to like us to fly down low so they could see us – it made them feel safer, I suppose. We'd ask them to lower their balloons, and they'd come back saying, 'No, you keep out the way!' So we'd say, 'If you don't lower the balloons, we're going back!' That usually sorted the issue.

I had something of a close shave on one sortie, and I didn't even have the Luftwaffe to contend with. It was a relatively simple, enjoyable and straightforward tasking and it came directly from Squadron Leader George Powell-Shedden – our CO, a quite amazing fellow. He'd flown with Group Captain Douglas Bader in the Battle of Britain, shot down at least four Huns and damaged his shoulder after baling out, having been shot down himself. He'd go on to be awarded a DSO and bar, and a DFC. After the war, he represented Great Britain as a bobsledder at the 1948 Winter Olympics in St Moritz. As I said, a quite remarkable chap.

We'd just taken delivery of a brand-new Hurricane at the squadron and the CO asked me to take it up and put it through its paces.

'Eric, old chap, why don't you take that up and see if it will do exactly what the factory says it will?' he asked. I didn't need asking twice. It was a run-of-the-mill job, a routine that we carried out whenever aircraft were delivered to us straight from the factory. We'd take them up for a test flight, fly some aerobatics and combat manoeuvres – a few tight turns, dives, rolls and wing-overs just to make sure the controls did what they should and responded how they were supposed to. 'Take it up, fly it, check the maximum height she'll fly at,' he said. It was all about making sure the aircraft were in acceptable condition really.

By now, I felt really at one with the Hurricane. I had acquired a further eighty hours' experience on it by then, enough formation flying, combat manoeuvring and gunnery practice to make me feel completely at home in the cockpit. Every day saw an improvement in the weather, and I looked forward to getting out of bed each morning just so I could take to the skies in this amazing aircraft.

Transition

The airframe glinted in the morning sunlight as I bade the CO farewell and walked out to dispersal, my parachute hooked over my shoulder. I nodded to the ground crew as I climbed on to the wing and settled into the cockpit. Sunlight glinted off the dials in front of me as I strapped myself in, and breathed in the familiar smells of oil, wood and fuel, which were somewhat more muted on this airframe given its newness. I signalled to the ground crew and started her up.

'Come on, Eric,' I chided myself. 'Enough musing, it's time to get airborne.'

It was another beautiful day as I pointed her towards the grass runway and opened the throttle, really lovely and balmy. As the wheels left the ground and escaped gravity, accelerating upwards, there was almost no breeze, no clouds – just endless miles of blue sky and perfect visibility.

I lifted my oxygen mask, which was hanging loose on my chest, and secured it over my nose and mouth as I pointed the aircraft upwards and increased the rate of climb. By the time I reached 20,000 ft, I was really enjoying myself. I did a couple of aileron rolls and revelled in the speed at which we spun through 360 degrees – less than a second. It was like being on the fast spin in a modern washing machine. I flew a loop, then an inverted loop, tensing my abdomen against the g-forces trying to impel my body's eight litres of blood south, away from my head and into my lower legs and feet. My vision cleared, and I felt normality return, as I levelled out and executed an Immelmann turn. 'No complaints about this particular Hurricane,' I thought, back in level flight. She dived, climbed, turned and performed with bird-like efficiency, and I again drank in the view, which extended to about fifty miles in each direction.

'They're pretty!' I thought, as I noticed little black clouds forming on my starboard side. Then another appeared just below me, and another, and another. They were all around me now, little puffs of black. 'Strange,' I thought, 'I've never seen those before.'

I thought nothing more of it and pointed the nose downwards, heading back to Valley, and executed a perfect landing, a real greaser, the wheels kissing the runway and leaving tracks behind them in the grass. I taxied back to dispersal and shut down, pushing back the canopy and lifting myself out.

Back at the squadron HQ, I saw the 'old man' and he called me over.

'Ah, Carter, there you are! Have you been over Liverpool, lad?'

'Er, I'm not sure, sir. I might have been but I wasn't really paying attention to what was below me – I was more concerned with how the aircraft was performing. Why do you ask?'

'Well, some bugger was up there – I've just had Group on the line. The AA guns thought it was a lone Me109 and opened up on it,' he said as he turned tail and walked away.

That was when I had a real sinking feeling in my stomach. 'You idiot!' I said to myself. 'Those weren't harmless little black clouds, it was flak! They were shooting at you!'

Walking back to the sergeants' mess, I noticed one of the fitters running over to me from dispersal.

'Did you get him, then, Sarge?' he enquired. 'You must have had a right set-to with Jerry up there going by the number of holes in the rear of the fuselage. And the rudder's riddled with them!'

A lucky escape, then. But then, I've always been lucky. That is, until Johnny and I were posted to the other side of the dispersal area at RAF Valley to lend a hand with 456 Squadron, which had only just been stood up on 30 June. It was established under the Empire Air Training Scheme as a night fighter squadron, equipped with black-painted Defiant turret fighters. Johnny and I knew this so neither of us wanted to go – news of life on night-fighter squadrons was rife in the RAF and nobody would have volunteered for them because it was such an awful job. The two of us were told to report to a location in Nottingham for an eyesight test, which we understood was to ensure we had the requisite vision for night fighters.

On arrival, we were shut in a dark room, the lights were turned off and then silhouettes of various ships and aircraft were held up against a bright screen – our task was to identify what they were. We'd made our minds up on the drive down in my Morris 12 and decided that we'd go out of our way to make sure we failed every single test we faced. And we did – we made sure of that. But the RAF wasn't as daft as we thought. When we got back to the squadron a couple of days later, the old man was waiting for us with some unwelcome news:

'Well, lads,' he said, 'you've passed all the tests so you're off to 456 Squadron with immediate effect. You'll be flying Defiants.'

And that was that. My God, I hated it! It was a horrible job; I was more scared of night flying than anything before or since. The Defiant was an awful aircraft to fly and it was universally unpopular with all pilots. It was underpowered, impossible to manoeuvre, and poorly armed; it was a turret fighter, so the gunner sat behind the pilot, manning the four machine guns, but it had no forward-facing guns – a bit of a handicap in a fighter and very disconcerting for the pilot.

Before we flew, we'd have to sit in a dark room for half an hour to allow our vision to adapt, which was not something we relished. It was a miserable existence, if I'm being honest, and we dreaded each night in a way we never did when we were at 615 Squadron.

I remember one sortie we flew early on. Bear in mind it was the middle of the night, with the blackout in full force, and no moon, so it was pitch black outside. There were no runway lights so we were literally flying blind. We were above Liverpool and we were vectored on to an enemy aircraft, although it was exceptionally difficult to see the thing. Every now and then, I'd get a flash of its exhausts, but with us flying in and out of cloud in the pitch black, it was an impossible task. Just to make life a little more interesting, we also had the barrage balloons to contend with; these were placed in all the major cities and sat at different heights, making it precarious and difficult for both enemy aircraft and our own – the cables securing them to terra firma would have sheared through our wings life a hot knife through butter. We were scrambled on a regular basis but none of the sorties we ever flew came to anything. We'd close in on the German aircraft, only to lose them in cloud and, given the impenetrable darkness, it was impossible for us to find them to line up on them. There was no night-vision equipment in those days!

Each sortie lasted an average of ninety minutes, which was basically the maximum endurance for the Defiant, so we'd be very low on fuel by the time we returned. The worst thing was if our low fuel status occurred while a raid on Liverpool or Manchester was in full flow. If that happened, and it did on a number of occasions, RAF Valley wouldn't put the landing lights on, for obvious reasons. However, that was of little use to us, up in a black sky with our fuel running out by the minute. I can remember returning to RAF Valley on a number of occasions and asking for the landing lights to be illuminated so I could land, only to be told, 'Negative, the raid is still on at Liverpool.'

One particular mission saw us flying circuits around the vicinity of the airfield waiting for a raid to finish so we could land. Over fifteen minutes later, things were desperate so I called, 'Mayday, Mayday, Mayday! Fuel status critical, we must land now!' and I was told, 'The raid is still on, you'll have to fly over the Irish Sea and bale out!' The water was only a few degrees above freezing so if we'd baled out, we'd have been dead in minutes – it was tantamount to hearing your own death warrant read out. We didn't have immersion suits like those the fighter pilots of today wear. I have no idea how or why providence intervened as it did but suddenly the runway lights came on – we were flying on fumes and fresh air by that stage. It wasn't just us, though – as soon as the airfield was illuminated, there were Defiants coming in from all directions, each one desperate to get on the ground before the fuel pumps sucked up nothing but air from the tank. That really focused the mind.

Luckily we didn't lose anyone in this manner, but we did sadly lose people to the Welsh mountains that delineated the area around the base at Valley. We had the Irish Sea on one side; a few seconds out in your navigation calculations and you'd fly into the side of Snowdon, which rises to over 3,000 ft. In the pitch black of night, that wasn't as difficult as you might think. One of my pals crash-landed on the beach at Harlech; although he managed to get his aircraft down on to the sand, his Hurricane flipped over and, unable to escape, he drowned. That's such an awful way to die; it still haunts me today.

If we were pushed, it wasn't unusual to find ourselves flying sorties for both 615 Squadron *and* 456. Back at 615 during the day, we'd spend the time out on dispersal waiting for the order to scramble in our Hurricanes. We passed the time by playing cards, listening to music and chatting to one another. At night, we'd cross dispersal and fly night missions for 456. They were tough days, sleep was short, and it was a thankless task. We existed in a sort of permanent fatigue, our limbs as heavy as our eyelids, our reaction times short and our vision of the world filtered as if through a veil. But then, there was a war on – people died. We really had nothing to complain about – we were just tired.

It was around this time that two events occurred which would affect me; one was a great positive, the other not so much! On 22 June, Hitler invaded Russia. And a week or so later, I met Phyllis, the woman who was to become my wife. On my nights off, the boys and I used to head out to Llandudno which, although our nearest major town, was a good 60 miles away. It was, however, the nearest place if we wanted to go to a dance, so we'd head to Llandudno's Winter Gardens and that's where I met Phyllis; I think it's fair to say it was love at first sight.

Luckily, our tenure at 456 would last only about six weeks, but when I headed off on leave around the middle of July, I had no way of knowing that then and besides, my head was full of the joy of release; it was my first leave since I'd headed off on basic training in 1940. I just threw a few things into my trusty Morris 12 and headed home to stay with my parents. I had thoughts of Phyllis on my mind all the way as I drove from RAF Valley to Birmingham.

However, if I thought I was in for two weeks of rest and relaxation, the Air Ministry had other plans for me. Little did I know, but Churchill had us earmarked for a secret mission. The stage was set, the players cast. I, and around 549 others, were about to learn just what lay in store for us.

5

Force Benedict

Hitler's invasion of the Soviet Union on 22 June 1941, code-named Operation Barbarossa after the medieval Holy Roman Emperor Frederick Barbarossa, changed everything – for me personally, but more importantly, the course of the war. Max Hastings describes the invasion as the 'defining event of the war, just as the Holocaust was the defining act of Nazism'.[1]

The Führer had myriad reasons why he wanted to invade Russia, but he was making plans to expand eastwards and open a new front in Russia even as the Luftwaffe's aircraft were fuelling up to engage the RAF on the Battle of Britain's 'Black Saturday'.

Perhaps unsurprisingly, the prime targets at the heart of the plan to invade the Soviet Union included Moscow, Leningrad, Kiev and Rostov. What was rather more difficult to understand at first glance, however, was the inclusion alongside these strategic objectives of Murmansk – a small, solitary port in the Kola Bay which lies on the extreme north-west of the Russian coastline.

Hitler took a personal interest in this port, seeing the seemingly innocuous city as a vitally important strategic target – and with good reason. He regarded it as the most dangerous Russian deployment centre in the far northern territory, as it provided Russia with a lifeline to the west, where goods vital for the Soviet war effort were traded and brought into the city. It may have been buffeted on all sides by frozen wastelands and vast areas of icy nothingness but, owing to the warm, swirling Gulf Stream waters channelling into the Kola Bay, Murmansk's harbour was ice free throughout the year, giving the Soviet Union a gateway into the Atlantic.

Murmansk's railway system also supplied a communications network linking the Arctic Ocean with central Russia. Furthermore, just 60 miles west, a veritable treasure trove lay in wait in the form of the nickel mines at Petsamo, and Hitler didn't want the Russians (who had just invaded Finland) to get to Varangeren Fjord (the point where Norway, Finland and Russia converge) and threaten his access to the Arctic Ocean. Doing so would also give them access to the ports that the Führer's forces held in German-occupied northern Norway. Knowing that Stalin could move men and supplies quickly from central Russia to the Finnish border by rail, he would have decided early on that Murmansk had to be captured at the very outset of any invasion of the Soviet Union.

But Hitler seems to have forgotten the maxim that those who forget the lessons of the past are condemned to repeat them. In 1917, America and Russia had formed an alliance against the Kaiser's Germany, and Murmansk, with its port and railway infrastructure, linked the two allies; Hitler failed to see that history was bound to repeat itself where he was concerned, with Murmansk, and the port of Archangel on the White Sea, taking in vast quantities of aid from Britain and the US, thus playing a major role in Russia's survival.

General Eduard Dietl, the commander of Hitler's Mountain Corps Norway, was charged with the task of getting his *Gebirgsjäger* [mountain infantry] across the 60 miles from the Finnish border into Murmansk. Dietl was brutally honest in telling the Führer of the problems confronting him caused by the unique environment of the tundra surrounding Murmansk, and the Arctic conditions that prevailed. He described the tundra belt that runs for 60 miles around the city as a pathless, stony desert with nothing but rocks and scree: a wilderness bordering on myriad lakes, rivers and rapids; a swamp infested by mosquitoes during three short summer months under hot sun and, in winter, nothing but a blast-frozen landscape swept by icy gales. According to Dietl, the 60 miles from the Finnish border to Murmansk were a hell on earth in which waging war was impossible.

Hitler, undeterred, ordered that 'Operation Silberfuchs' [Silverfox], the code name for the assault on Murmansk, should go ahead as planned and that the *Gebirgsjäger* were to embark on this course a week after first occupying the Petsamo area. However, he did take one bit of Dietl's advice, deploying six divisions to cut the railway lines into Murmansk at three separate locations in the more favourable conditions that prevailed farther south.

As German troops massed along a front on the Russian border reaching from the Baltic to the Black Sea, and Dietl made plans for an Arctic campaign that he'd briefed Hitler was doomed to fail, everything had to be done with total operational secrecy owing to the non-aggression pact signed by Germany and Russia in 1939. Despite this, Stalin's vast intelligence regime was reporting the massive build-up of German forces along his border, but the Soviet dictator refused to act for fear of provocation. Much as Britain's prime minister Neville Chamberlain had following Britain's declaration of war on Germany in September 1939, Stalin was playing for time, not by choice but out of necessity; he simply didn't have the advanced war resources such as the latest tanks and fighter aircraft required to begin an offensive. A large proportion of Stalin's arms and equipment were obsolete, and although a massive upgrade was in force, it was still at a fledgling stage; for example, his vast army had only about 1,500 of the latest KV and T-34 tanks.

Hitler, on the other hand, had few problems. With the exception of the Battle of Britain, for which the Luftwaffe was bearing responsibility, he was riding on a wave of successes. His blitzkrieg technique had proved successful since 1937, when, following a call for aid by General Franco in the Spanish Civil War, German forces had destroyed Guernica, and nothing had been able to withstand the might of the German military machine that rolled across Europe in 1939 and 1940. First, the *Anschluss* [annexation] of

Austria into the Third Reich in March 1938, then Czechoslovakia, swiftly followed by Poland, neutral Denmark, Norway and Luxembourg, then the Netherlands, Belgium and France. Following the aberration that was the defeat of the Luftwaffe in the Battle of Britain in the summer and autumn of 1940, 1941 brought continuing success. Rommel, dispatched by Hitler to take over the campaign in North Africa, pushed the British ever farther back towards Egypt, while a rapid German thrust south through the Balkans overwhelmed Yugoslavia, opening the way for the occupation of mainland Greece and Crete. Hitler must have felt invincible as his forces massed to take on the might of the Soviet Union.

Such was the secrecy around Operation Barbarossa that even those German soldiers who were grouped along the Russian and Ukraine borders didn't know their real reason for being there. German intelligence went to great lengths to convince the troops there that they were being rested prior to the invasion of England, with detailed maps printed and distributed in their tens of thousands, while assault code names for 'Operation Haifisch' [Shark] and 'Operation Harpune' [Harpoon] identified special operations. English interpreters joined units to further increase the credibility of the ruse and briefings were carried out to explain in great detail the targets and plans for the invasion. German propaganda poured out a steady stream of anti-British abuse, leaving Soviet Russia out of the equation for once.

Finally, at 2300 Berlin time on Saturday, 21 June 1941, Adolf Hitler gave the order for Operation Barbarossa to be put into action. Four hours later, at 0315, Russian border guards on the Bug river bridge at Kolden were summoned by their German counterparts to 'discuss important matters'. As they approached, a German MG-42 machine gun opened up, cutting them down.[2] Fifteen minutes later, on the dot of 0330, Wehrmacht artillery opened up along the full length of the frontier with a barrage of devastating firepower. The first shots had been fired in what was to become the biggest battle in the history of war. Behind the shells, almost four million Axis troops, ranged across a front stretching some 1,800 miles, began the advance into the Soviet Union, supported by some 600,000 motor vehicles and three-quarters of a million horses.[3] Operation Barbarossa had begun.

Shortly after 0430, the German ambassador, Count von der Schulenburg, handed Stalin's foreign minister Vyacheslav Molotov a note to the effect that the German government had declared war on the Soviet Union, but this message wasn't passed to Soviet forces until 0800. Stalin's armed forces had been under orders not to respond to provocation, so the initial bombardment and advance by Axis troops was unopposed. As they rained fire on Soviet positions moving forward, the Russian soldiers were hamstrung by their orders and unable to retaliate. They lacked the combat experience of the German soldiers, so all they could do initially was cower in fear.

The confusion and three-and-a-half hour delay in broadcasting new orders to Soviet forces, telling them to counter-attack, cost Stalin dear. Unopposed, German armour was able to drive wedges of more than thirty miles into Russian defences, giving huge momentum to the panzer divisions. Russia was utterly unprepared for the onslaught confronting it; many of its front-line units found themselves unable to communicate – some lacking radios, others because some German engineers had crossed the border ahead of the invasion force dressed in civilian clothing to cut the communication lines. Compounding the problem was the fact that the Red Army's formations along the western border of the Soviet Union were poorly deployed. It lacked effective and charismatic leaders – a great many of its best commanders had been killed in the purges of 1937/38 and replaced by incompetent lackeys.[4]

The Luftwaffe established air superiority from the off, taking advantage of the confusion to destroy hundreds of Russian Air Force aircraft immobile at their airfields. By midnight on 22nd June, the Russians had lost 1,811 aircraft, 1,489 of which were destroyed without ever leaving the ground.[5] This figure arguably represents the largest single blow ever delivered in a surprise attack against a branch of an armed service in a single day. The Luftwaffe cleared a path ahead of the panzer and mechanised infantry units and made the most of the mayhem on the ground.

The news of the German invasion was broadcast to the world almost as soon as the artillery barrage began at 0330 but it can't have come as a surprise to Winston Churchill. Intelligence sources told him that a German invasion of Russia was imminent, and had been informing Stalin of major activity by the Luftwaffe, which had recently been moving its aircraft from the Balkans up to the Russian frontier. Churchill sent a series of personal telegrams to the Soviet leader as early as April 1941, warning of Hitler's plans, although there is some evidence that Stalin hadn't actually received all of them as intended. A document dated 14 October 1941 backs this theory up. It details messages sent by Churchill to his ambassador in Moscow, Sir Stafford Cripps. Marked 'Most Secret – To Be Kept Under Lock and Key', the document quotes Churchill's personal advice to Stalin from 3 April 1941, which at that time was to be delivered to the Russian premier personally by Stafford Cripps. Churchill writes to Cripps,

> *Following from me to M. Stalin provided it can be personally delivered by you:–*
>
> *I have sure information from a trusted agent that when the Germans thought they had got Yugoslavia in the net, this is to say, after the 29th March, they began to move 3 out of the 5 Panzer divisions from Romania to Southern Poland. The moment they heard of the Serbian revolution this movement was countermanded. Your Excellency will readily appreciate the significance of these facts.*[6]

The document also copies advice from Foreign Secretary Anthony Eden to Sir Stafford Cripps and states,

> *My telegram No 278 (of 3rd April: information to be conveyed to M. Stalin): If your reception gives you the opportunity of developing the argument, you might point out that this change in Germany's military dispositions surely implies that Hitler, through the action of Yugoslavia, has now postponed his previous plans for threatening Soviet Government. If so, it should be possible for Soviet Government to use this opportunity to strengthen their own position. This delay shows that the enemy forces are not unlimited and illustrates the advantages that will follow anything like a united front.*[7]

It goes on,

> *. . . obvious way of Soviet Government strengthening its own position would be to furnish material help to Turkey and Greece and through latter to Yugoslavia. This help might so increase German difficulties in the Balkans as still further to delay the German attack on the Soviet Union, of which there are so many signs.*
>
> *. . . You would not of course imply that we ourselves required any assistance from Soviet Government or that they would be acting in any interests but their own. What we want them to realise however is that Hitler intends to attack them sooner or later, if he can.*[8]

Churchill copied the file to his foreign secretary, Anthony Eden, and Lord Beaverbrook, a close friend and confidant who was then Minister for Aircraft Production. In it, he is scathing about Stafford Cripps' performance and, in a withering attack, blames him personally for a considerable dereliction of duty. He writes,

This file is really worth looking through in view of the statement that Stalin made to Lord Beaverbrook [this would have been in September, when Beaverbrook was part of a British delegation to Moscow] about not remembering when he was warned. This was the only message before the attack that I sent Stalin direct. It had to be somewhat cryptic, in view of the deadly character of the information, the fact that it came from the Head of the Government and was to be delivered personally to the Head of the Russian Government by the Ambassador were all intended to give it special significance and arrest Stalin's attention.

Churchill goes on in even stronger terms,

It was astonishing that the Ambassador should have had the effrontery to delay this message for sixteen days, and then merely to hand it to Vyshinsky [Andrey Januarevich Vyshinsky, Soviet deputy foreign minister under Molotov]. It may very well never have reached Stalin at all, or merely have been put casually before him. That Sir Stafford Cripps should think the fact that he had been writing a long personal letter about a war to Vyshinsky, and that this would be more likely to make an impression than a direct message from me only shows his lack of sense of proportion.

Churchill left his audience in no doubt about his opinion of Cripps . . . 'Sir Stafford Cripps has a great responsibility for his obstinate, obstructive handling of this matter. If he had obeyed his instructions, it is more than possible that some kind of relationship would have been constructed between me and Stalin. Let me have this back.'[9]

There's evidence that Stalin often ignored his advisers. For example, he rejected explicit intelligence about Barbarossa from Soviet agents in Berlin and Tokyo, scrawling across one report from Beria, the chief of Stalin's secret police, the NKVD, 'You can tell your "source" from the German Air Headquarters that he can go and fuck his mother. This is not a source, but a disinformant. I. St'[10]

Churchill was officially notified of the news of the invasion at 0800 on the morning of Sunday, 22 June. With Germany committed to such a large operation, it meant the pressure on Britain was partly lifted, giving Churchill some room to breathe. Despite his regular communications with Stalin on various matters, the fact remained that until just a few hours previously, Russia had been an enemy of Britain. With the invasion, everything changed in an instant; now, she was an ally. While that fact wasn't likely to be viewed as positive by a British public distrustful of the communist state, Churchill instinctively knew that, without British aid and support, Russia would fall. Churchill was as distrustful of communism as Hitler, but his desire to defeat the Nazi leader trumped *everything*.

There was no time for him to mull the situation over, or discuss it at length with cabinet colleagues; Churchill planned to broadcast to the nation later that day, so it was his decision, and his decision alone, to go ahead with an offer of assistance to Stalin. Having made the decision to give Russia all the aid that Britain could provide, he also resolved to apply maximum pressure to President Roosevelt for the US to do the same.

When he sat down to broadcast to a waiting nation at nine o'clock on Sunday, 22 June, he didn't pull his punches, but he saved his most florid style for his description of the new common enemy:

I see advancing upon all this [the Russian homeland and people] in hideous onslaught the Nazi war machine, with its clanking, heel-clicking, dandified Prussian officers, its crafty expert agents fresh from the cowing and tying down of a dozen countries. I see also the dull, drilled, docile, brutish masses of the Hun soldiery plodding on like a swarm of crawling locusts. I see the German bombers and fighters in the sky, still smarting from many a British whipping, delighted to find what they believe is an easier and a safer prey.

He then stressed that there was '. . . but one aim and one single, irrevocable purpose'. 'Any man or state,' he continued, 'who fights on against Nazidom will have our aid . . . It follows therefore that we shall give whatever help we can to Russia and the Russian people.'[11]

There was initially very little response from Stalin to this stirring rhetoric. A few extracts from the speech were published in *Pravda*; Churchill was asked to receive a Russian military mission. In return, a similar British mission was rapidly assembled and dispatched, arriving in Moscow on 27 June, led by Lieutenant General F. N. Mason McFarlane, CB, DSO, MC, the pre-war attaché in Berlin, who had allegedly recommended the assassination of Hitler. The senior air member of the Mission was Air Vice-Marshal A. C. Collier, CBE, with Group Captain I. C. Bird as his 'wingman'.[12]

Churchill was more accurate than he could possibly have known when he uttered the words in his broadcast about the Nazi war machine advancing in hideous onslaught, for they showed an almost freakish prescience. The war *we'd* fought against Hitler's forces was a world away from the war he was engaged in prosecuting in the east, which he referred to as a *rassenkrieg* [race war]. It was a war of extermination, without mercy or concern for human life. By the end of the first day of action, Stalin's forces were in complete and utter disarray. Hitler's forces were extraordinarily efficient in the execution of his generals' plans, and both brutal and swift in their actions. The Russians had been caught completely by surprise and were utterly unprepared for the blitz-krieg tactics of the Wehrmacht and SS, which steamrollered their way across huge swathes of Russian territory.

Entire armies were swallowed up and destroyed in the first weeks of the invasion, while Stalin's soldiers surrendered in their hundreds of thousands. The sheer scale and numbers are almost incomprehensible, as were the inhuman atrocities visited upon each side by the other – and in the case of the Russians, on his own people by Stalin and his agents. By the beginning of July, there was talk among Hitler's generals of the campaign having been won in just fourteen days. Some three million Soviet POWs would be captured in 1941, most of whom would not be accorded the protection of the Geneva Conventions; they would never be returned alive.[13]

By the beginning of July, the unstoppable Nazi war machine had taken Riga, having rolled through Russian-annexed Poland and the Baltic states. Göring's Luftwaffe was utterly dominant in this theatre, having achieved total air superiority and all but neutralised the Red Air Force. If Russia fell, Hitler's dream of a Nazi hegemony would be complete, stretching from France in the west, and encompassing almost every piece of land to Siberia. Churchill believed that Hitler's Russian conquest of Russia could be over within two months. Hitler would then be in a position to attempt an invasion of Britain before the end of October.

By 10 July, most of the city of Smolensk, just 260 miles west of Moscow, was in German hands, although a fierce battle raged in the northern part of the city which continued for a further two months. Encircled Russian armies refused to surrender and every single inch of territory yielded came at enormous cost in both manpower and materiel; territory was fought over street by street at a cost to the Germans of almost a quarter of a million men.

Smolensk was just one battle, however, and by mid-July it was clear that the Russians were retreating on all fronts. Stalin had his hands full, and it was not until 18 July that he made a direct response to Churchill's initial and follow-up messages of support. In a theme he returned to endlessly, Stalin suggested that the best help Britain could provide would be the opening of a Second

Front, in fact two fronts – one in northern France and one in the Arctic. This approach was noted by Churchill to be the first example of Stalin's 'monotonous disregard for physical facts'. At that time, Hitler had forty divisions in France alone, and the entire coastal area of northern France bristled with guns and fortifications.[14] We had stood alone against Hitler's forces for more than a year, so our own forces were stretched almost to breaking point.

Nevertheless, on 20 July Churchill replied in detail in another telegram directly to Stalin and said: 'We are also studying as a further development the basing of some British fighter air squadrons on Murmansk . . . some [aircraft] of which could be flown off carriers and others crated.'[15]

That same day, staff in the Air Ministry were studying two documents. The first, a long report of a reconnaissance visit to northern Russia by Group Captain F. L. Pearce, gave comprehensive details of infrastructure, logistical support and airfield characteristics for potential bases in and around both Archangel and Murmansk. A shorter note – signed off, also on 20 July 1941, by Group Captain A. D. Davies – provided the planning assumptions for the movement of an 'air force contingent' (at that time expected to comprise a Beaufighter and a Blenheim squadron as well as two Hurricane squadrons). The plan, at that stage, had all the Hurricanes being flown off a carrier. The others would be assembled at Archangel after transit as crated cargo. Group Captain Davies estimated that 'from the time the executive order is given' the squadrons would be ready to operate in forty-one days.[16]

Two days later, Sir Charles Portal, who had recently been appointed as Chief of the Air Staff, went to see Winston Churchill with an outline of the Air Ministry's plan to send a Hurricane wing to Murmansk.[17] Churchill told him to proceed at once.

The result of all these discussions was 151 Wing, Churchill's 'gift' to Stalin. The CO's very brief directive, issued by the Air Ministry, is marked 'Secret' and gives the mission the code name

'Force Benedict'. The directive appoints him as '. . . Force Commander of the R.A.F. in North Russia (No. 151 Wing)'.[18] The force's primary role, as directed, was to be '. . . the defence of the Naval base at Murmansk and cooperation with the Soviet forces in the Murmansk area'.[19]

6

An Assembly

I'd only been on leave at my mum and dad's house in Bourne-ville for a few days when a telegram was delivered for me. Dated 28 July 1941, it was terse, abrupt and direct. It said, 'RETURN TO UNIT IMMEDIATELY. STOP. ADJUTANT 456 SQUADRON. STOP.'

I was in the process of packing my stuff up when there was a knock at the front door. A police constable stood there.

'I'm looking for Sergeant Pilot Eric Carter.'

'Er, that's me. What can I do for you, Constable?'

'I have a message for you saying you're to report back to base immediately; you're wanted by your CO.'

Clearly something was afoot, so I said goodbye to my parents and jumped into my trusty Morris. When I got back to RAF Valley, though, it wasn't the CO of 456 who wanted to see me, but Squadron Leader Powell-Shedden at 615, who told both Johnny and me to pack our things up; we were being posted to 81 Squadron at RAF Leconfield for overseas duties.

Unknown to us, a similar scenario was being played out at RAF bases up and down the country, with squadron bosses being asked to send one or two pilots and/or ground crew to join either 81 or 134 – the two new squadrons being stood up to form 151 (Fighter) Wing.

On 27 July, a Fighter Command Movement Order instructed No. 17 Squadron, at that time on convoy protection duties, based in Scotland, to detach: '. . . one flight of 9 operational pilots and ground personnel plus the Squadron Leader and Adjutant, and move [them] to RAF Leconfield, by p.m. 28th July, to form the nucleus of No 134 Squadron, coming under 151 Wing to proceed overseas at short notice.'[1]

Similar manoeuvres gave birth to 81 Squadron, in this case with the nucleus of the squadron coming from 504 Squadron. That meant Artie Holmes, and his good pal Basil Bush [known as 'Bushy'], who had by now both received commissions, along with Wag Haw and his pal Ibby Waud were all Yorkshire-bound, as were Neil Cameron and Tim Elkington, plus a host of others. The transferring squadron commanders were Squadron Leaders Tony Rook for 81 and Tony Miller for 134.

So far so simple. But for the disparate mass of the rest of the forming wing, coming from far and wide, they had a merry old time getting to Leconfield.

Pilot Officer 'Scottie' Edmiston, recently transferred to Hurricanes after a highly successful tour on Defiants with 151 Squadron at Digby (he had one confirmed and five probables to his credit, including four at night, during just two months), responded to a call for volunteers for the Middle East.

Another traveller – like me, with a wingman – was Flight Sergeant (later Group Captain) Peter Knapton, a Hurricane pilot on 257 Squadron at RAF Coltishall since May 1941. On 28 July he was called in – with a fellow sergeant pilot, Hector Keil – to see the CO. This was the legendary Canadian squadron leader Howard Peter 'Cowboy' Blatchford. He'd made a name for himself during the Battle of Britain by being awarded the DFC after ramming a Fiat CR42 fighter when he'd run out of ammunition. He got so close that he took the pilot's head off with his propeller; when he returned to base, his airscrew was nine inches shorter than when he'd left, and his Hurricane's nose cone was covered in blood.

With averted eyes and apparent guilt in his tone, Blatchford said, simply: 'Keil and Knapton – you're posted to Leconfield for overseas service.' Peter Knapton found out years later that the guilty voice was because he'd been ordered to send two sergeant

71

pilots to the newly forming wing. The only way he felt able to do this was to put all sergeant pilots' names in a hat and draw out two. 'We did not know about this new method of RAF posting at the time,' reflected Peter in his memoir of the subsequent adventure.

RAF Leconfield was a fighter station in the East Riding area of Yorkshire. One of the RAF's newest, it had been built in 1936. A few hours after we arrived, we were all mustered in an empty hangar – some five hundred ground crew and support staff, and thirty-eight pilots. We were a mixed bunch of experience and inexperience, drawn from the RAF Volunteer Reserve, and the older, more established Royal Auxiliary Air Force (both of our squadron bosses, and many of our officers, were ex-Royal Auxiliary Air Force). We were also a mix of all nationalities, like the League of Nations. Four Australians served with the wing, including Sergeant Pilots Nat Gould, Bart Campbell and Nobby Clark. Hector Keil was from Rhodesia, Paddy McCann was from Belfast, David Ramsey was Canadian, there were a couple of Poles, and the boss was from New Zealand. Some, like Johnny and myself, had operational flying experience but had fired few shots in anger. Others like Artie Holmes, Wag Haw and Tim Elkington had flown in the Battle of Britain and had several kills to their names. Artie and Tim both knew the terror of being shot down and had deployed their parachutes. For others like myself, the parachute was something we sat on when we flew; I had no particular wish to have to clamber from the relative serenity of my cockpit into the maelstrom of violent noise and slipstream outside it, and to wonder, will my parachute deploy properly? If it does, will a German pilot try to shoot me as I descend to earth?

The bulk of the pilots in 81 Squadron had fought together in combat, so they'd forged a tight bond with one another. Thus Johnny and I felt very much outsiders, although we can't have been the only ones. We'd soon come to know one another; whatever we'd done, wherever we'd come from, we were now part of the same family, the two squadrons under 151 Wing with our new CO, a highly regarded test pilot and former New Zealand rugby player, the somewhat wonderfully and improbably named Wing Commander Henry Neville Gynes Ramsbottom-Isherwood, AFC.

Our CO had arrived at RAF Leconfield on 28 July. I remember him as square jawed, short and tough – much as you'd expect of a scrum-half. Flight Lieutenant Hubert Griffith, the wing adjutant, was a journalist and author of some repute, and someone who had made various trips to Russia before the war, so he understood the culture, language and people. According to him, Isherwood was: '. . . thirty-sixish, grey-haired, with a mouth that shuts like a steel trap. He is a test-pilot of long standing, and has probably forgotten more about flying than many young R.A.F. pilots have yet learnt. Also, he seems to like a joke.'[2]

I'd got chatting to another sergeant pilot who had introduced himself to Johnny and me as 'Nudger' Smith. Another chap with Nudger was introduced as 'Avro' Anson, and, as we were standing around talking, I saw two others walk over towards us.

'Hi, Wag, Ibby,' said Nudger to the two new arrivals. 'This here's Eric Carter – Ginger to everyone for obvious reasons,' he added, nodding towards my crop of ginger hair. 'And this here's Johnny – he and Ginger were together through training and at 615 Squadron.'

'Hello, Wag, nice to meet you,' I said. Then, 'Well, it's obvious why I'm known as "Ginger" but it's been bugging me – why does Smith go by the name of "Nudger"?'

'That's because he swore that if he ever got shot down and got the chop, he'd come back and "nudge" the lads,' Wag said, winking.

I heard other names being uttered and saw around us other pilots we'd soon come to know. There were the two Canadians, Jimmy Walker and Dave Ramsey, and Dicky Wollaston was an officer who was good pals with Peter Knapton.

After a short time, we all came to attention as Isherwood walked in. He stood us at ease as he addressed us:

'Now see here, you fellows,' he said in his unfamiliar, clipped New Zealand accent. 'We've been brought here to do a special job. I am sworn to secrecy about what it is, but there must be no talking on or off the camp about what happens to us from this moment on. All leave is cancelled forthwith. Nobody is allowed off the camp. All outgoing mail will be censored. The first thing is inoculations,' he went on, turning to the wing adjutant. 'All right Griffith, carry on.' His address had been short and without preamble. He immediately struck me as a no-nonsense fellow.

To a collective groan, Flight Lieutenant Hubert Griffith handed us over to a medical team lurking at the back of the hangar, who immediately went into action with hypodermic needles and a sinister assortment of multicoloured bottles. They scratched smallpox paste on our biceps and squirted a wide variety of revolting diseases into our buttocks and arms. The effects were both rapid and catastrophic; dead arms and bruised bottoms were the least of our worries. Fever, vomiting, dizziness and fainting smote us all. Both 81 and 134 Squadrons to a man retired to bed cursing their fate and disappeared from the face of Leconfield for forty-eight hours. There could have been no surer antidote to careless talk.

When we surfaced again, each man was issued with a mosquito net, the officers with a .45 Webley revolver and ammunition. The mosquito nets were a clever ruse to suggest that the wing was heading for a hot climate, a ruse that we were to discover later went as far as issuing us with hot-weather kit, and adding tropical climate air intakes to the Hurricanes we'd be shipping out with. The guns, on the other hand, were not a ruse; they were deadly serious.[3]

While we were *hors de combat* following our inoculations, life went on for the wing executive. The CO turned out to be an impressively 'hands-on' commander with a 'can-do' attitude, as evidenced by a request by the Air Ministry for his attendance at a conference in Whitehall. He was at Leconfield when the call came in around midday and the conference was due to start at 1500. My instinctive reaction would have been to say, 'Bugger off! Do you think I'm living just around the corner?' but then, perhaps that's one of the reasons he was the CO and I was a lowly sergeant pilot. His reaction was to somewhat coolly have lunch in the mess, following which he took a Spitfire and flew it to Northolt. From there he took a car to the Air Ministry, where he arrived five minutes *early* for the conference. Not bad considering he'd come all the way from Yorkshire. Even more impressive, though, was that he was back having drinks before dinner with his command team at Leconfield in the anteroom by 1800.[4]

They were a characterful bunch, our officers. Among the pilots were a pair of Rooks. One was a squadron leader and the other, his cousin, a flight commander. Rook major was tall, about 6 ft 1 in, with what Hubert Griffith described as 'a ferocious up-twirling black moustache and a chin like Philip IV of Velasquez. He looks almost too much like a stage fighter pilot to be true but has a very creditable record in the Battle of Britain.' Rook minor was even taller, about 6 ft 4 ins, and apparently insisted on referring to his cousin as 'Sir' whenever they were in the mess.[5] Another character was Flight Lieutenant Ross, who had to be one of the smallest pilots ever to fly a Hurricane – it's no exaggeration to say that he was only about four feet tall in his stockinged feet. Apparently, at one particularly raucous party in the mess, he was hoisted on to the enormously tall mantelpiece in the anteroom. He was unable to get down unaided as it was about twice as high as he was, so he was forced to stay there and make a speech to the assembled company. He did this with perfect nonchalance, as though he had been making speeches from mantelpieces all his life.

One of the most colourful officers was Neil Cameron, although he was a sergeant pilot when he arrived at Leconfield. That said, he'd had word that his commission, offered then withdrawn after his 'low-flying' incident during training, was back in the offing. Realising that, as a sergeant, the accommodation he'd be offered en route to our overseas posting would be of a lesser standard than that enjoyed by officers, he took matters into his own hands. Even though leave had been cancelled, he thought he'd apply for a few days nonetheless and, much to his surprise, it was granted. He then left for London and arrived at the Air Ministry to make a case that the commissioning procedure must be accelerated, but the civil service wasn't to be hurried, even in wartime.

As he describes in his autobiography,

> *This put us in a bit of a quandary. It was clear that we were destined for overseas somewhere but we did not have in our hands the actual commissioning authorisation. We decided that the only answer was to pay a call on Moss Bros in Covent Garden, persuade them that our commissioning was real and get the necessary uniforms and other kit. They were sympathetic to our persuasion and we left the shop fully kitted as pilot officers.*

After celebrating a little, they took the train back to Yorkshire. Their only hope was to put a bold face on the situation and hope that their papers would come through before they left the UK. Cameron carries on,

> *The CO seemed pleased to see us in our new rank and went out of his way to make us feel at home in the Officers' Mess. Happily, before we left England, the commissioning papers came through and we were made honest men, but it had been touch and go. The peacetime air force would have*

been deeply shocked, but times were not normal and
occasionally action had to be taken which was a little
unorthodox.[6]

Such behaviour clearly has its rewards. Neil Cameron later went
on to become Marshal of the Royal Air Force and Chief of the
Defence Staff.

7

Convoy

We'd been told we would be sailing overseas, but we weren't told where we were going, nor how long it would take to get there; we weren't allowed to take any leave, we weren't allowed to make any phone calls home, and we were told to visit the quartermaster and draw kit for the Middle East so, quite naturally, we thought that was where we were going. We soon realised that the Middle East was not our planned destination when two interpreters – who both spoke fluent Russian – joined 151 Wing. Then rumours (unusually, all true) started to surface that the wing adjutant, Hubert Griffith, was a Russian expert with experience of the country. It wasn't long before Russian dances were being performed in the mess!

It takes a lot of effort to keep just a few pilots airborne – those of us who flew the aircraft were but the tip of a veritable iceberg of support staff. I've already explained that 151 Wing comprised two squadrons – 81 and 134 – but it also had a Headquarters Unit. The two squadrons each had their own squadron commander, each their own flight commanders, their thirty or so pilots to fly the fighter aircraft, and then there were around one hundred airmen who worked on the ground to keep us in the air. The wing headquarters had its wing commander (the commanding officer or CO of the whole force), his wing adjutant (Hubert Griffith in our case, responsible for all staff and administrative issues), personnel responsible for medical kit, equipment, signals, engineering and maintenance. Then there was the transport section with its drivers and mechanics, the staff of cipher officers, and the run-of-the-mill ordinary aircraft hands – that is, non-technical personnel responsible for taking care of all the general fatigues and chores around camp. In all, for Wing HQ, there were about 350 bodies, so adding these to wing and squadron personnel, you're talking about some 550 people. And that's without our kit, equipment, aircraft, vehicles and other assorted kit. It was a logistical nightmare.

It's astonishing looking back just how quickly, and relatively efficiently, things happened. I mean, just think for a moment about what was involved. I think the sheer pace is indicative of just how *important* this mission was. From Churchill first mooting the idea of providing aid to Stalin by way of aircraft on 20 July, the squadrons being stood up, the CO being appointed, a base being organised for us and us all arriving there took just eight days. The British government had conceived, planned and organised Force Benedict, a military mission of two squadrons of aircraft, pilots and ground crew in a little more than a week. So, having been brought together in great haste, with a war on, and Stalin needing assistance, we kicked our heels. And then we kicked them some more.

The busiest man on 151 Wing at this time was Hubert Griffith, the wing adjutant. To him fell the legwork and the veritable mountain of paperwork that a new wing about to deploy on overseas operations generates. Also to him fell the unenviable task of finding ways to keep us occupied while arrangements were being made for ships to convey us and our Hurricanes to Russia, together with a convoy to escort us. One Saturday morning, he had the universally unpopular idea of a small route march, which, he suggested to the CO, was the perfect thing to 'keep the chaps fit' before we undertook what was likely to be a somewhat long sea journey. Isherwood thought this was a first-class idea and ordered that *everyone* should take part – including all of us pilots. You can imagine how *that* went down!

In the early hours of 12 August, we were roused from our beds and mustered in the hangar in full uniform with all our kit. We were loaded on to motor transport and driven to a completely empty train that stood waiting to receive us at Beverley station. You have to bear in mind that the blackout was in force, so once the train started moving, there was nothing to see outside. We sped through every station without stopping, but they would have offered us no clue even if we'd gone through at walking pace with searchlights cutting through the inky black that enveloped everything – all place names had been removed during the Battle of Britain to make life difficult for the German invasion force that we had been expecting. So we did what all servicemen and women do whenever they're headed somewhere and there's nothing else to do – we slept.

Time's elastic when you sleep so I've no idea how long we'd been travelling, but we eventually pulled into a siding. It was still pitch dark when we jumped off the train and were led along the track and into a large hall which, in turn, led to a covered corridor connected to a gangway and on to a ship. A glimpse of the Liver Building told us we were in Liverpool, and a short time later, a group of us stood at the ship's rail as we heard the gangways being hauled ashore. That was it; no way off, no way on. Ropes were cast off, our screws churned white foam from the Mersey under our stern and, without any fuss, she slipped her moorings and cast off into the night, destination, for some of us at least, uncertain.

Our new home was the SS *Llanstephan Castle,* which, before the war had been a luxury cruise liner plying the route between Europe and Africa for the Union Castle line. Built in 1914, by Fairfield of Glasgow, she'd been designed for the East African Service between England and Natal via Suez. She'd been requisitioned during the First World War, in 1917, when she carried troops across the Atlantic, and in 1919 she brought back the prime minister of South Africa, General Louis Botha, from the signing of the Treaty of Versailles.

In yet another sign of just how important our impending mission was, she'd been hastily converted into a troopship specifically to move elements of 151 Wing. I say converted, but you'd be hard pushed to tell. Most of us were in the lap of luxury. While the officers among us occupied two-berth first-class cabins, we sergeant pilots were hardly hard done by in our tourist-class cabins. We were three to a cabin – I shared mine with Johnny and Sergeant Pilot Ken Bishop, another good pal of ours in 81 Squadron. We dined with the ship's crew in their dining quarters, while our officers dined with the captain and his officers in the ship's lavishly appointed dining saloon, adorned with white pillars, mahogany walls and a sweeping double staircase that led to the lounge, and on through to the gym, squash court and swimming pool. Neil Cameron's self-commissioning jaunt when he sneaked off to London and bought himself an officer's uniform had paid off handsomely!

Prior to us embarking, the ship had recently been restocked in South Africa so the kitchens were operating on a peacetime scale with delicacies scarcely seen or unknown back in England for a year or more. Grapefruit, jam, butter, meat, fish and eggs, and the choice of at least half a dozen dishes for breakfast. There was also a duty-free bar. And each morning, we had tea in bed brought to us by the steward! We could scarcely believe our luck – wherever we were destined, whatever lay ahead of us, we were sailing there in conditions of opulence that some of us had never known, and that we were unlikely to experience again. It all lent a touch of unreality to everything. Billeted in such luxury, it was hard to believe we were on our way to war.

Stretching that belief even further was the fact that the *Llanstephan Castle* also carried some twenty-four civilian passengers. These included the members of the Polish Legation and their ladies, and a Czechoslovakian mission, with both parties heading to Moscow. There was Vernon Bartlett, MP for the Bridgwater constituency in Somerset, the American journalist Wallace Carrol, and Feliks Topolski – a Polish artist of some renown who seemed to be everywhere at once, always sketching and making notes. Finally, there was the rather delightful Mrs Charlotte Haldane, wife of the notable geneticist and communist J. B. S. Haldane. Charlotte was an interesting lady – she was accompanying us as a war reporter for the *Daily Sketch* newspaper and had caused something of a scandal in the 1920s when, already married to her first husband, Jack Burghes, she conducted an adulterous affair with Haldane, whom she'd fallen for while interviewing him for the *Daily Express*. To obtain a divorce from her husband, Charlotte sought advice from a private detective and together they planned for her to spend the night with John Haldane at London's Adelphi Hotel. The case received national publicity, as a result of which Haldane was expelled from Cambridge University for 'gross immorality'. The following May, the couple were married.

Feliks Topolski was travelling on the liner as an accredited war artist for both Polish and British governments, but he was also on contract to *Picture Post*, which published many of his drawings of 'Russia in War' after his return. The episode is covered in his autobiography[1] and a number of the drawings of his time on the *Llanstephan Castle* are in his book *Russia in War*.[2] Among them, there is a lively sketch of 'An improvised concert on the after-well-deck'.[3]

That image depicts a vigorous foreground figure, wearing flight sergeant crowns, who is energetically playing the spoons – or something very like them. Sergeant Pilot Peter Knapton recalls that concert in his own notes of the voyage: 'Topolski made a series of sketches of RAF personnel and one was a brilliant impression of Flight Sergeant "Doughie" Baker who played two bone clappers in one hand while dancing down the deck.'[4]

Topolski's *Fourteen Letters* makes it pretty clear it was a pair of spoons. On 29 August there was the first of a number of farewell parties. Topolski's diary recalls how 'A cockney sergeant dances a wooden puppet, plays on spoons – the heights of charm, of the comic's gestures; little legs twisty/mincing, rhythmical; the bunched shoulder blades the wittiest; pursed lips narrowed/ twisted cutely – a miracle of East End style.'[5]

Teresa, Topolski's daughter, recalls that the editor of *Picture Post* had a letter from a lady immediately after the picture of the spoons-playing flight sergeant had appeared. 'Thank you,' said Mrs Baker, 'I knew my husband was off somewhere but he wouldn't say where – now I know and I'm ever so pleased he's all right.'[6]

The sea was quite rough for the first couple of days but I soon got my sea legs. We sailed into Scapa Flow on 14 August, and I've never seen so many ships in a single place. It was as if most of the Royal Navy's fleet was at anchor here, and I saw at least three aircraft carriers. We didn't move off again until late evening on the 15th with a heavy escort, in a convoy with two cruisers, four destroyers and a couple of corvettes.

To pass the time, we did a lot of strolling on deck, initially. Being on a ship was still a new experience for me, although there wasn't much to observe. One day segued seamlessly into another with an endless expanse of ocean stretching in every direction. It was still relatively warm and the sea was millpond calm now, so we were in the habit of sunbathing on deck most of the day, while listening to a gramophone that was playing a steady stream of dance music. Funny how a term can take on a different meaning over time – the dance music we listened to was a world away from the dance music that teens and twenty-somethings listen to now. I was lucky enough to see a school of whales and dolphins spouting one afternoon, which was a real privilege. A few of us worked out that we were heading north because the sun hardly set. We'd walk around the deck at midnight and the rim of the sun would set just beneath the horizon, yet, within thirty minutes, it was on the point of rising again. *That* took some getting used to!

We still had no idea where we were going, but Artie Holmes, in a display of the sort of daring and chutzpah that saw him commissioned, befriended the ship's two radio officers, Icke and Vyle. He spent considerable time with them and they eventually confided in him that we were headed to Iceland. On 20 August, we arrived there having navigated the vertiginous rock walls either side of Seyðisfjörður to see a mammoth inland fjord. The sun was just setting as we arrived, creating a beautiful vista, with the snow-capped headland and mountains bathed in a delicious gold and red hue. It was truly breathtaking. Already moored on the lake when we arrived was an assortment of various Merchant and Royal Navy ships, while in the distance, the lights of some far-away town were twinkling.

The Wing HQ staff, most of 81 Squadron's pilots and most of the airmen were with us on board the *Llanstephan Castle*, but it didn't take us long to work out that the majority of the 134 Squadron pilots and assorted other personnel were missing. That night, we found out why. While the other sergeant pilots and myself dined, the officers were up on deck being addressed by the CO, Wing Commander Isherwood. He explained that when Hitler had launched his attack on Russia in June, Churchill and President Roosevelt had promised Stalin aid in the form of arms and equipment. Churchill's contribution was to include shipments of Hawker Hurricanes for the Red Air Force, which had been decimated in the earliest days of Operation Barbarossa by the Luftwaffe, and which was desperately short of up-to-date fighters. Our mission was to deliver the first batch of what would eventually be some three thousand Hurricane Mk IIBs to the Russian Air Force.

The much-loved, and vastly more manoeuvrable, Spitfires were coming on line quickly back home, so we had lots of Hurricanes going spare. The Mk IIB had a revamped and improved Merlin engine and was armed with twelve machine guns in place of the more usual eight. Our role was to teach their pilots to fly the aircraft, and their crews to maintain the engines, radios and armaments. Also, until the Russians were fully trained and operational on the Hurricanes, we would be defending the airfield and escorting Russian bombers over the German lines. We'd be putting our lives on the line to fight for a country that had, until a few months ago, been an enemy of Britain; I wasn't entirely sure how I felt about that.

The mission objective was for us to deliver the first batch of Hurricanes, defend the port of Murmansk and train the Russians to fly and maintain the aircraft. Simple. We'd leave all the equipment we had brought with us behind for the Russians, and possibly one or two of the engineering, wireless and armaments technicians. It was reckoned that we'd probably be on our way home by the end of October at the latest, although I have to say a great number of us worried about the truth behind that statement. For starters, nobody seemed to have given any thought to how, or exactly when, we'd be getting home. Aside from that obvious obstacle, how could anyone possibly know what the picture on the ground would be then? What if Murmansk was captured and fell into German hands? What about the weather? It was only going to get colder, and fog, thick ice and snow would feature. We would be fighting *at all costs* to defend Murmansk, but that sounded very much like a suicide mission to me. Just to confuse the issue a little more, Churchill was obviously keen to maintain diplomacy, because once we arrived in theatre, while the CO would still maintain full operational control of 151 Wing, it would be under the aegis of the Soviet commander of the Army Air Force of the Northern Front, Major General for Air Kouznetsova.

Some of the Hurricanes were crated up in the holds of the cargo ships in the convoy moored on the lake alongside us. They had preceded us by separate routes to Iceland. Having flown Hurricanes, it was difficult to imagine them boxed up, but then the crates were appropriately sized to take them – some 30 ft 2 ins x 10 ft 6 ins x 9 ft 3 ins and each one weighing some five tons.[9] The remainder were fully assembled and ready to go, along with the missing pilots and ground crew, on the aircraft carrier HMS *Argus*, which was also on the lake near by. Now I knew where Bushy, Wag and Ibby were; they, along with Tim Elkington, Neil Cameron, the two Rooks Tony and Mickey and a host of others were on the *Argus*, a few hundred yards away from us, out on the lake. That night, we exchanged greetings in Morse by torchlight.

Our convoy was to be met in the Arctic Ocean by a Russian battleship, the *October Revolution,* and escorted to Archangel, where the crated aircraft were to be unpacked, assembled by squadron technicians and then flown across the White Sea to Murmansk – by us. So we'd soon discover if they had been put together properly. Apparently, Wing Commander Isherwood had originally been pencilled in to test-fly the Hurricanes once constructed – his background was as a test pilot, after all – but instructions came in a signal from the Air Ministry that he was forbidden to fly over Russia because of the risk to the overall mission; if he was shot down and captured, it might have enabled the Germans, by torture or other means, to learn the strategy of this and subsequent convoys taking the Arctic route to Russia.

Shortly after our convoy left British shores, a secret cipher message arrived in the Air Ministry at 0345 on 14 August. Sent by AVM Collier, the Russian-speaking head of the British Mission in Moscow, it opened with the following discouraging words:

> <u>Para One</u>. *Your X.722 8/8. Russian Naval Staff confirm that 24 Hurricanes can land at Vojenga repeat Vojenga* [sic: a transliteration of Vaenga] *ex carrier and that whole British force will be based at this aerodrome only. Russians state categorically that direct new railway from Archangel to Murmansk is not yet working. They strongly recommend erection of 16 cased aircraft at Archangel and flight thence to Vojenga. Vojenga under air bombardment daily and*

*unsuitable for large scale erection. Naval staff will make all
preparations for work to be done by R.A.F. party at
Archangel.*

*Para Two. Russians recommend that ground personnel
equipment supplies and M.T. shall be transhipped at
Archangel and moved by sea to Kem thence by rail to
Murmansk and Vojenga. Journey from Archangel to
Vojenga should take about five days.*[10]

No doubt this all came up in the briefings between the CO and
the senior officers of the wing while we'd been at sea.

Something imperceptible had changed when we awoke on our
first morning in Iceland. I'm not sure it was even tangible, but we
were left in no doubt that somebody back in Blighty was taking
Churchill's promises to Stalin seriously. I awoke well before the
steward knocked to deliver our morning cup of tea courtesy of
the clatter of countless winches pulling up anchor chains. The
ship didn't look any different, but what had hitherto been a floating luxury hotel had suddenly turned into a fighting ship. We
were most definitely off to war now.

We slipped away from the fjord leaving Iceland in our wake,
our convoy having grown substantially from when we arrived the
previous day. As we steamed north, various ships fell into station
as if ordered by some unseen hand, our pace governed by the
slowest vessel in the convoy. Minesweepers headed the pack, the
destroyers playing sheepdog. Life for those of us from the wing on
board fell back into its routine, but there was a heightened sense
of industriousness and discipline about the ship's crew, who went
about their duties in a controlled, purposeful manner. They were
still friendly and accommodating towards us, but our interactions
were briefer and less frequent than before.

Feliks Topolski, Charlotte Haldane and the other civilian
passengers weren't there to freeload their way to Moscow; many
of them were experienced speakers, so Hubert Griffith decided to

offer the 550 officers and men a series of lectures to pass the time. Although these were entirely voluntary, almost every one of us on board took advantage. The main dining saloon was the largest space on board with accommodation for 250 people, so each lecture took place at 1100 with a repeat at 1500 for those unable to make the first one.

There was little to trouble us as we sailed, and aside from the daily Commanding Officer's inspection of quarters, the routine was idleness and well-being, so the lectures were a welcome and interesting diversion. Any romantic visions of Russia being some sort of earthly paradise that we may have had were quickly dispelled when Hubert Griffith gave us a lecture on the subject. Given that he was a fluent Russian speaker who had both visited and lived in the country before the war, we listened intently to what he had to say because most of us knew nothing of the distant land we were heading to and that we would be fighting for. The main gist of this long and informative lecture was the fact that until just twenty-five years earlier – a single generation – Russia was the most backward country in Europe, and not by a little bit; he quoted from the memoirs of the last French ambassador to the court of the tsars, M. Paléogue, who described the country as '. . . like the rest of Europe before the Reformation of the sixteenth century, before the renaissance of the fourteenth century'. Griffith backed this up with a whole raft of facts and gave us a brief historical analysis of illiterate, peasant Russia. He said, 'In the year 1914, 90% of the Russian population was illiterate – 90% of all the Russian peasant soldiers going to fight against Germany could not read, could not spell out the simplest placard – and did not know if the "Germany" they were fighting against was a man or a woman or a thing.'[7]

He pointed out that the Russia we were going to had advanced enormously in the past twenty-five years. It was now industrialised, organised and with a population educated enough that it was able to field millions of troops to fight on almost equal terms with Hitler. But he didn't mince his words when he described what we were likely to find when we arrived there: 'It's possible that we will have a camp of wooden huts, set down in a mud-flat, and seeing the geographical situation that we will be in, we will have to grin and pretend that we like it.'[8]

The following day, we crossed 67½ degrees into the Arctic Circle. The weather was noticeably colder than it had been, and the sea and sky merged into one purple-black hue. The water, which had been choppy on our voyage since leaving Iceland, became rough, and whenever we ventured out on deck now, we held on tightly as our convoy of ships lurched into troughs and crested the summits of waves, which crashed noisily over the rails. At the 75th parallel, the whole convoy slewed 90 degrees to the right and began heading east in an attempt to avoid detection by Jerry submarines and recce aircraft from German-occupied Norway and Finland. Artie later told me that Icke had informed him that, if we were torpedoed now, there would be no point in trying to get out of the water; it was so cold, we'd have been dead from hypothermia within two minutes. It was no bad thing that we sergeant pilots didn't know of that fact at the time.

Once we were north of the Arctic weather station at Bear Island, the southernmost island of the Norwegian Svalbard archipelago, we met the reinforcements for our naval escort. If we'd had any doubts that we were headed into the lion's den previously, they vanished here. The sheer size of the armada that awaited us was astonishing in both concept and scale, and a clear sign that we were approaching dangerous waters. Their presence was paradoxically both reassuring and horrifying. Seeing them there really concentrated our minds. Fighting ships dotted the horizon like jewels on a chain.

Waiting for us to join them were the cruiser HMS *Shropshire*, the aircraft carrier HMS *Victorious*, five destroyers including *Electra*, *Impulsive* and *Active*, plus a further two cruisers. Our six merchantmen – *Lancastrian Prince, New Westminster City, Esneh, Trehata*, the fleet oiler *Aldersdale*, the Dutch freighter *Alchiba*, and not forgetting our humble liner the SS *Llanstephan Castle* – with their cargoes of fifteen crated Hurricanes, transport lorries, wireless tenders, stores, equipment, provisions and spirits for 550 RAF men [beer was too heavy and bulky] were being escorted by no fewer than twenty-four naval craft, each one bristling with enough armaments and weapons to start a small war on its own.

The convoy was so large, it had its own name: Operation Dervish – and our ship was also the commodore ship, with Captain J. C. K. Dowding in command. Though we did not know it then, we had just formed the first of what would prove to be seventy-eight Arctic convoys that would continue ferrying vital supplies and provisions from Britain, Iceland and the US to Russia until the end of the Second World War.

Two days out from Archangel, we were due to rendezvous with the *October Revolution*, the Russian battleship. That would release our escort to head back across the Arctic to meet the next convoy, which was due out of Greenland and loaded almost entirely with Hurricanes. The *October Revolution*, meanwhile, would act as our guide south through the minefields guarding the entrance to the River Dvina.

For several days, there was nothing to see from the ship but a world of dull and unmitigated dreariness. It was impossible to see where the sky ended and the sea began; they were both one big morass of steely grey. As a group, those of us on the *Llanstephan Castle* withdrew from the outside world – the habit of communicating with the other ships in our convoy using Morse messages sent by torchlight or signal lamps fell by the wayside very quickly. On board, we organised table tennis and darts tournaments, while others played all manner of card games or read whatever books were around.

Food continued to play a starring role for everyone on board; Ken, Johnny and myself had made a good pal in one of the cooks.

One night, he brought us three pheasants; where he got them from is anybody's guess. We got one each, followed by tinned fruit and cream. On other nights, he gave us roast chicken, even turkey, but always followed by the fruit and cream desserts and, on one occasion, he even produced some strawberries. Our officers weren't exactly enduring hardships on the dining front either. The wing's senior medical officer Squadron Leader Jackson's menu card for dinner on the night of 30 August is signed by members of the Polish and Czech missions and bears his portrait, sketched and signed by Topolski. It reveals that after the varied hors d'oeuvres, the consommé and the suprême of turbot, diners could choose from three main meat courses, have two sorts of potatoes, green beans and salad before either '*Pouding Soufflé Orléans*' or '*Chartreuse of Green Figs*'.[11]

The lectures continued; Johnny, Ken and I went to a fascinating one conducted by the flirtatious and dynamic Charlotte Haldane, entitled 'Domestic Life in Russia'. It was a real eye-opener, and the room was, as usual, packed. She writes very warmly of her audience in *Russian Newsreel*, her book about her experiences in Russia. She says, 'The questions asked at the end of my lecture showed a very high level of intelligence; a good grasp of political and international affairs. These boys had brains and were using them. I was proud to be going to Russia with them.'[12] Pilot Officer Dicky Wollaston recounted to Peter Knapton that Ms Haldane was rather taken with him [Wollaston] and he had been spending time with her in her cabin. I wouldn't like to suggest what they got up to in there, but I doubt they were discussing the weather. Let's just say that Dicky was engaged in 'international affairs'.

A series of lectures were given by the wing's senior medical officers. These encompassed such need-to-know information as general bodily hygiene, diseases, frostbite, snow blindness, care of food and water . . . oh, and VD, which made us wonder just what awaited us at the other end. Russian women? I'd never so much as seen a picture of one, but the medical staff obviously thought it prudent to warn us of the risks if we were to indulge in the sins of the flesh while on ops.

Another popular pastime to while away the hours on our voyage to Russia was learning the language. Flight Lieutenant Hodson, one of 151 Wing's intelligence officers, was fluent in Russian and held lectures twice a day. He had been born, and lived much of his life, in the Russia of the tsars before the Bolshevik Revolution. It was a difficult language to learn, although we soon managed to master the alphabet and some basic phrases and words. That was as far as it went for many of us; for my part I was just content to be able to say 'please' and 'thank you' or drink a toast to those who were to be our new hosts. Perhaps the most important phrase we learned, though, was, '*Я английский язык. Я не понимаю русский*'. It translates as 'I am English. I do not understand Russian.'

Among our passengers and cargo was an American Army Air Corps officer and some fifty-one Curtis Tomahawk P40 fighters. Peter Knapton did some research on this fellow and writes in his unpublished memoirs of the trip,

The young United States Army Air Corps officer was going to Russia to advise the Soviet Air Force on the assembly and operation of the Tomahawk fighter. His lone mission must have played a significant part in the battle as the Tomahawk was a good, strong fighter, very suitable to the rough conditions on the Russian front. I cannot recall the US officer's name but from American Historical Research Records, it is probable that it was either Captain Thomas or 2nd Lt Cook. The latter name does seem familiar. He disembarked at Archangel and with a small American team started to assemble the first 51 P40s. These aircraft were to be the first of 1800 fighters and light bombers supplied by the US Government over a period of nine months (October 1941 – June 1942).

*In a subsequent report from the American team in
Archangel, they praised the 50 Russian mechanics who
assembled the P40s under their guidance. According to the
US officers, the Soviet mechanics were superior to their
equivalent in the US Army.*[13]

Everything was going well on board the SS *Llanstephan Castle* as
we sailed ever farther towards our objective, but that all changed
when we were just outside our rendezvous point with the *October
Revolution*. The world outside was a mass of low, thin cloud that
seemed near enough to touch; it covered all around it like a blanket, obscuring both the horizon and the near distance, which was
fortunate for us, because we could hear a twin-engined aircraft
flying directly above us. Every now and then we'd get a glimpse
of blue through the thin cloud, so we knew it was a German
reconnaissance aircraft – most likely a Ju88 – and it was hunting
for us. The Germans must have known where to look – it was too
much of a coincidence that they just happened to know the exact
time and position of our rendezvous with the battleship – leading us to conclude that the convoy's progress had been leaked by
someone on the Russian side. That was a little discomfiting;
what were we sailing into?

All engines were shut down to prevent the telltale sign of smoke
from the ships' funnels giving our exact positions away in what
was effectively a deadly game of cat-and-mouse. Radio silence
was observed throughout, so each ship just sat, drifting, listening,
waiting. Eventually, the German aircraft had to cut and run for its
base in Finland – its fuel load was always going to be a factor in
how long it could stay aloft – and we were, if only temporarily, off
the hook.

The upshot of it was that the commodore decided we would go
it alone through the Russian minefields. We hadn't been able to
communicate with the *October Revolution* owing to the radio
silence, so he decided to release the Royal Naval escort that had

guided us this far so it could turn back and head to its next objective. It was a judgement call based on the fact that the Ju88 had failed to get a visual confirmation of our position owing to the low cloud, so it was unlikely the Luftwaffe command would commit to sending waves of bombers for a convoy it couldn't see.

The message came down, 'All personnel are to wear lifebelts and warm clothing continually, day and night, and to stay within reach of their own lifeboat.' The commodore said, 'Good luck all,' to which some wag in our merchantman's crew, breaking the tension, retorted, 'And you'll bloody well need it! It's about time the RAF got its feet wet.'

With the escort released, we fell into line astern with two minesweepers leading us, clearing a narrow path for the rest of the convoy to follow through safely. The tension was unreal; the water had a language of its own and spoke silently to us through its appearance – cold, black, deep and uninviting. We'd enjoyed our voyage to date; we'd got our sea legs and were savouring the laid-back life of luxury we'd become accustomed to in the past couple of weeks, so this was a rude awakening of the worst kind. We were miles from home, with enemy forces all around us, surrounded by freezing-cold water. Were we to take a hit, it would be instantly cold, cruel and dangerous, and probably the end of all of us.

For all that, though, our luck held as we steamed south through the Barents Sea towards Russia and on through a gap and into the White Sea – misnamed, I thought, as I contemplated the black waves that rolled towards us on our voyage through it. Low cloud was both our constant companion and safety blanket; we never heard another enemy aircraft, and thanks to our minesweepers living up to their name and finding and destroying two mines, the entire convoy got through the minefield unscathed.

But we weren't in the clear just yet as we still had to navigate our way across the White Sea, which began as a relatively narrow 31-mile-wide channel that ran inland for 100 miles or so, before opening out both left and right into a stretch of water some 300 miles long. Westwards it reached Kandalaksha, almost on the Finnish border, and 30 miles east to the River Dvina, on which lay our final destination of Archangel. To the right side of the channel, the low-lying land was mostly bogs and lakes, a result of some six feet of snow that lay over winter and thawed in the spring with nowhere to drain away. A hundred miles to the west of this bogland lay the port of Murmansk. It was from Vaenga aerodrome, near Murmansk and just 20 miles east of the German lines, that 151 Wing was to operate.

It took us two anxiety-filled days and nights to navigate that channel into the White Sea and, on 1 September, we turned into the River Dvina for the final 15 miles of our three-week odyssey. The services of a Russian river pilot were engaged for this final leg, along which the riverbanks were stacked high with timber. Pine logs cut from inland forests floated downriver, directed by men in spiked boots who walked across the floating logs as if it was the most natural thing in the world. As most of us stood watching from the deck, it occurred to me that I don't think I'd ever seen so much wood in various stages of production. It was being cut, seasoned and stripped everywhere we looked. There were few buildings, but those I saw were all of primitive, rudimentary design and made, predictably, from wood. They were a resourceful lot – we later learned that the only tools used in their construction were cross-cut saws, hammers and axes.

As we came ever closer to Archangel, it became clearer and clearer that distance lent enchantment to the view. What appeared from afar to be a massive fortress turned out to be a decrepit customs house. A majestic opera house turned out to be a tawdry stucco structure which had taken the place of the architecturally perfect Russian cathedral, with its gilded domes and mosaic façades, all destroyed during the Bolshevik anti-God campaign of 1917.

We also got our first sight of Russian women, all of whom appeared to be dressed in blanket shawls, heavy skirts and clogs.

The material was shapeless, making the women appear squat and broad, and I can't have been the only man on board who wondered just why the medical team had bothered to warn us of the dangers of VD. As I stood there wondering, my thoughts were violently interrupted by the unmistakable sound of rifle fire, and it was being aimed at us! We were quickly hastened away from the rails, but not before one of the rounds found a target, and our secret mission to Russia had its first casualty; a member of the ship's crew had taken a round through the arm. What a time to find out that our uniforms resembled those of the Germans! It served as a reminder to me that, just a few weeks earlier, we and the Russians had been enemies.

It appeared to some that we still were.

8

From Little Acorns . . .

The wooden wharf which awaited us at Archangel gave us immediate and significant problems. Its uselessness was all the more pronounced given that the *Llanstephan Castle* was a good 50 feet from the riverbank when she dropped anchor owing to the shallow depth of the water there. Before we could leave the ship, a temporary wharf would have to be hastily assembled. That evidently wasn't a problem in Russia as suddenly several hundred Russians appeared seemingly from nowhere and began to build one. Other than that, nothing else of note happened for at least an hour. It was all rather surreal looking out from the ship that had been our luxurious home at such a featureless, barren landscape. It all looked so . . . primitive. We couldn't help but wonder what awaited us at our eventual destination.

A short time later, a Russian admiral's launch swung alongside us. His yacht was probably the smartest thing in all of northern Russia on the evidence so far. A newly built vessel, it was about the size of a Royal Navy sloop, a wonder of gleaming white paint, polished brass and, in the admiral's cabin, equally polished wood. As well as the rather young-looking Russian rear admiral, Air Vice Marshal Collier was on board. He was the Russian-speaking head of the British Air Mission that had flown ahead of us to Moscow to arrange and coordinate the specifics of our trip with the Russians. With him from Moscow was his colleague, Group Captain Bird. Also present were two Royal Navy liaison officers. They were shortly joined on board by Wing Commander Isherwood, the wing's wireless and engineering officers, and Hubert Griffith. As I say, it was a size-able yacht.

The maxim says that no plan survives first contact with the enemy, but in Archangel the plan that the CO and the wing's executive officers had worked on so carefully during the course of our three-week voyage didn't even survive getting off the ship. It collapsed spectacularly in on itself as the meeting unfolded.

During the voyage, the CO had been working out a plan of action should AVM Collier and his party fail to show. His inten-tion was to shift the bulk of the main party by road to Murmansk, using its own vehicles, but he soon realised on arrival that there were no roads at all from the banks of the River Dvina. Trains were no good either – the Kandalaksha–Murmansk railway had been bombed the night before we arrived by the Germans and put out of action. At the meeting, it was hastily decided that the only thing to do was to utilise all air and sea resources and make use of the railway as and when it was repaired.

A small engineering party would be sent to an island aero-drome at Keg-Ostrov in the mouth of the River Dvina, a few miles outside Archangel, to assemble the Hurricanes that had arrived crated in our convoy. Artie Holmes, Dicky Wollaston and Mickey Rook would test-fly the aircraft as they were assembled, while the rest of us pilots would wait to ferry the Hurricanes to Murmansk once they were all completed.

One of the things the CO had to ensure was that all the pilots didn't travel together – if they did, and their vehicle was hit by enemy fire, it would have jeopardised the whole mission, so he decided to split the wing into five groups.

A party of 200 souls under the wing commander would be transported on the two Royal Navy destroyers HMS *Electra* and HMS *Active* and would depart within forty-eight hours. Two days later, yet another group was to go by Russian tramp steamer to Kandalaksha and from there by train to the airfield at Vaenga.

Finally, two more parties would make the entire journey by train once the bombed rail link had been repaired.

As if we didn't have enough problems already, another presented itself when unloading of the wing's equipment stowed in the cargo hold of the *Llanstephan Castle* began. The fitters', riggers' and armourers' toolkits and other equipment had all been lumped together in boxes without labels and packed in the lowest of the ships' holds.

So while the CO dealt with the problems of unloading and transport that confronted him, the aircraft carrier HMS *Argus*, carrying Neil Cameron, Tim Elkington, Wag, Ibby and the rest of the wing's pilots, plus the remaining Hurricanes, ploughed its way through the waves en route to Murmansk. Conditions aboard the *Argus* were about as utilitarian and spartan as it got. Space on board was at a premium because the *Argus* was a converted merchant ship that, to use the current vernacular, wasn't really fit for purpose. It had been captured from the Italians in the First World War, given to the Royal Navy and, to put it simply, clearly wasn't designed for the job it had been pressed into service to do. Most of the ship's superstructure had been cut away to allow for the installation of the rather flimsy steel flight deck, which was just 360 ft long.

From time to time, Ibby and Wag would go below the decks to where their new Hurricanes were stowed, although the wings had been removed to accommodate them and would have to be bolted on before flight. They were still sufficiently in love with the idea of flying that they'd sit in the cockpits, feel the controls, and imagine what would confront them once they finally got to Vaenga and started flying patrols over Russia. Wag had combat experience from the Battle of Britain but he was still plagued with insecurity; would he cut it in Russia? Was he really as good as everyone else? Ibby, on the other hand, was like Johnny and me; he was yet to shoot anyone down, so for all of us, Russia would be a good opportunity for us to build up our combat experience.

Tim Elkington's diary records that on 18 August,

> *. . . the First Sea Lord gave us a briefing which told us that we, as 151 Wing, had been promised by Churchill in response to Stalin's demands for support. Our role was to be the defence of the naval base of Murmansk and co-operation with the Soviet forces in the Murmansk area. We were to instruct the Soviet authorities in the operation and maintenance of our aircraft and ground equipment, which was then to be handed over to them.*

Midway through the voyage, the twenty-four pilots on the *Argus* attended a briefing where they learned that they were to fly off the ship's flight deck and land at Vaenga. Not a single one of them had ever attempted anything remotely approaching a carrier take-off before, and they were hardly eager to try once they'd paced it and realised, with mounting horror, just how short 360 ft really was. The Navy provided a Fleet Air Arm officer to instruct them just how to effect the take-off, although the exercise was somewhat academic as he could offer them only theory, which they already knew. One thing he told them was that they should give the ramp at the end of the flight deck a decent thump to help the aircraft get airborne. There could be no practice attempts, though; their take-offs had be to right first time, or not at all. There were no second chances. This preyed on their minds for the rest of the journey.

During the briefing, they were informed that, given the far northern latitude they were in, the normal magnetic compasses in the cockpits wouldn't work accurately – certainly nowhere near close enough for accurate navigation. The two squadron commanders, Tony Rook of 81, and Tony Miller of 134, said that the plan was for them to get airborne and as soon as three of them were up, they would do a circuit of the *Argus*, pick up a destroyer that would deploy on the horizon, fly down the length of it and, at the same time, set their gyro compasses. This would be the means that they would employ to reach the Russian coast, where they would turn right and navigate to Vaenga aerodrome, which should be a few miles inland on the left. Finally, they were told to keep an eye out for any bandit aircraft in the vicinity.

The *Argus* sailed through a blanket of fog for most of her voyage north, and there was no sign of it abating as they finally made a turn south towards the Russian coast, where she took up her position on the night of 6 September, slightly out to sea. There was insufficient wind for the Hurricanes to attempt a take-off, though, so the carrier described slow circles in the sea as she steamed round and round waiting for things to improve.

The first six aircraft to go had been brought up to the flight deck earlier in the night; there was only room on deck for six at a time, so they would have to depart before the next six could be brought up. The pilots were awakened at 0200 with breakfast for anyone up to eating it so early in the day. Few took advantage, simply preferring to make their way up to the flight deck in readiness. They were wearing battledress, fur-lined flying boots and Mae Wests. Most had gone down to the hangar deck the previous evening and placed their helmet, goggles and oxygen masks in their respective cockpits along with any other items of kit they'd need for the flight. While the first six pilots got themselves strapped in and ready to go, the others sought sanctuary from the vantage point of the safety nets. The sea was calm and there was a gentle breeze blowing. The pilots felt the vibrations as the captain of the *Argus* ordered the engines up to full – the carrier would need to go full ahead if the Hurricanes were to have any chance at all of getting airborne. They'd need every single one of her 17 knots, plus whatever wind there was, in order to take off.

Tony Miller, the 134 Squadron boss, led from the front and was the first to go. He cycled his Hurricane's Merlin XX engine up and let the brakes off, his aircraft sprinting down the deck. He did exactly what the Fleet Air Arm officer had suggested and pulled hard back on the stick as he reached the wooden sloping ramp at the end. The Hurricane leapt into the air in a perfect take-off and the rest of the pilots breathed a sigh of relief. Then they noticed that the undercarriage had been damaged by the ramp and wouldn't retract. They realised that they'd have to find a way to get airborne before they hit the ramp. One down, twenty-three to go.

The second aircraft to go let off the brakes and went for it; the watching pilots crossed their fingers and looked intently at the receding image of the Hurricane as it charged down the flight deck and, as per the instructions from the Fleet Air Arm officer, its pilot yanked hard back on the stick and got its nose well up. The audience gasped as the aircraft clipped the ramp and promptly disappeared over the edge of the carrier. Convinced both aircraft and pilot had plummeted to a watery grave, they looked around at one another, shocked, just as the aircraft's nose reappeared above the ramp, swiftly followed by the rest of the fuselage as it struggled aloft and climbed out to join up with Tony Miller's circling aircraft. It hadn't escaped completely unscathed, though – a substantial piece of the propeller sat on the ramp, sheared from the rest of its components as it made heavy contact with it. The next aircraft to depart suffered exactly the same fate. Its pilot too managed to keep it aloft, but its under-carriage hung uselessly beneath the aircraft. It was a depressing start to the operation and a very sad and sorry Vic formation of Hurricanes that eventually struggled towards Vaenga.

Neil Cameron was in the second six aircraft to depart, and the pilots, having learned from the mistakes made ahead of them, got away without trouble. Wag was due to leave in the third wave and watched with interest as he saw his Hurricane 'H for Harry' being brought up from the depths of the carrier. The ground crew worked quickly and expertly in preparing it for take-off and, within minutes, Wag was climbing into the familiar cockpit. It was comforting being inside the aircraft once again, awaiting his turn to depart. He hadn't flown for well over a month, and he drank in the familiar smells, and the feel of the controls as his hands and feet rested on them. He reminded himself that the aircraft wasn't fully armed as he remembered the boys telling him that only six of the Hurricane's twelve machine guns had been fitted, in order to save valuable weight. With such a short flight deck, every ounce saved could be the difference between lifting into the waiting sky, or tipping nose first into the inky-black depths beneath the ramp.

Wag watched his number-one roar down the deck ahead of him and get airborne without mishap. As the ground crew manoeuvred his aircraft into position and signalled to him, he selected partial flap, opened the throttle and cycled up the mighty Merlin XX engine, holding the machine's urge to sprint forward in check with the brakes. As soon as his ground crew signalled, he released the brakes and shoved the throttle fully open. The ramp beckoned him from the end of the flight deck, mocking him, daring him to overcook it and to mess up the take-off. He aimed for a spot just before it and pulled the stick towards his stomach, grinning to himself as he felt the aircraft lift off perfectly and climb skywards, slipping the chains of gravity in a climbing turn.

Looking around as he retracted the flaps and the wheels, he spotted his number-one circling the *Argus* and together they climbed up to 1,300 ft as the final Hurricane in their stick caught up and completed the Vic formation. Slightly ahead and to their right, they could see the destroyer lined up, pointing the way to the Russian coast, and, as they flew down its length at altitude, the three pilots set their gyro compasses to zero as a directional aid. Soon after passing over the destroyer, they flew into thick fog, closing up into tight formation to maintain visibility with one another and dropping down towards sea level, barely skimming the wave tops in order to fly in clear air. Twenty minutes later, the weather above them cleared and they gained altitude just as they caught their first glimpse of the Barents Sea. Ahead, on the horizon, they saw land. It was barren and devoid of any sign of human life, a featureless landscape that seemed drained of colour, reflecting the steely greyness of the clouds above. Visibility was good despite the cloud, and Wag pumped the throttle in order to maintain speed as the formation banked towards starboard and flew along the coastline in search of Vaenga.

It wasn't difficult to spot, despite the grey cloud that hung over everything like a pall. Wag saw the Hurricanes that had landed ahead of him lined up below, including two which were lying on their bellies, having made crash landings as a result of the earlier accidents with the ramp at the end of the flight deck. He could see a group of men standing around them; Russians by the look of them, he thought.

From the air, it appeared to be a sizeable base, oval shaped and about three or so miles in length running east to west, which, Wag assumed, was a result of the direction of the prevailing winds there. There were no paved runways; indeed, there were no identifiable runways of any sort, and no hangars or other buildings of the type you'd usually find at a major operational airfield, which is what Vaenga was supposed to be if the briefing he'd had was correct. The surface looked to be covered in a grey, sandy-coloured substance. He joined the circuit and lost height as he throttled back, adding a touch of flap on the approach. He felt the aircraft buck and kick on landing, a result of the undulating, rough, bumpy surface that served as some form of runway. As he turned off and parked the aircraft with the others at dispersal, his aircraft was instantly surrounded by Russian fighter pilots from the three squadrons already based there.

Wag shut down his Hurricane, pulled back the canopy and climbed out on to the wing. Then he jumped down on to Russian soil for the first time. He looked around, smiled, and drank deeply of the clear, cold air. At last, after a journey that had been signed off by Churchill just six weeks earlier, the first RAF Hurricanes were in Russia.

9

The Erection Party

The small engineering party that had been sent to the small island aerodrome at Keg-Ostrov to assemble the crated Hurricanes soon acquired the name 'The Erection Party' – with all the ribald comment the term encourages. It was led by Flight Lieutenant Harry Gittins, the wing's engineering officer, assisted by his No. 2, Warrant Officer Hards, and their labour force of rank-and-file technical airmen. Harry Gittins was a regular RAF officer, a cheerful, upbeat fellow with a keen sense of humour. He was a little older than his peers, very capable, organised and calm. He'd need to be, given the difficulties his team would face.

The party left the *Llanstephan Castle* after breakfast one morning in early September and was transported by boat to the airfield at Keg-Ostrov, which was about an hour away on the other side of the river, opposite Archangel. There, they found the crated Hurricanes awaiting them, dumped outside hangars on a rough, uneven mudflat. That in itself presented the immediate problem of how to shift each 4½-ton crate into its hangar.

However, just to make life a little more difficult, the team discovered that many of the essential tools they needed to assemble the aircraft – including the unique airscrew spanners, vital for fixing on the heavy three-bladed propellers – were missing.

Fortunately, engineers across the world are fluent in a common language in which words aren't necessary to communicate certain practical matters. Flight Lieutenant Gittins quickly established a rapport with his Russian opposite, who improvised. Gittins provided him with some rough drawings and an airscrew as an example and the Russian simply machined a replacement, then did the same for all of the missing tools. In the event, Flight Lieutenant Gittins and his marvellously named Erection Party had the fifteen crated Hurricanes erected and ready for flying in just nine days, a feat which greatly impressed the Russians. It showed them that we meant business right from the off. Gittins kept a diary of the events, which makes for interesting reading. He recorded that their midday meal on that first day consisted of cabbage soup, beef steak and rice followed by stewed fruit. They resumed work afterwards at 1330 with one group unpacking a second Hurricane from its crate while the wireless radio team erected a base station using the empty crate that the first Hurricane had been transported in to house it. The Russians provided petrol and oil supplies and, by 1430, accumulators were being charged. Just an hour later, the second aircraft was being pushed up into its hangar.

Russian tea was served at 1630 in a glass without milk, accompanied by dark brown bread and butter so pale it looked like lard but wasn't. By 1830, the third Hurricane was being pushed into a hangar and, shortly afterwards, the WT station was complete. Owing to a shortage of heavy lifting tackle, they stopped work at 1900 and enjoyed a supper of fried fresh pike, minced meat cutlets and cocoa.

A short time later, they were moved to their billet – an ancient river paddle-steamer that resembled something straight from the pages of Mark Twain's *Life on the Mississippi*. In true naval fashion, the airmen occupied the lower decks while the officers' cabins, dining saloon and kitchen were up above. The boat came to be known as the Winkle Barge. That first night, Gittins was woken by two airmen whom he describes as being 'covered in bumps and blood' who said they'd been eaten alive by insects. He went down to their cabins and 'found the whole place alive with bugs. I made the men put the lights on in their cabins and told them to leave them on all night.' There was little else he could do as he had no medical supplies to hand, but he made a note to ask the Russians whether they could disinfect the vessel at the earliest opportunity.

His main problem the following morning related to the lifting tackle that he'd used the previous day – on reflection, he considered it wasn't really up to the job without causing undue risk, so the Russians again stepped in and saved the day by providing him with three 1,000-kilo cranes, some cable and bolts which he used to lift the aircraft until it was standing on its undercarriage. During the morning, a number of high-ranking Soviet army and navy air arm officers visited the hangar to watch the proceedings. The whole operation was causing quite a stir locally because, to the Russians, the Hurricane was like a new toy which they couldn't get enough of. Generals would stop by to watch as the Hurricanes were constructed, while lower-ranking personnel and pilots would stroke the wings lovingly, taking in their form. They were extraordinarily efficient in the handling of their own aircraft, but the Hurricane was a new one to them. They knew its reputation, and were hungry to experience its performance.

Later that afternoon, a further two aircraft were hoisted on to their undercarriages by the cranes. Tail units were fitted, while the armourers got busy with the machine guns. It rained that evening, so Gittins decided not to start unpacking further aircraft as he lacked the facilities to erect them. Instead, he split the working party into three gangs and carried on fitting tail units and mainplanes. Russian tea was again taken at 1630 and, by 1900, two Hurricanes had wings loosely bolted into position. He made good on his commitment to ask the Russians for some temporary accommodation for his men so that the Winkle Barge could be disinfected and, much to everyone's delight, they found a house which, when he went to inspect it at 2030, he found to be clean and comfortable. The only downside was that it was situated about four miles from the aerodrome. Much to his surprise, the Russian authorities immediately offered to provide two lorries and a car, which turned up at 2300. They all piled into the transport and headed for their new digs after working for almost thirteen hours.

By 0700 the following day, the men had arrived back from their temporary accommodation and were enjoying a breakfast of smoked salmon, breakfast sausage and potatoes. I know there is a lot of mention of food here, but you have to remember, it was something of a fascination for all of us, given the dull, scarce offerings that rationing back home in England had given us. The feasts on offer since we'd left was eye-wateringly good.

Good progress was made on three aircraft until 1215, when the men had a lunch of potato soup, meat rissoles and coffee. That afternoon, a fourth and fifth aircraft were unpacked from their crates and pushed into the hangar. Yet more Russian tea, and again at 1630. In his diary, Gittins highlights the supper that they were given that night, calling it 'the weirdest dish yet'. It was called *Byelooga,* and he describes it as minced meat wrapped in white cabbage leaves. The food that the party were being given was of a very high quality – at least a match for anything we had on the *Llanstephan Castle* – but the diet was considerably richer than the majority of the men had been used to, particularly to stomachs that had become used to the pared-down culinary existence of life back home. Consequently, a number went down with 'tummy troubles' which were severe enough to warrant the dispatch of the *Llanstephan Castle*'s medical officer.

On the party's fourth day, they began filling the already constructed aircraft with oil and coolant. They unpacked the sixth aircraft and moved it to the hangar while work continued on the other five, getting them ready for ground testing. Later that day, Johnny and I were taken to Keg-Ostrov to see how things were progressing with the aircraft that we'd eventually be flying to Vaenga. We'd been bored back on the ship, which lacked a lot of its atmosphere with so many of the wing having left, so it was good to get out – even more so to be back around the Hurricanes – and it just made us more keen than ever to get airborne and on our way. That said, I've always had quite an interest in engineering and maths, so I was particularly interested by Gittins' account of the problems that he'd had with the missing tools. I was enthralled by what he was telling me, and I felt really privileged to actually be there when the Russian engineering officer arrived with the new airscrew tool and the other missing bits of kit, enabling the lads to fix five propellers and inlet sparking plugs to the partly assembled Hurricanes. Gittins and I were talking afterwards and he said to me, 'I've asked the authorities for some petrol and they've promised me it will be here by 1800 so, if you're lucky, you'll be able to see us fire the engines up for the first time. Interested?'

I certainly was, and my luck was in too because, bang on time, the petrol (benzene) was delivered with a chamois-leather funnel and a pump to extract it from the barrels. Johnny and I watched as some of Gittins' men fully fuelled the first aircraft.

The excitement among our Russian friends was palpable; they were really keen to see the first Hurricane engine actually running. At 2035 the chaps turned the engine over by starter battery until the oil gauge showed movement. Gittins later told me, 'We had to do it like that as we had no facilities for making a priming pump.' Then, at 2037, the main switches were thrown and that Merlin XX engine just sprang into life as if it had been shut down only an hour earlier. Inside the cockpit, all of the instruments read correctly. It was great. And there were plenty of cheers and clapping on the part of the spectators.

The erection of the Hurricanes by Gittins and his men had become something of a focal point for the Russian high command and several generals and colonels came to watch them being assembled. They would dine in the officers' dining room on board the Winkle Barge, which had become something of a draw at mealtimes, during which a particularly close relationship was forged between the RAF and the Russians, particularly those commanding the battles on the northern Russian front. When that first Merlin roared into life, for example, a large supper party was held to celebrate this 'momentous' event. Russian officials there included General Grigorieff, Colonel Eelegin of the Naval Air Service and Admiral Kuznetsov, commandant of the Keg-Ostrov aerodrome. On the British side, AVM Collier, the Russian-speaking head of the British Air Mission in Moscow, and Group Captain Bird were there for the RAF.

At the end of Gittins' first week at Keg-Ostrov, some engineers specialising in oil and petrol arrived and were firing questions at everybody concerning fuel and oil. We'd been using aviation fuel of a much higher octane than the Russians and they wanted to know all about it as it noticeably improved aircraft performance.

Back on the SS *Llanstephan Castle*, meanwhile, those of us left behind to kick our heels were finding the time slow in passing so, after much negotiation, arrangements were made for us to go ashore and visit Archangel. Initially, only the officers were permitted to go. My memory of events at that time is quite sketchy as, while we were waiting to go forward to Vaenga, I became quite lax in updating my diary. Artie Holmes, though, writes quite colourfully in his own diary of what Archangel was like. It's probably better that I let his diary tell you of what we found; it wasn't pleasant.

The weather here is still warm and mild. The mosquitoes are thriving in this humidity. It is dark now by 8pm, and growing very cold at night. The local inhabitants are mainly of the peasant type, poorly clad and fed. They look dour and disinterested. They seem to carry on their work mechanically, without enthusiasm or ambition. They rarely smile – which I suppose is understandable. Finally, and unforgivably, they smell!

Their cigarettes, which are one third a hollow cardboard mouthpiece so that no tobacco is thrown away, are responsible to a great extent for the smell. Russian tobacco has a flat musty odour, lacking the sweet fragrance we enjoy from a Virginian leaf. It has the tang of a smouldering wet mattress. This, combined with body odour, vodka breath and clothing stops you dead on a still day or in a warm room.

When the very cold weather arrived about a month later, we learned that the peasants then sewed themselves into their quilted suits and stayed in them for the winter. They were very obedient and a small group of officers handling a large work force could achieve prodigious results.

Archangel was depressing. The river front, its most attractive section, with its white wooden buildings, was shoddy and in need of paint, with many dirty, broken windows. Dogs are rare. When you see one, it is lean like a wolf, scavenging for food. There are no cats. Perhaps the dogs have eaten them.

As the Russians have coupons for necessities, and are forbidden to buy luxuries without permission, stocks are trashy and uninteresting. The only cinema in Archangel has wooden seats and no ventilation. Upholstered seats would very quickly become 'alive'. We have been forbidden to drink Russian water unless it is boiled. We are advised to add sterilising tablets with which everyone will be issued. The local drinking water is from the river and being near a town can scarcely be termed fresh!

While passing a little shed of a house, an old man sitting cross-legged and apparently dozing at his front door suddenly started shouting at me as I approached. I could not tell whether he was a fiery Bolshevik cursing me to damnation, and ready to throw a bomb at me, or was spouting a stream of anti-Hun propaganda for my benefit.

111

I grinned at him in as friendly and encouraging a manner as possible to reassure him that we were both on the one side against the common enemy.

Just then he rose to his feet, surprisingly nimbly, advancing with hand outstretched for mine. I seized it gladly, and shook it warmly. Suddenly, and to my surprise and somewhat to my concern, he started dragging me into his house. Whether he wanted to show me to his wife, or offer me vodka, or to slit my throat once he had me prisoner, I shall never know because I did not go in to find out. I dug my heels in and broke free of his strong grasp, freeing my right hand ready for my revolver. To my friendliest smile he replied with an ugly leer so I went on my way. Back at the boat, I asked Flight Lieutenant Hodson, who spent much of his childhood in Russia what this was all about. He said: 'Politics? Robbery? Genuine hospitality? Who knows? But it's fifty-fifty we'd not have seen you again if you had gone in.'

Artie writes too about a trip to Archangel at night on 2 September and describes the Russian guide provided as 'A charming olive-skinned girl in her early twenties. She had learned English at university in Kiev, yet never before spoken to English people. Her speech was fluent and easy, her vocabulary extensive, with no trace of an accent. She would have made an ideal BBC announcer.' He says, 'A dozen of us went with her in the launch. We saw nothing of what was in the streets as she led us straight to a Russian restaurant. This was to be our "night out" in return for bringing them forty Hurricanes. It was our first initiation to Russian food.'

He describes a bizarre night in which the food was awful, the vodka plentiful and potent, and their being joined by a team of male interpreters who quizzed them extensively about their lives in England, the war in Europe and, particularly, what their role was to be in Archangel/Murmansk. Artie and the others eschewed both the vodka and the food, and refused to answer any of the interpreters' more pointed questions. Interestingly, he says that Hodson later informed them that he'd discovered that the restaurant to which they'd been taken had been in the NKVD headquarters, that their conversations had been bugged, and their behaviour observed through two-way mirrors.

Peter Knapton recorded his own memories of Archangel in his personal diary of the time. He writes,

> *Soldiers were singing and marching and the town had the air of a frontier post. I think Tolstoy or Lermontov would have recognised the general situation.*
>
> *Our favourite haunt in the town was the Cafe Sevair [Cafe of the North], a rather seedy restaurant with a small dance floor and a two-piece band. The clientele would have fitted in well to a le Carré spy story, e.g. Soviet Army and Naval officers and the odd woman 'who happened to speak English'. We drank Peevo, a rather weak sour Russian beer, with vodka chasers, and ate garlic sausage, borsch, schee (a vegetable soup) and damp, dark brown bread.*
>
> *The lavatory in the restaurant was foul and was one of those two-step no-seat affairs where everyone misses. A babushka sat outside the door of the lavatory behind a table arranged with scent sprays. As you left, she gave you a quick squirt. The smell was cheap and nasty. We nicknamed it 'Stalin's breath'.*
>
> *In later years when I was assistant Air Attaché in Moscow, a Russian General on hearing that I had fought on the Northern Front and had been in Archangel remarked that, 'If Northern Russia is the arsehole of the world, Archangel is half way up it.' I have some sympathy with his observation.*

Events start to collide around 7 September, as Flight Lieutenant Gittins and his party at Keg-Ostrov sent a radio message to notify Artie, Mickey Rook and Dicky Wollaston that the first three Hurricanes would be ready for test-flying the following day. We also heard that the carrier party would be flying their Hurricanes off the carrier at the same time. This meant that the ground crews that left on the Russian destroyer with Wing Commander Isherwood on 4 September had all arrived safely and were ready to receive us.

Word must also have reached the Germans that we had arrived, as we heard on the wireless that they were claiming they'd shot down some English aircraft over Leningrad. We had a good laugh about that; we were the only RAF contingent in Russia at that time. What the broadcast indicated was that the Germans had intelligence that we were there, but they weren't sure where. Perhaps they thought that we would broadcast a denial and give them a clue as to where we might have been. They were so naive.

Neil Cameron describes a party that took place on the night of the 8th following an invitation from Admiral Kuznetsov to a local club at 2100 in order that all of the wing's officers could meet their Russian counterparts. About 150 were present, all dressed in their best uniforms and finery. I'll let Neil describe what followed:

> *The white clothed tables were groaning with bottles and the inevitable caviar (which I still love regardless), and the festivities soon got under way. The first toast was made by the Admiral in Russian Champagne. I cannot remember the exact designation of the toast, but I think it was to the king of England. The reply which came from our Wing Commander was to Joseph Stalin. The eating started. The next toast soon followed which was made with a well-filled glass of vodka. The British team sipped in appreciation, but the Admiral was on his feet again with the challenge that the English must drain their glasses in one and made*

the accusation that he did not think that the English could drink. This was a severe challenge and I knew that we were in for trouble. And so it went on during the evening and into the early morning. The toasts were numerous and the drinks mixed in the most suicidal fashion. We were all called in turn to make a toast – those who could still speak – but it was very clear that the Russians were holding their drink rather better than those the Admiral called the English. Soon after midnight, the English began to slip under the table, but not before the Wing Commander and the Admiral together had given a superb display of Russian dancing between the two long tables! I suppose 'passing out' is the expression and it was done with some dignity, but certainly cars and an ambulance had to be called to take away the most severely wounded who were being helped to their transports by our senior medical officer and his Russian colleague. When inebriated, the Russians seemed to insist on kissing each other. We had to rescue the Wing Commander from the embraces of three officers before we could leave.[1]

Back at Keg-Ostrov earlier that morning, three of the Hurricanes which Flight Lieutenant Gittins and his party had assembled were pushed out of their hangars, ready for air testing. Around the same time as they were being wheeled out, Artie, Mickey Rook and Dicky Wollaston set off in a motor launch for the aerodrome along with Group Captain Bird from Moscow, and Flight Lieutenant Hodson, who would be acting as an interpreter. Best-laid plans of mice and men and all that . . . they didn't make it. Keg-Ostrov is located in the mouth of the River Dvina, just where it empties into the sea, and they encountered some really rough water. In his diary, Artie explains, 'Suddenly a wall of water as high as a house swept right over us, completely submerging our bows. It tore away our windscreen and stopped our engine.

Immediately, the boat lost way and wallowed out of control across the waves. We waited for the moment when we would take aboard a great torrent of water and be buffeted under.'

Somewhat fortuitously, they managed to restart the engine and somehow made it back to the safety and refuge of the *Llanstephan Castle*, where they dried out. The following day, they tried again. Over to Artie again:

September 9th. Today, they took the three of us out to Keg-Ostrov again, this time in a tug. That morning, five Hurricanes were ready for us to test. There was tremendous excitement both among our boys and their Russian counterparts. Russian admirals, generals, colonels, their Air Ministry representatives, technical experts, engineers – all were there to get their first glimpse of a Hurricane going through its paces. Mickey gave me the first to test, making me the first pilot to fly a British war plane in Russia.

Group Captain Bird briefed us that the Russian delegation were expecting to see something exceptional from the Hurricanes. They had heard about their successes against the Messerschmitts, Dorniers and Heinkels, in the Battle of Britain. Now they wanted to see just what they could do. This was carte blanche to give the Hurricanes all they'd got! If we'd flown like this at a British airfield, we'd have been court martialled. The cloud was below a thousand feet, so the three of us were able to circle the aerodrome in cloud then spiral out of it at full throttle, sweeping at ground level across the grass straight at the delegation, then climbing up over their heads a hundred yards short of them.

Flight Lieutenant Gittins never stopped talking that night about how well his aeroplanes had performed and about the muddy uniforms of the Admirals and Generals through flinging themselves headlong on the ground as the

Hurricanes roared over. We tore out from behind hangars at them, vertically banked above their heads, until red Very lights from the control tower indicated they'd seen enough. We did a couple of rolls and went into a tight formation to land in a Vic of three.

Artie says that when they climbed out of their cockpits, they didn't know whether they'd be bound for Siberia or their own beds that night. As it happened, the admirals and generals took them indoors and between them a great many lavish toasts were made with vodka. They didn't test the other two aircraft that day; I wonder why!

Artie continues,

On subsequent days, at the Group Captain's invitation, we finished a test by beating up the Llanstephan Castle. This delighted the officers and crew, who had never up till now seen anything near their ship but hostile aircraft, dropping bombs or torpedoes, and strafing their decks with cannon fire. Now we came in at sea level, broadside on and well below her decks. I could look up through my windscreen as I approached at 300mph and see the excited men at the rails waving furiously down at me. Then most of them would dive flat on the deck as my Hurricane went into a vertical climb to skim over the funnels and mast tops and disappear into cloud. One day, a Russian sentry on the quayside dropped his rifle and dived under a pile of timber.

The local people of Archangel were very happy about the performance of the aeroplanes we were sending them. But they were convinced the pilots flying them were drunk, drugged, mad or all three. We were gratified at this reaction. It meant the success of our mission, if the Russians had favourable first impressions of our fighters, for it was well known that Stalin had asked Churchill for Spitfires!

Back on the *Llanstephan Castle*, those of us left were getting increasingly frustrated. Things seemed to be moving at a snail's pace and I was desperate now to get airborne and over to Vaenga. In the meantime, we were joined on the ship by one Lieutenant Lee, a Fleet Air Arm pilot who'd been shot down in flames by an Me109 during a dive-bombing attack from his aircraft carrier, on Petsamo. His flying kit was completely destroyed by fire and the salt water, but the only thing the Russians had to give him was a commissar's uniform and hat, so they gave him that. Soldiers then saluted him on all sides. He became immensely popular on board because his uniform could get us in anywhere so he was forever being dragged off on shopping expeditions to Archangel.

When word finally came, Mickey Rook, Dicky Wollaston, myself and the rest of the pilots said farewell to the *Llanstephan Castle* for good, and left for Keg-Ostrov to fly the fifteen Hurricanes to Vaenga. Harry Gittins and his 'Erection Party' had done an astonishing job, when all was said and done, particularly so given the challenging conditions they were working in. It rained frequently, turning the aerodrome's ground into a muddy, uneven morass. They were billeted four miles from their place of work, and many of them suffered from tummy troubles as a result of the rich Russian food they'd been eating. And they'd been on continuous 'parade' in a technical working sense because everything they'd done had been under the ever-present watchful eyes of high-ranking Russian officers. In that regard, Gittins' team were acting as ambassadors for the RAF throughout.

Yet they managed to uncrate, lift and lower on to their undercarriages fifteen Hurricanes in just nine days. They had fitted their wings and tailplanes, armed, fuelled and tested them, and prepared them all for their flight to Vaenga. And despite missing tools and vital equipment, each aircraft was expertly assembled, without so much as a single missing screw, misaligned panel or faulty bulb.

Before we left Keg-Ostrov, the Russian officers there threw a farewell party for us. We were handed large glasses of high-strength vodka and they seemed intent on getting us all drunk. They partied hard, the Russians, and I think they wanted to see every one of us shovelled into bed in a vodka-fuelled haze with a Russian girl. Mickey Rook was a good leader, and I was growing to like him immensely. He kept a watchful eye on us all and he had a caring manner about him. We were given jars of caviar to eat with bloody great spoons. I was a bit dubious at first but Mickey laughed and said to me, 'Go on, Ginger, it's good for the "working parts", lad!' so I stuffed it down. It tasted a bit oily, but it wasn't at all unpleasant, and I have to admit, it did go down well with the vodka.

Ah yes, the vodka . . . Mickey told us all to go easy, and if we accepted more than a single glass from our hosts, it would be on pain of death! 'One each, boys, but only if you want it, and nobody – but nobody – has a second! Those Russians will have a big laugh if any of you chaps prang one of the aircraft on take-off. Got it?' he said, grinning.

Looking very dapper in my new RAF
uniform shortly after being awarded
my 'Wings' in 1940.

Left: With a 615 Squadron Hurricane
at RAF Valley not long after being
posted there.

A Luftwaffe Messerschmitt Me110 fighter pilot's view of the white cliffs of Dover in October 1940 during the 'Blitzkrieg' aerial bombardment of London.

A Hawker Hurricane pictured on its way to engage German bombers as they crossed the south coast of England during the Battle of Britain, summer 1940.

Hurricane cockpit. The primary flight instruments show altitude, heading, speed and rate of climb or descent. Note the 'spade' type control column – the button fired the aircraft's guns when depressed.

Prime Minister Winston Churchill with his unlikely ally, the Soviet leader Joseph Stalin.

The aircraft carrier HMS *Argus* was a converted merchant ship that had been captured from the Italians in World War I. The rather flimsy steel flight deck, at just 360ft long, was about 30ft shorter than required for Hurricanes to safely take off.

The cargo hold on HMS *Argus*. 'From time to time, Ibby and Wag would go below the decks to where their Hurricanes were stowed. They were still sufficiently in love with the idea of flying that they'd sit in the cockpits, feel the controls.'

Wag Haw was granted a commission after his return from Russia, seen here with his unique combination of awards: the DFM and Order of Lenin. Wag was later awarded a DFC.

Squadron Leader Anthony Rook, Officer Commanding 81 Squadron. During the Battle of Britain, his charges at 504 Squadron included both Wag Haw and Ray 'Artie' Holmes.

Wing Commander Henry Neville Gynes Ramsbottom-Isherwood, AFC, the man appointed to lead 151 Wing. He had a keen sense of humour and was highly regarded both by his fellow officers, and the War Office.

Brothers in Arms: My best friend and wing man Johnny Mulroy, who I met in training, shows an air journal to two Russian sailors.

Neil Cameron (left), Tim Elkington, the diminutive Jack Ross and Rex Furneaux. Neil's stance describes him perfectly. Tim had his gloves made in the UK by Moss Bros to protect against the cold at high altitudes.

Aircraftsmen from Harry Gittins' Erection Party take a break at Keg Ostrov. Behind them is one of the crates used to transport the Hurricanes to Russia. They were more than big enough for use as accommodation. This one is being used as the W/T headquarters.

'The Kremlin': The Wing's officers were accommodated in an imposing two-storey building constructed in red brick that rather appropriately resembled a large country house.

RAF Airmen lower the coffin of my friend, Sergeant Pilot Norman 'Nudger' Smith into his grave at the Russian Naval Cemetery in Severomorsk. A firing party of Soviet sailors stands by on the right to give the salute.

Wag (right) and Ibby with Russian fighter ace and Hero of the Soviet Union Boris Safonov (left), who scored 20 kills before his death in combat in May 1942.

81 Squadron pilots pose for a picture outside the flight hut. To the left, a board shows the readiness and availability of each Hurricane. From left to right, J Walker, AJ McGregor, the CO Tony Rook, Canadian David Ramsey, 'Gin' Sims, Ken Bishop and Wag Haw.

134 Squadron pilots share a brew while sitting in readiness to scramble. From left, Hector Kiel (foreground), Squadron OC Squadron Leader Tony Miller sits under the phone, Nat Gould is pouring the tea. Neil Cameron looks on while Nobby Clarke sits to his left.

10

Acclimatisation

Back at Vaenga, Wag removed his flying helmet. He looked around – other Hurricanes from the *Argus* were taxiing into dispersal, their pilots revving up before cutting the engines. He looked at his watch: almost seventy-five minutes had elapsed since he'd tentatively launched from the precariously short flight deck on HMS *Argus,* and made the uneventful flight to the wing's new home. Throwing his parachute pack on to his shoulder, he opened a large compartment in the Hurricane's fuselage and pulled out his parachute bag, containing his clothes and personal kit.

Neil Cameron approached him and smiled. Wag was immediately struck by the differences between Neil and himself, and the Russian pilots who were now poring over every inch of the Hurricanes that they would soon be flying. They all wore flying helmets even though they were not flying, something he would soon learn they did every time they went on duty. They all had shaven heads, and were dressed in heavy, thick leather coats with their sidearms worn at their sides. Wag looked at Neil, with his longish hair, suede flying boots and the new barathea uniform which he had somehow persuaded out of Moss Bros in London, against regulations.[1] The differences were as between chalk and cheese.

Ibby joined them and together they wandered over to a larger group of 81 Squadron pilots. Wag missed the start of the conversation, but heard one of them say, 'Well, chaps, that was one hell of a reception committee they had lined up for us! I heard there was a Russian Air Vice Marshal there with all his senior officers watching us come in. I bet they pissed themselves laughing when they saw the first two Hurricanes to touch ground in Russia crash landing! What on earth must they have thought?'

The aerodrome on which the pilots found themselves was really a sandy strip that had been carved out of pine forest, and on it were two Russian bomber squadrons and two fighter squadrons, which swelled to four once all of the RAF Hurricanes arrived. 151 Wing's Operations Record Book (known colloquially as 'the 540' after its official form number) for September 1941 paints a detailed but rather dull picture based on the thinking at the time.

As I recall it, Murmansk (Vaenga) aerodrome was large enough to be used as two separate aerodromes with 134 Squadron using the north end of it and 81 Squadron the south. Russian bombers were able to take off using either half of it. Its surface consisted of rolled sand which, whenever it was wet, became very bumpy – that made a central section of the aerodrome unusable. As the 540 says, 'It remains always an aerodrome on which experienced pilots have to exercise care in landing and taking off.'[2]

The camp was built on a sandy plateau covered with a silver birch plantation and surrounded by low hills about fifteen miles north-east of Murmansk. Brick barrack blocks, HQ offices, the mess and other facilities were set at wide intervals with as much as 500 yards between them, making them naturally camouflaged and well dug in. This made them much less vulnerable to air attack, but the downside was that it made transport difficult – the nearest part of the aerodrome itself was about half a mile away from the camp, and the furthest dispersal point was almost a mile and a half away. Given that both us pilots and the ground crew would have to cover that ground several times a day, you can see the logistical problems that were thrown up. Just to compound the problem, the 'roads' were of a type hardly known outside Russia – there were no highways as such, just one metalled road that ran a mile through the camp. The widely dispersed buildings and huts were connected only by very rough paths and cross-country tracks. To make matters worse, the heavy autumn rains that had made life difficult for Gittins and his Erection Party at Keg-Ostrov also made life difficult here. They'd rendered the paths and tracks through the birch trees a muddy morass, with potholes that were axle deep in places.

Wag and the rest of the pilots were picked up by an antiquated bus driven by a man in a Russian naval uniform and smoking an enormously long cigarette. They were dropped off at a square building on the far side of the airfield, surrounded by trees, which turned out to be the communal mess where breakfast awaited them. The mess itself was brightly lit, spotlessly clean, and the vista greatly improved by Russian waitresses in gipsy skirts and blouses. It got even better when they saw the menu: meats, caviar, cheese, black bread and – the boys couldn't quite believe this one – champagne. In quite astonishing quantities. Wag found an empty table and sat down, joined by Ibby and Nudger Smith on either side of him. Ibby poured them all a generous glass each and raised a toast.

'Enormous cheers and here's to our Russian allies – God bless 'em!' he said with a wide grin on his face.

'Cheers yourself, mate' said Wag and Nudger in unison.

Farther up the mess, Wing Commander Isherwood sat impassively. His poker face betrayed no emotion – not then, not ever – so it was impossible to know whether he was delighted, extremely unhappy or somewhere in the middle. He was a somewhat remote figure to most of us pilots, businesslike, and never using more words when speaking than the minimum required to convey his message. To compensate for him registering no emotion whatsoever, though, the pilots decided to make hay while the sun shone; champagne with breakfast wasn't something any of them had ever seen in any RAF mess before, and they weren't likely to, either. They wondered whether this was a one-off, or whether it was to be a regular breakfast drink while they were there. Just in case, though, they made sure they drank their fill. Who knew when the action would start? It would be strictly business from then on – and who knew when it would stop?

Once the pilots had eaten their fill and drunk the mess dry of champagne, a truck was laid on to transfer them to their accommodation. Wag and Ibby were already close friends from training, and they'd become good pals with Nudger over time, so the three of them naturally decided to share a room. There were plenty to choose from in the brick-built block, but all the rooms were completely bare of furniture except for three beds. Spartan didn't come close. Additionally, each room featured a hole in the wall which went straight through to the outside. The holes served as rudimentary fireplaces where the fellows could burn wood, and a tin flap provided the only protection against draughts when the fireplaces weren't in use. There were no wardrobes – kitbags or parachute bags provided storage for personal kit – and there was no running water either; that had to be fetched from a tap outside. Canvas bowls on wooden legs provided the only washing facility, and the loo consisted of no more than a hole in the ground, and a plank. That was always going to be an unsavoury experience – the boys looked at each other in horror when they found it. It's rather accurately described in the Wing 540: it simply states, 'outside sanitation of the most primitive kind for both officers and airmen'.

The wing's officers were accommodated in a much more imposing two-storey building constructed in red brick that rather appropriately resembled a large country house. The ground floor served as Wing HQ and included an operations room, orderly rooms, sick quarters and stores, while upstairs, large bedrooms accommodated three officers to a room. The bedrooms all opened on to an uncarpeted corridor which multiplied and amplified all sounds made in it. As Hubert Griffith describes, 'the cough of a fly at the other end of the building becomes like the banging of a door. Hence any larking about or singing late in the evening by one room full of young pilots can keep half the officers of the Wing awake. Hence, larking about and singing after a certain hour in the evening have to be severely rationed. Beds, blankets and sheets (spotless) are provided by the Russians.'³ Fixtures and accessories were again non-existent, with bare floors, and nothing to decorate the walls. There was an anteroom and bar, but they were similarly spartan. At least the rooms were clean. Within days, the HQ had become widely known simply as 'The Kremlin'.

One element of life that was the same for officers, NCOs and airmen alike was the sanitation – or lack of it. Neither the officers' nor the airmen's accommodation had running water, and as for the officers' loo . . . From afar it may have been a more grand affair than that afforded the other ranks, but appearances can be deceptive. The rotunda-style toilet was unique and redolent of a revolving door. An octagonal affair, it was open to the elements at the sides, with eight seats of separate cubicles arranged around a central vent, and built over a pit. Inside, there were two steel bars to rest your feet on while you squatted. It was the Russians who were blamed for the fact that said steel bars were always covered in faeces. It was said, although nobody every hung around long enough to find out, that by mid-October the limit for gentlemen before frostbite set in on the private parts was three minutes.⁴

Wag, Ibby and Nudger made themselves at home as best they could, but there wasn't much they could do to brighten things up in their living quarters so they set out to find the sergeants' mess. Like every other building in the camp, it was a fair walk through the trees – a good half a mile, and it was what they found in the trees that brought home to them for the first time just how close they were to the front line – Russian sentries. They were armed with pistols and rifles and stationed outside both the living quarters and the mess, as well as at regular intervals among the silver birch trees. The distance between their accommodation and the sergeants' mess may have been off-putting to the ignorant, but to

Wag, Ibby and Nudger the reward made it worth all the drudgery – gin was only 4s 6d per bottle (around £8.50 in today's money).

The mess was only a few degrees less spartan than their living quarters, but that crucial difference was just enough to lift it above bland and boring. From outside it was just a long wooden hut, styled, it seemed, on the latest in German POW chic. Inside, things were little better – simple trestle tables and wooden chairs that had seen better days. I suppose you'd call the decor – such as it was – 'distressed' in today's terms. But there was a bar at one end and it was warm inside, courtesy of the hut's double skin and, crucially, a wood-burning stove that was blazing away. Anyway, who pays much attention to the decor provided a bar provides the necessities of life – being clean, warm, spacious, and with the booze priced to attract custom? You make your own entertainment in a bar, and provide your own atmosphere.

It took a few days for the pilots to acclimatise, both to life on the aerodrome and to the weather and conditions in the Russian Arctic. The mildness of a few days earlier had been replaced by a biting cold, but it wasn't the sort of cold that ate its way through to your very core. The climate this far north was crisp and dry, a long way from the damp cold that permeates every cell in your body such as was the norm back home. One of the jobs they turned their attention to first was the focal point of every fighter pilot's life, the flight hut, which was located on the eastern fringe of the aerodrome behind dispersals. It was more like a rather spacious dugout than the huts we'd all been used to at RAF stations back home but it was no less suitable for that. The Soviets had no radar system at Vaenga so that was another difference; there was no question of us being vectored to intercept German aircraft as we were used to.

As it was the place we'd all be spending the majority of our time on duty in, they wanted to make it as comfortable as possible. The Russians had already done most of the legwork, adding ventilation shafts and a staircase. Inside, we had cast-iron wood-burning stoves with a chimney pipe through the roof, which would glow a dull red, with a steady diet of pine and birch logs, and for reading, relaxing or sleeping when we weren't flying, there were two-tier bunk beds round the walls. The lads installed the wind-up gramophone player they'd had with them on the *Argus,* and brought over a selection of records that had survived the voyage to the Arctic undamaged. The Ink Spots were big then, and it reminded them of home listening to them sing 'When the Swallows Come Back to Capistrano', or 'Whispering Grass', which was another favourite. We had quite a few on board the *Llanstephan Castle* too, so the record collection swelled quite considerably when we arrived.

The Russians were very fond of dugouts, a theme that extended to their hangars as well as our flight hut. The Hurricanes would be vulnerable on the ground, so we needed somewhere secure to store them where they'd also be accessible when we needed to scramble. Wing Commander Isherwood pointed this out to the Russian general at the aerodrome. No problem, said the general. So the wing commander asked him when this was likely to be completed. The general replied by midday tomorrow. Thirty-nine hangars to be dug out to a width of 40 feet, roofed and covered in turf, and it was already late afternoon.[5]

The Russian solution to our problem was a marvel of innovation – soil was excavated so that the aircraft could be parked partly below ground level, and the shelters were constructed with silver birch trees that were cut down specifically for this purpose. The roof was then covered with branches and topped off with turf to blend it in with the surrounding ground. We were stunned to discover that the work was carried out in a single day by a labour force constituted of a seemingly endless number of people, who appeared to emerge from the trees the following morning. Neil Cameron described them as 'a sad looking gang of over a thousand of all nationalities from the length and breadth of Russia'.[6] Carrying nothing more technologically advanced than picks and shovels, they set to work digging out hangars wide and deep enough to accommodate the Hurricanes. Back home, it would have been a major undertaking, with the task accomplished in weeks. But the lads had never seen anything like this; the labour force worked like robots, toiling for hours without stopping for food, drink or rest at any stage. They worked on endlessly until the job was complete and then they melted away again into the forest just as silently as they'd arrived. By the end of that day, the job was done.

Neil Cameron wandered into their accommodation one day by mistake. He described it as 'a huge barn-like structure with hundreds of bunk beds going up to the ceiling. The smell was horrific (shades of the Gulags as we came to know them)'.[7]

While the pilots were making themselves at home in the first few days and acclimatising to their new environment, no such luck befell the engineers at the aerodrome. The Wing 540 records that the armourers had forgotten to pack a key part for the Hurricanes' machine guns, which were without fire and safety mechanisms attached. A message was sent back to the Air Ministry and arrangements were being made to fly out the missing parts on a Catalina flying boat, but even so, it would take a good few days for them to arrive in Vaenga. Rather than the whole wing remaining non-operational, two aircraft from each flight were stripped of guns, enabling each flight to have four aircraft with eight guns operational.[8]

This was disappointing news for the pilots, who had been looking forward to the significant additional firepower provided by twelve guns on each aircraft, but it wasn't going to affect operational flying in any way. Then the Russians came to the rescue again, with a splendid piece of engineering; having been shown what was required, they went away and simply made replacement parts so that, within forty-eight hours, all of the Hurricanes were operational again, with twelve machine guns on each.[9]

The first operational sorties began on 11 September with

front-line patrols carried out by eight aircraft from 134 Squadron, and eight from 81 Squadron. It was a good day for flying, with broken cloud and good visibility. No combat took place, and no casualties occurred on the patrols; it was as much an opportunity for the pilots to familiarise themselves with the area and test their guns over a nearby lake. Wag Haw led a section of three in Vic formation, and from 3,500 ft they were able to get a good perspective on the local area. Murmansk Sound was clearly visible, as was the outline of Fisherman's Island, the name given to the Rybachiy Peninsula. Murmansk itself had seen intense bombing by the Luftwaffe since the beginning of Operation Barbarossa and three-quarters of it had taken the brunt of the blitz.

Wag had no desire to instigate combat if he could avoid it, so he turned his section to port in order to avoid Petsamo, which had been dead ahead. Petsamo was where General Dietl's *Gebirgsjäger* were attempting to fight their way to Murmansk itself, so there was no point poking the hornets' nest until the pilots had familiarised themselves with the local geography. Wag knew how disorienting aerial combat could be from his experience in the Battle of Britain and, as the aerodrome lacked radar, he couldn't exactly radio them for a bearing. He didn't fancy his chances if he had to bale out, either – there appeared to be no signs whatsoever of human habitation down below, just an endless vista of lakes, peat bogs, swamps, forest and tundra.

Thirty minutes in the air made him realise that navigation wasn't likely to be anywhere as difficult as he'd first thought, at least when it came to finding his way back to base. He had a frame of reference for this, and it was one of the first lessons he'd learned as a newly minted fighter pilot in the skies over southern England during the Battle of Britain. All he had to do was fly north to pick up the coastline, or fly west and hit the Kola inlet, just as he used to do on the south coast back home. He was in the groove now, really loving being back in the air, at one with his machine, and just enjoying the feel of his hand on the stick and his feet on the rudder bar, the aircraft doing his bidding. Sixty minutes after taking off, Wag led his formation into a turn and headed back to base. It had been a good first patrol.

Neil Cameron flew one of the first patrols for 134 Squadron, flying a Vic formation with Flight Lieutenant Jack Ross (the mannequin on the mantelpiece from the party at Leconfield) and one of the Soviet fighter squadron commanders, Major Koharienko. He was a Georgian fellow and, according to Neil Cameron, a great personality who didn't seem worried by the fact that without a shared language, they couldn't communicate between aircraft. However, that was the least of their problems; while flying at altitude over the front line, where they attracted anti-aircraft fire from German units below, Neil's engine kept cutting out. After all of the aircraft had returned from the sortie, they discovered that two other Hurricanes from 134 Squadron had experienced the same problem.

The cause of the problem was quickly diagnosed – it was the Russian aviation fuel, which was of a far lower quality than the British fuel that the Merlin XX engines powering the Series II Hurricane were designed for. Although the engine in Neil's aircraft suddenly lost power at altitude and subsequently cut out, he was able to restart it by resorting to frantic hand pumping.

Among 151 Wing's technicians was Henry Broquet, a young airman who had grown up in Guernsey and, before the war, had learned to fly. He'd joined the RAF on the outbreak of the war and had a particular interest in fuels, so as soon as the engineering officer was made aware of the issue surrounding the low-octane Russian fuel, he seconded Henry to work with a team of Russian scientists who were trying to solve the problem. In the meantime, the Hurricanes were obliged to operate below 16,000 feet, and limited to ground attack and bomber support.

That near-disastrous first sortie can be attributed to the differing Western and Russian oil production industry philosophies of the time. This may all sound very technical but we had to sort the problem out quickly before we lost planes and pilots; it wasn't something anyone had anticipated.

The bulk of Russian oil output, second only to that of the USA in the 1920s and 1930s, was used for heating, lighting and heavy industry. Their use of fractionation refining produced only small quantities of petrol, which was of inconsistent quality. By contrast, Western technology utilised catalytic and thermal oil refining to produce much higher-quality petrol, and in 1923 incorporated lead tetraethyl as a performance booster. In 1941, so called high-octane Russian aviation petrol contained certain compounds that caused 'waxing', which saw it morph into a partially crystalline state at low temperatures. The addition of lead tetraethyl didn't solve the problem.

The issue wasn't limited to the Merlin XX engines that powered the Hurricanes; the fighters that the Soviet Air Force were using at the time suffered from the same problem, so despite having a ceiling of over 20,000 ft, they were limited to operating at altitudes no greater than 15,000 ft. Therefore solving the fuel problem became a priority.

They'd been aware of the issue long before 151 Wing had arrived in Russia, hence the visit by the Russian fuel and oil specialists to Gittins and his team at Keg-Ostrov, and the non-stop questions on British fuel. The Russians were a leading authority in the fields of organic chemistry, catalysis and metallurgy, so they firmly believed that a solution was possible. They had experience in assessing the use of metal catalysts, which they knew stabilised and improved the oxidation and combustion of hydrocarbon fuels. While low-cost, lead-based compounds were widely used in the West, tin featured heavily in the work of the Russians and had already been the subject of many 1930s patents.

Russia was, and still is, one of the world's leading tin producers. Tin was known to have outstanding stability and vastly superior catalytic properties, compared to lead-based alloys and compounds, for the reduction of fuel-degrading reactions between various hydrocarbons and other fuel contaminating compounds which, in turn, have an adverse effect on combustion efficiency. These degrading-reaction products also contributed to the 'waxing' effect experienced by the 134 Squadron aircraft, and which had plagued the Russian fighters of the time. The Russian technicians working on the problem were therefore uniquely placed, and Henry Broquet's contribution was to corroborate their work and advise on the response of the Merlin XX engine.

After those first patrols flown by the two RAF squadrons on 11 September 1941, numerous stoppages were found in the machine guns following the test firing over the lake shortly after take-off, so it was decided that the aircraft affected would be non-operational until the necessary tools and equipment arrived. Fortune, however, shone on the engineers for once, and the problem was resolved far sooner than anyone had anticipated as, unexpectedly, one officer and 100 men arrived that evening, having travelled by train from Archangel. They were followed by the MT vehicles for the wing, and overnight stores of all descriptions began to come in, so working parties were detailed to await the trucks as they arrived. The tools that the engineers needed to rectify the problem with the machine guns were readily identified and the work carried out before first light. We needed to be sure that if we were scrambled to engage the Luftwaffe in action for the first time since the Battle of Britain – this time in Russian skies, in defence of Murmansk – the guns would work first time, every time.

11

First Blood

It snowed in the early hours of the morning on 12 September; nothing heavy, just a few flurries which settled on the cold ground of the aerodrome. Although the wing was still only partly staffed, the CO had declared that the two squadrons were ready to start offensive patrols and begin the first escorts of Russian bombers. Ever since the wing's arrival in Russia, a signal had been transmitted daily to the Air Ministry in London by Wing Commander Isherwood giving brief details of the events of the previous twenty-four hours. In the early hours of the 12th, the signal went out as usual with the welcome news that the wing was ready for action as of first light.

As well as those back in Whitehall, this news also delighted the pilots, who would finally get a chance to get airborne! Wag, who had long-held dreams of being a fighter ace, was positively champing at the bit, desperate to get into action again.

The morning of the 12th dawned with good visibility. The light dusting of snow from earlier in the night lay across the aerodrome as the pilots woke up to their first fully operational day in Vaenga. The first patrol of the day was carried out by three pilots from 134 Squadron, who, although they sighted German bombers, lost them again in cloud and failed to make contact. 81 Squadron had a little more luck on the second patrol of the morning when Artie's mate Bushy got his guns on an Me110 and damaged it. 134 Squadron were airborne again twice before lunch to provide escort cover for Russian bombers, but once again, the pilots landed without having fired their guns.

It was some time after lunch. The majority of 81 Squadron's

132

officers had gone to the mess to eat, leaving a rump of six pilots in the flight hut on readiness should they be called to action. With no radar in the sector, the only 'early warning system' was the Soviet Army. As soon as the German bombers took off and started to group over their own airfield, Russian observers would radio the number and type of aircraft, their position and course to their anti-aircraft posts. The AA crews would launch effective fire the moment the Luftwaffe's aircraft came into sight and the AA bursts would alert the Russian fighter pilots, who were sitting in their cockpits ready to scramble. They would then take off and head towards the flak bursts. For us, they'd amended the system slightly and would signal a warning to the base at Vaenga which would then phone the flight hut to scramble the pilots.

The pilots on readiness that lunchtime included Wag Haw, who was the leader of 'Red Section', 'A' Flight, with the Canadian pilot officer Jimmy Walker as his wingman, 'Red two', and Nudger Smith as 'Red three'. Ibby Waud was leading 'Blue Section', 'B' Flight with Flight Sergeant Basil Rigby as 'Blue two', plus one other as 'Blue three'. If the call to action came, they'd scramble as two Vics, but in the meantime they were taking it easy in the dugout – well, as easy as you can ever take it when you are on readiness, waiting for the field telephone to ring. You can never fully relax because every minute that passes is potentially only moments away from you being scrambled to action, so you spend the entire time poised and ready to sprint. It's as if every cell in your body is primed and ready for action, so you're buzzing and constantly fidgeting. If the call comes, then it's every man for himself and a mad sprint for the aircraft, which are waiting and ready for take-off.

Every second counted, so Wag and the others sat around in their flying kit, wearing their Mae Wests loose and untied. Their helmets sat waiting, ready for them to pull on in the cockpit of their Hurricanes. Time dragged, but it was nothing new to them; it wasn't really any different from lying around on dispersal during the Battle of Britain the previous summer, except then the weather was good and they were lying on the grass of England's green and pleasant land; here, it was somewhat colder, and it was a foreign field they were there to defend. Otherwise, everything was the same. They sat around chatting, playing cards, playing chess, but not really able to concentrate fully on whatever task they were engaged in. They were just going through the motions. The reality was, they were just waiting for that call.

Music always helps to pass the time, and the wind-up gramophone they'd brought from the *Argus* was in constant use, although, with only twelve records to choose from, there wasn't a great choice of music available. Wag picked one at random from the limited selection and put it on the turntable without looking at it. As he wound the player up and set the needle on the record, he heard the first notes of guitar strings being plucked and then the double bass kicked in and he heard the unmistakable vocal harmony of the Mills Brothers' four voices as they sang.

Wag sat and, for the umpteenth time since he'd left England, wished for a piano. He'd heard the song countless times and for him it was evocative, bringing back vivid memories of his time at Hendon the previous summer when they'd play it frequently. That seemed a world away now.

Nudger had been outside for a pee. Waiting around on readiness did that to you; there was nothing worse than being caught short once you were up in the air, and the constant anxiety of waiting for the phone to ring often manifested itself in an urge to pee. He had no sooner put his head through the entrance, though, when the field telephone exploded into life with its unmistakable ring. Wag snatched it up. 'Red leader' he answered.

'Red leader, bandits reported in the area around Petsamo. Fly due west and look for Russian flak bursts which will assist you in locating the bogies.'

'C'mon boys, we're on!' he shouted as he leapt from his seat, but the others were already on their way out. He tied his Mae West up as he ran, and shouted out the information he had to the rest of the section. He climbed on to the wing and into the cockpit of his Hurricane, Z4018, and pulled his helmet on, plugging the RT lead from it into its socket and doing the same with his oxygen supply. His ground crew were ready outside with the accumulator trolley plugged in, delivering power to the aircraft. He pulled his harness tight around him, becoming part of the machine as he did so. As his finger pushed the start button, the Rolls-Royce Merlin XX roared into life with a flash of flame from the six exhausts on either side of the cowl ahead of him and a cloud of black smoke was breathed out, momentarily covering the cockpit. He pulled the canopy closed and, checking to see whether the rest of the formation was present, opened the throttle wide and led his section skywards.

He trimmed the flaps and raised the gear as his Hurricane climbed aggressively to altitude. He looked to Ibby in Z4006 on his port side, who gave him a thumbs-up. It was then that he noticed the formation was one short – they'd left one behind so the section consisted of just himself and Ibby, plus Jimmy Walker in Z5157, Nudger Smith in Z3746, and Basil Rigby in Z5207. Not to worry; they could deal with whatever threat there was between them. He led the formation of five Hurricanes, two on either side of him, due westwards as they continued to gain height. The sky was a steely grey as they levelled off at 5,500 ft, halfway between Murmansk and the coast. Wag turned down the luminosity of his gunsight, which was too intense against the dull vista outside the windscreen. Within a matter of minutes, he saw the telltale black powder puffs of Russian flak ahead and slightly to starboard.

He looked around him in every direction, as he knew the rest of the formation would be doing, searching for bandits . . . and almost immediately, he saw them. There . . . five black dots on the horizon ahead of him, passing from left to right across his sights.

'Bandits dead ahead!' he yelled to his section over the RT, open-ing the throttle wide and turning the gun button on his control stick to 'fire', as he pulled back gently on the control column to manoeuvre into a position from which to launch an attack on the German aircraft. As the distance closed with the targets, they morphed from black specks into five Messerschmitt Me109s. They were the fighter escort to a Henschel 126 two-seat recon-naissance aircraft and, to his amazement, they turned *away* from the attacking Hurricanes instead of towards them. The black crosses on the wings were clearly visible now; five targets, five potential victims to five predators. Five against five . . .

Wag gave a quick glance above and behind, and saw nothing but empty space. 'Tally ho!' he shouted over the RT, as he broke away into the vast panorama of sky, diving into the battle arena. He locked on to one of the 109s below and slightly ahead of him now. He looked at it through the gunsight, the target getting larger . . . Wag hit the 'fire' button with his thumb and all hell was let loose; he felt his Hurricane momentarily shudder from the massive recoil of the twelve machine guns as they spat .303 rounds out at 160 rounds per second. They made a noise like tearing calico.[1] He gave a ten-second burst and watched the tracer rounds lighting a path to the target, the De Wilde incendiary ammunition igniting and flashing as it hit the 109.

Everything happened in an instant. It was mayhem. Suddenly, the 109 filled his windscreen and instinctively he broke hard right to avoid hitting it. His rounds had hit their target, though; the 109 started spewing black smoke, and he watched in fascination as oil streaked across the German pilot's canopy. Wag's Hurricane passed so close he could even hear the 109's engine as he somehow got away with it and avoided a collision. Wag pulled the stick over and added a touch of rudder to stop him slipping as he watched the 109 he'd just hit burst into flames and begin spiralling earthwards.

Wag's wingman, the Canadian Jimmy Walker, was above and a way back as he watched the battle between his section leader and the 109 unfold. Then he spotted another 109 on Wag's tail and immediately dived after it, giving it two bursts from the Hurricane's machine guns of a few seconds each. He watched as the rounds found their mark and the 109 turned turtle, bursting into flames. Jimmy watched with a mix of delight and horror as it plummeted earthwards and crashed into the ground in a huge explosion.[2]

As Wag had shouted 'Tally ho!', Ibby Waud, leading Blue Section, had his eye on the Henschel that the 109s had been escorting. He described the action later:

A great deal happened in seconds. The damned fools turned away from us instead of turning in towards us. They must have been straight out of the Operational Training Unit or maybe they'd been sent to the Russian front for being continually pissed. I was flying next to Wag as he opened fire on a 109. It burst into flames immediately, an appalling great ball of flame. I found myself catching up with Wag's 109 as it rolled over on to its back. It was an awesome sight, the 109 drifting along inverted, with flames and debris pouring out of it. Black crosses, flames and smoke, one could almost smell them. The pilot must have been dead in the cockpit.

As the flamer disappeared from my sight – this all taking seconds – the Henschel somehow drifted across my gun sight, right to left. Such a pretty little aeroplane, but plastered with black crosses all the same, and instinctively I locked on to him and fired a short burst from the quarter. Another damn fool pilot, this one; he turned prettily, stuffed his nose down and dived very steeply towards the west; he must have been in a panic to get away, but he did quite the wrong thing in diving down in a dead straight line. He could have turned that Henschel in little circles on a pfennig and if he had done that, I wouldn't have had a chance of getting him. As it was, he presented a perfect

100% dead astern target. Diving after him, I had a tremendous overtaking speed, but I opened fire and kept the button pressed all the way in. As I closed in, a huge plume of white smoke poured out of him. (God, did I do that?) I passed over the top of him with what seemed like inches to spare, drawing in my breath in near-horror because I nearly collided with him.

I immediately abandoned any interest in the Henschel, pulled the stick hard back and opened the throttle up to maximum. I was concerned with the main action – the 109s above me – and clambered back to regain height and rejoin the party. But where was it? I looked around almost desperately, but could see no aircraft at first. I saw a Hurricane and a 109 circling round each other in classical combat style. I had the advantage of height and speed and was determined to keep it. Then began a cat-and-mouse game of diving down to attack the 109 and pulling up to superior height again.

I started the first attack immediately and probably too hastily; the 109 might have had a chance to fire at me as I passed over him for the first time. But I made myself a difficult target. Thrashing both the engine and my own guts, I pulled up sharply again to regain height, twisting like a snake in the cockpit to keep the 109 in view. Then a second dive, and a second burst of fire at him, this time from the front quarter. Again, I climbed and turned sharply, nearly screwing my eyes out of their sockets to keep the 109 in sight and make sure I still had the advantage. This combat was now taking an uncomfortably long time. Then suddenly the 109 broke away sharply to make a run for home, and made off towards the west. I still had the height over him and kept him carefully in view as he flew along the bed of a dried-up river, right down at nought feet and going like a bat out of hell. I positioned myself carefully

*above and behind him. Surely he could now see me coming?
But he didn't deviate and once again I was presented with a
perfect target from dead astern.*

*Steadily overtaking, I put the red dot of my gun sight on
the centre of the 109 and fired continuously all the way in.
Why the hell didn't he turn around towards me? Flying
straight and level, he was now signing his own death
warrant. But he just kept on going, flat out (and desperate
to get away I imagine).*

*As I closed in, I saw a thin stream of black smoke
starting to pour from him. He veered to the left – not a
proper turn, he just skidded away, left wing down a little
– and crashed right into the bank of the river. There was a
tremendous flash under my port wing as he exploded on
the ground. It was yet another awesome spectacle.*

*Once again, I immediately opened up to maximum revs
and climbed to regain height, twisting around to look for
other aircraft. I was still obsessed with the thought there
would be 109s above me but for some time I saw nothing.
But then, right ahead of me, a little dot, an aircraft twisting
and turning like myself and at the same height. Was it a
109? I flew towards it and soon realised (with some relief)
that it was a Hurricane. It turned out to be Wag!*[3]

Wag had seen the Henschel that Ibby had shot down veering
away with thick black smoke billowing from it, but then, having
already shot down one 109, he became involved in combat with
another. After a few viciously steep turns and controlled stalls at
speed with each pilot trying to outmanoeuvre the other's aircraft,
neither was able to get the advantage over the other in order to
get guns on. Eventually, the 109 broke away and accelerated into
a steep dive in an effort to run for home. Wag considered going
after him but his attention was diverted at that moment by a
Hurricane which Wag realised, to his shock, was trailing thick

smoke and losing altitude. It was heading in the direction of Vaenga and the Kola inlet but it looked to Wag as if it was out of control.

Diving down to get a closer look, he pulled alongside the stricken Hurricane and realised to his horror that it was his good friend and room-mate Nudger in the cockpit. One of the 109s must have had a good go at it because there was a huge hole just behind the cockpit. Nudger appeared to be trapped inside his machine, unable to get out, and it dawned on Wag that the canopy must have been jammed as one of the rounds exploded. He saw Nudger struggling desperately to move it but he was unable to and Wag was repulsed by the realisation that he was looking at the inevitable death of one of his closest friends. He felt impotent, unable to do a thing to help him, and he was struck by the thought of his own mortality. A fleeting thought, but he wondered how Nudger felt at that very moment, trapped with the awful knowledge of the time and date of his own death, feeling the seconds ticking by to his inevitable demise. Wag was unable to leave; although he couldn't help, he couldn't bear the thought of his friend dying alone, so he flew alongside Nudger and watched agonised as he saw his friend's aircraft crash into the ground.

12

An Arrival and an Aftermath

A short time before Wag and the rest of the pilots were scrambled at 1505 that afternoon, Mickey Rook and those of us with him at Keg-Ostrov finally said farewell to our hosts and fired up the waiting Hurricanes. It felt great to be back in the cockpit, and I felt a shiver run down my spine as I completed my pre-take-off checks and fired up that mighty Merlin XX engine once again. Finally, after all the days spent killing time, waiting for the Hurricanes that Harry Gittins and his crew had built to be tested and signed off, we were ready to fly them to Vaenga.

My excitement at being back in the pilot's seat again was tempered, however, as I was feeling a little apprehensive about the flight ahead of us. Vaenga lay 300 miles away from us to the north-west, placing it at the absolute limit of endurance for the Hurricane. Gittins and his team had done everything they could to maximise the range of our aircraft, from setting the carbs to maximum economy to preserve fuel, to stripping each of the nine aircraft of their guns and ammunition. Weight is expensive in terms of fuel so anything we could do without was taken off the aircraft. Even so, we'd still have to go easy and keep the aircraft trimmed to be as lithe as possible.

It had been arranged for a Russian bomber to head our formation, meaning we wouldn't need to navigate our way to Vaenga, and there'd be no confusion or risk to us from Russian ground forces which might mistake us for Germans. As helpful as it was, it added to my worries because I was one of the first to get airborne, which meant I had to circle the aerodrome for almost ten minutes waiting for the rest of the formation to take off so that we could form up together behind the Russian bomber. Eventually, though, we were on our way, and as we flew across the White Sea, I noticed the ships down below us firing Very lights, which the bomber responded to with the colours of the day. It was quite magical to watch, and took my mind off the monotony of the flight.

I'd been so engrossed in what was going on down below us, however, that I didn't notice I'd subconsciously been applying pressure to the rudder bar on the left side, with a touch of right aileron, causing my aircraft to 'skid' as it flew. Ordinarily, it wouldn't be too much of an issue, but the way I was flying meant that the aircraft wasn't nose first, so it was presenting a side of the fuselage, and inducing drag. That meant that I was using more fuel to combat the added effects of the drag to make progress. That really worried me; added to the fact that we were using the lower-octane fuel supplied by the Russians [the solution worked out by the Russians with Henry Broquet hadn't been fully rolled out by this stage] it meant it would be really touch and go whether I'd have enough fuel on board to get me to our destination. The terrain beneath me didn't exactly fill me with confidence that I'd survive in the event of a forced landing either; it was relentlessly desolate, with no signs of human habitation as far as the eye could see.

Somehow, by constantly trimming the aircraft to ensure the leanest profile possible, and constantly looking at the fuel gauge and willing it to show positive, I made it. After about an hour or so's flying I got my first view of the aerodrome that was to be our home from several thousand feet up when I saw a few Hurricanes tucked in between trees on the airfield boundary. It looked cold, desolate and barren. As we made our approach, I could see other Hurricanes in the pattern, and as we came in to land, they slotted in between us. The airspace was busy, and I wondered what had happened, of course having no idea at that point that my colleagues in 81 Squadron had just shot down four of Jerry's aircraft and that we'd also lost one of our own.

Wag joined the circuit just as the last of our formation landed, and we were already on our way to the accommodation by the time he'd shut his aircraft down and was hanging around dispersal in a daze. He knew that they'd got the better of the patrol that they'd engaged; he'd seen the 109 he'd shot up go down in a blaze of fire, so that was a confirmed kill, and he'd seen Ibby bag the Henschel too, but he had no idea at this stage that Ibby had also downed a 109, nor that his wingman, Canadian Jimmy Walker, had also bagged one. Once they'd been debriefed, they sat down to write their combat reports. Written in spare, functional language, these contain only the most salient details of each dogfight and, once completed, become part of the Wing Operational Record Book or Form 540.

Wag's write-up goes:

At 1525 hrs. on 12.9.41 whilst leading a patrol of five Hurricanes over the enemy lines I intercepted five Me.109 E's escorting a Hs.126. My height was 3500 ft. The e/a were approaching from ahead and slightly to the left, and as I turned towards them, they turned slowly to their right. I attacked the leader as he turned and gave him a ten second burst from the full beam position. The e/a rolled on to its back, and as it went down burst into flames. I did not see it crash owing to taking evasive action, but Red 2 confirms that it passed him in a 70 degree dive at 500 ft., smoke and flames still pouring from it.

Jimmy Walker's report fills in the missing bits:

I took off at 1505 hrs. as Red 2. While flying on patrol at 3500 ft. sighted 5 109's and one Hs.126. Followed Red 1 into attack at about 1522 hrs. Broke away and engaged two of the 109's concurrently in head on attack. When about 500 ft saw the a/c Red 1 was attacking go past me breaking

*into flames and heading straight for the ground. Climbed
up and saw a 109 on Red 1's tail, headed in and gave the a/c
a couple of bursts of a few seconds each. The 109 broke
away and fell towards the ground pouring out smoke.
Followed him down and saw him roll over – then regain
upright position he then burst into flames and crashed.
Returned to base with Red 1, landed at 1550 hrs.*

Ibby reports that he was leader of Blue Section, and had followed
the actions of Red Section. He continues:

*I found myself in a favourable position to attack the
Hs.126, and after delivering a short burst from the beam it
turned and dived away steeply westwards. I followed,
overtaking rapidly and fired a burst at 50 ft. range. As I
passed over the top of the e/a a thick cloud of white
smoke poured from it. This was observed by Blue 2 (Sgt.
Rigby). I did not see what happened to the Henschel, as I
broke away and climbed again to 4000 ft. and had to look
out for Messerschmitts, and take violent weaving action.
From my height I saw a Me.109 and a Hurricane going
round in a circle at ground level. I dived, and using my
advantage of speed and height, was enabled to deliver a
rear quarter attack, followed by a front qtr-attack. I then
got on the tail of the e/a and again closed to 50 ft. range
and passed over the top of the e/a. As I delivered my last
attack I saw smoke coming from the e/a, which was flying
very low and just after I passed over it, I saw it crash in
flames. I did not see the other Hurricane again and
presumably it was Sgt. Smith, who was missing from the
engagement.*

Basil Rigby kept a brief diary of his time in Russia and in it he
describes the day's action:

Did a patrol and sighted enemy. Only five of us sighted six enemy. One Hs126 and five 109's. In the ensuing fight we shot four down, ie the 126 and three 109's. But poor old Smith was hit and all the way home was losing height. I circled above him also another Hurricane. We saw him try a crash landing, but in this country such are almost impossible. He was killed and his kite destroyed by fire.
This was a dampener on our first success. I was No 2 to Ibby Waud who shot two down. I stayed on his tail and did my job. This was my first fight and at the time I did not feel any fear – much – but given a bit more time on the way home I was quite glad it was over! Pity Smith was killed, but I suppose it's all in the foul cause of war.

It wasn't until they'd all been debriefed and completed their combat reports that they could begin to relax. Back in the flight hut, Wag realised just how successful their afternoon had been. Four confirmed kills for the loss of Nudger. That hurt, despite the elation that he felt personally for having got one. He was delighted, however, for his mate Ibby, who now had two kills to his name from the one patrol.

Wag lay back in one of the chairs; they could relax a little as they'd been downgraded to thirty minutes readiness. He was mentally and physically exhausted; they'd pulled a lot of G in those dogfights, and the physical exertion of throwing his aircraft all around the three-dimensional arena of the sky had taken a heavy toll.

'That dogfight, my friend, feels like the equivalent of a week's labour!' he said to Ibby, who had flopped down in the chair next to him, but he felt a little flat as what had happened to their friend Nudger interrupted his thoughts. He knew it was something they'd have to deal with but he wasn't looking forward to returning to the room that he and Ibby shared with their now dead friend. Also, Nudger's personal effects would have to be packed up, and there would be a Norman Smith-shaped hole in their lives that would be impossible to fill – but then, that was war. He'd also lost friends in the Battle of Britain. It was just another thing you had to deal with along with everything else this blasted war presented.

Ibby too felt drained. He was thinking about the two aircraft he'd shot down – more specifically, the pilots that he'd just killed. Were they men just like him? he wondered. Did they have families at home, wives and children who would never see their husband or father again? His elation at shooting them both down was tempered by the fragments of memory he had, the glimpses of the faces of the men he'd killed frozen in time to solitary images that he knew he'd carry with him for ever.[1]

Soon, though, their natural ebullience returned, and the two friends abandoned their thoughts and began to talk about what they'd just experienced.

'I can't believe those dumb Luftwaffe pilots turned away from us,' Wag said, 'when they'd so obviously seen our formation. The stupid bastards must have thought we were Messerschmitts because otherwise they'd have turned into us.

'They were obviously going fairly slowly to escort the Henschel which isn't a very quick machine, but they should have had the sense to "break" knowing for certain who we were.'[2]

'Well, I'm bloody glad they didn't,' replied Ibby. 'Those German pilots must have crapped themselves when they saw the British Hurricanes with RAF markings coming down on them.'[3]

They talked about their friend Nudger. Wag told Ibby he'd seen him go down and that he'd seen that the side of his Hurricane had been shot away shortly before he crashed. They worked out that it must have been their friend who had been circling the 109 which Ibby had dived on and chased up the valley. They'd felt a unity that went beyond mere friendship, those three. They had a kinship founded on the fact they were all Yorkshire lads – Nudger had come from Leeds – and they'd spent so much time together at

Leconfield and throughout the voyage. Although Nudger had been a sergeant pilot, the same as Wag and Ibby, he hadn't joined the VR before the war broke out and come up that way – he was too young. Sergeant Pilot 936292 Norman 'Nudger' Smith[4] had been just seventeen when he joined up and just nineteen when he'd been killed. They wondered whether he'd make good on the threat that had given him his nickname – to give them a 'nudge' now he was dead. They thought of his parents, receiving the telegram notifying them their son had been killed in action, followed by the letter that the CO would be writing to them. Ibby thought he should feel glad about the fact he'd shot down and killed the pilot of the 109 that had killed their friend, but he didn't. There was nothing glorious about killing people who, like Ibby and his pals, had been sent by politicians to fight on their behalf.

Later that evening, two sections of aircraft from 134 Squadron took off on the sixth and final patrol of the day and intercepted three enemy bombers escorted by four Me109s. They'd been on their way across the front lines to attack Archangel, but when the 134 Squadron pilots bounced them, the Luftwaffe bombers immediately dropped their loads to make them more manoeuvrable. Then they turned tail and fled, without causing any damage, and the 134 Squadron pilots returned to base without having fired a shot.

It had been a busy day and the wing had really made its mark. The Luftwaffe in the area had had it easy up until now, but the RAF were the new sheriffs in town and they'd made a statement of intent to the Germans across the front line. The conversation in the messes of the Wehrmacht, Waffen SS and Luftwaffe that night must have turned on the fact that '*einige Jagd-staffeln*' of RAF Hurricanes, squadron number and wing number unknown, had dropped in on their sector of the front with a vengeance.[5]

I'm sure Wing Commander Isherwood took great pleasure in drafting his signal to the Air Ministry later that night with details of the day's actions. His draft signal now resides in a file of Sir

Charles Portal's papers relating to 151 Wing at the National Archives in Kew. It reads:

> *Enemy bombers were sighted by the first patrol of three aircraft of 134 Squadron but they avoided combat. In the second patrol, one Me 110 was attacked and damaged by two aircraft of 81 Squadron.*
>
> *Three aircraft of 134 Squadron gave escort cover to Soviet bombers but there were no engagements. On the fourth patrol, three aircraft of 134 Squadron gave cover to Soviet bombers but there were no engagements. Four Me 109s and one Henschel were intercepted by four aircraft of 81 Squadron in the fifth patrol. Two Me 109s were destroyed, one probably destroyed and the Henschel was damaged.*
>
> *In the sixth patrol, five aircraft of 134 Squadron intercepted three enemy bombers which were attempting to attack Archangel, the enemy evaded combat and dropped bombs ad lib without causing damage. The four Me 109s escorting the bombers evaded combat.*
>
> *Casualties for day:– Own, one aircraft, Sgt Pilot N. I. Smith killed. Enemy:– Three aircraft destroyed, one probable,[6] one damaged.[7]*

It had been a remarkable day really, with the wing carrying out its first offensive patrols. Not defensive, in response to the Luftwaffe attacking the base, probing, looking for a way forward. No, the wing had been actively patrolling with the intention of looking for trouble, and finding it. It had also carried out important escort patrols protecting Soviet bombers in the first dual operation since they'd arrived in Russia. On those occasions, their role had been to conduct patrols whose primary mission was to shepherd the aircraft of their allies safely up to their targets and back, rather than seeking desultory combat as the opportunity presented itself.

SECRET CYPHER TELEGRAM   WX.1400

TO:- AIR MINISTRY RFTD AIR ATTACHE MOSCOW.
FROM: 151 WING.

<u>IMMEDIATE</u>   <u>RECD. A.M.C.S. 1545 HOURS 13.9.41</u>

A.6 12/9. DAILY STATE OPERATION. BOTH SQUADRONS ENGAGED
ON AERODROME DEFENCE PATROLS. 6 PATROLS CARRIED OUT. FIRST
PATROL 3 AIRCRAFT 134 SQUADRON - ENEMY BOMBERS SIGHTED EVADED
COMBAT ON CONTACT ?. SECOND PATROL (CORRUPT GROUP) AIRCRAFT
81 SQUADRON ATTACKED ONE ME. 110 AND CAUSED DAMAGE (CORRUPT
GROUP) POSSIBLE. THIRD PATROL 3 AIRCRAFT OF 134 SQUADRON
GAVE COVER TO SOVIET BOMBERS, NIL ENGAGEMENTS. FOURTH PATROL
3 AIRCRAFT 134 SQUADRON GAVE COVER SOVIET BOMBERS NIL
ENGAGEMENTS. FIFTH PATROL 4 AIRCRAFT 81 SQDN INTERCEPTED 4
ME. 109'S AND 1 HENSCHEL - 2 ME. 109 DESTROYED, 1 PROBABLE
1 HENSCHEL DAMAGED. SIXTH PATROL 5 AIRCRAFT OF 134 SQDN
PROVIDED COVER TO HURRICANES FROM ARCHANGEL - 3 ENEMY
BOMBERS ENGAGED BY A.A. GUNS FIGHTERS GUIDED TO COMBAT BY
A.A. BURSTS ENEMY EVADED (?) AND DROPPED BOMBS AD LIB WITHOUT
CAUSING DAMAGE - 4 ME.109 ESCORTING BOMBERS ALSO EVADED
COMBAT, AIRCRAFT STATE 134 SQUADRON 6 AS 8 GUN FIGHTERS 81
SQUADRON 8 AS 6 GUN FIGHTERS. AIRCRAFT OF 81 SQUADRON ON
FIFTH PATROL CARRIED 6 GUNS. 6 AIRCRAFT AS 6 GUN FIGHTERS
ARRIVED FROM ARCHANGEL NON-OPERATIONAL. REMAINDER MAIN PARTY
ARRIVED MID DAY 12TH SEPTEMBER. CASUALTIES ENEMY
3 DESTROYED ONE POSSIBLE ONE DAMAGED CASUALTIES OWN 1
AIRCRAFT SERGEANT PILOT 935292 OR 936292 N.I. SMITH KILLED.

TIME OF ORIGIN 1830 HOURS/12.

ADVANCE   COPIES TO:-   S. OF S., C.A.S., F.O.4 (2)
                                          ACTION.

This image of the signal sent on 13 September shows the actual text differs slightly from that which Isherwood drafted.

With no radar to act as an early-warning system, or a guide to vector them on to German aircraft, the RAF pilots had been guided towards combat by accurate Soviet anti-aircraft fire. Four enemy aircraft had been destroyed for certain, while another had been fired at and those rounds had all found their target. The wing had lost one of its own pilots in Norman 'Nudger' Smith, a loss that was keenly felt.

Later that day, the Wing Headquarters party under Flight Lieutenant Hubert Griffith arrived after a mammoth 600-mile, four-day journey by locomotive from Archangel to Murmansk and then on to Vaenga. On the journey, the train they'd been travelling on had halted for a short time opposite a Russian hospital train coming down the track they'd been travelling on. This gave Griffith a chance to try out his Russian language skills, which he'd been honing in England, and he was delighted to find that as well as understanding what he heard, he was understood in turn when conversing. One positive note was the overwhelming positivity of the Russian troops they came across, who all gave the universal thumbs-up sign when Griffith had pointed out that 'we are the Royal Air Force arriving'.

They were extraordinarily lucky to have made the journey unscathed, as the Luftwaffe was heavily focused on the Kola Peninsula, particularly in the region of Murmansk and Archangel, in an effort to accelerate General Dietl's aim of capturing it. The railway lines that the wing adjutant and his party had used were Stalin's main resource for bringing reinforcements and supplies to the front line, and had previously been heavily bombed. Yet in the four days it took Hubert Griffith and the one hundred or so men travelling with him, there wasn't a single raid on the area.

When Artie Holmes flew in with five reserve pilots in the final six Hurricanes a few days later, shortly followed by Gittins and his Erection Party, the wing was finally at full strength. After our separate journeys by air, land and sea, from the *Llanstephan Castle,* the *Argus* and Keg-Ostrov, this was the first time since we'd departed from Leconfield in late summer that we were all together again, here in the Arctic Circle. The reunions went on all afternoon and into the evening. We were finally at full operational strength and ready to undertake the mission we'd been sent by Churchill to carry out – to defend Murmansk *at all costs*.

13

Reunited

September 13th was our first full day at Vaenga for Johnny, myself and the others who had flown in on the previous day, so we spent the morning getting ourselves organised and doing the rounds. I'd got to know Nudger Smith only at Leconfield and had rather liked him, so I was greatly saddened by the news of his death, although the overall mood within the wing was upbeat and positive, with everyone buoyed by the successes of Wag, Ibby and Jimmy.

Being newly arrived, Johnny and I were a little concerned at the proximity of the base to the front line. We'd heard that there were regular air raids on the aerodrome by the Luftwaffe, but that wasn't a major worry because it had been taken into account in the design, which saw the buildings placed far apart. My biggest concern was that we might be overrun, but Wag put my mind at rest when he told me that there were 'hundreds, maybe thousands, of Russian soldiers hidden in the surrounding woods'.

I wasn't greatly impressed by our accommodation – Johnny and I were unlucky enough to choose the only room in the block infested with vermin. My hair was quite short so it wasn't a major issue for me, but Johnny shaved all his hair off in a panic and then, seeing his bald head in the mirror, wound bandages around it. Johnny was highly conscious of how he looked – his vanity extended to his having had his uniform tailor-made back in England – so it really upset him. There was no way we could stay in the brick-built accommodation, so I had a word with the wing's transport chief. He and I had become good friends – we were both from the same part of Birmingham, so we had an immediate connection there to start with. He'd made his home in one of the 30 ft x 10 ft x 9 ft crates that the Hurricanes had been shipped over in and there was plenty of space, so he invited us to move in with him while our room was fumigated.

We were both surprised by just how far away everything was – we walked over half a mile from our accommodation to get to 'the Kremlin', which is where the operations room was situated. That, at least, looked a little more like the RAF stations back home – once inside, we could have been at any RAF base in England for all we knew; the walls were covered in the familiar blackboards displaying the names, numbers and letters of all the wing's pilots and aircraft.

One plus for Johnny and me was the food; well, not just the food – the Russian waitresses were an absolute delight. Some of them were really pretty so we certainly looked forward to meal-times. Their names were Mirosa, Norah, Anya, Ira, Lucie and Ryeesa, and they delighted in teaching us the names of the food items they served us. That said, they steadfastly refused all our attempts to teach them English, though!

The food was richer than we'd been used to but there was smoked salmon and vegetable soup, too. Maybe it was simply down to the fact we'd finally reached what was to be our permanent home for the next month or so and we were relaxed, but I really enjoyed our first few meals in the mess. One of our most favourite foods was the thick slices of cold ham that were always on the menu, although one day we went in and it had been taken off the menu. We learned that the Germans had captured the crossroads, which meant Russian food supplies couldn't get through. However, a few days later, the Russians launched a counter-offensive and won back the crossroads, and a few days after that the ham reappeared, only this time it was supplemented by some even tastier ham that had been taken off the Germans. From then on, ham was our very rudimentary war barometer, which we found highly amusing. If there was ham at breakfast, it meant we were winning. The more serious aspect to that was that if the Germans held the crossroads and managed to break through the Russian line, they'd have cut off the Kola Peninsula. That meant the entire wing would fall into German hands too.

Despite the vast and impressive range of food, fresh fruit and greens were in desperately short supply; in fact, they were utterly non-existent here, so to ensure we stayed fit and healthy, we were issued with vitamin tablets each day.

One of the things that really surprised me on that first day was the sheer logistical nightmare of trying to feed over five hundred of us when the largest dining hall at Vaenga could accommodate only 100 at a time. This obviously imposed huge pressures on the Russian waitresses, and it meant that feeding times for us were staggered over quite a wide time frame for each meal. As senior NCOs, we had our own sitting, as did the officers, and we were delighted to discover at supper on that first evening that large decanters of red wine were placed on the tables. I don't think any of us had eaten as well as we had over the past couple of months in years!

It was a quiet day from an operational perspective; six patrols were carried out over the course of the day, although none of them saw combat. There were no casualties to the wing either, although two of the Hurricanes broke their propellers as they were taxiing; that should give some idea of just how lumpy and uneven the ground was on dispersal. That put two machines out of action for a while. When the rest of the flight returned from one patrol, it was found that the oil around the guns on one aircraft had frozen, and another Hurricane landed with the pilot reporting that his windscreen had frozen at 8,000 ft.

The 14th dawned with thick cloud; it was cold, heavily over-cast, really grey and dull – rather like the mood of the wing as we prepared for Nudger's funeral later on that day. There was hardly any flying – just four patrols with no combat – and nobody felt much like doing anything, but however difficult things are, you don't have a choice. The wing had to carry on operating as normal. It must have been doubly hard for Ibby and Wag – especially Wag, who had seen their room-mate and good pal die first-hand. They were both to be pallbearers, a duty which I think weighed heavily on them but which they wouldn't have turned down even if they could. I think all of us at some point before the funeral must have remembered Norman's promise to come back from the dead and give everyone a nudge in the arm. He was forever doing that when he was alive; he'd come up behind you and give you a nudge in the arm with his knuckles. It got old very quickly and could be quite annoying sometimes. What any of us would have given to feel it just one more time.

All of the pilots were there for the funeral service that evening, along with the CO and most of the Wing Executive. We were driven out of the aerodrome around 1730 in a series of three-tonners provided by the Russians. I was travelling with Wag, Ibby, Basil Rigby, Avro Anson and others, and nobody said much; we were all content to be alone with our thoughts. There wasn't much to see as we made the short journey from the aerodrome, through the village of Vaenga itself (literally nothing to see here) and on to Murmansk itself.

After journeying for nearly an hour and driving up some steep hills, we arrived at a village situated on the high ground overlooking Murmansk Sound. As the pallbearers carried Nudger through the village to the grave, which was in the Cemetery of Soviet Heroes, his coffin was draped side by side with a British White Ensign that, in a touching gesture, the Russians had made and dyed unasked, and the flag of the Soviet Fleet Air Arm. Many of the villagers had turned out and bowed their heads as the coffin passed while Russian soldiers in fur hats saluted. The RAF had sent a guard of honour and a firing party, and the Russians too had sent one. The Royal Navy also provided a guard of honour. The funeral service, which was in English, was conducted by

Flight Lieutenant Fisher, the wing's signals and welfare officer. Wag thought a Hurricane should have been detailed to fly across the landscape in a final salute; it would have been better that way.

Not much happened of note on the 15th; the wing's Operations Record Book details five patrols, no combat, no casualties, and goes on to say that 'The Jerries appear to be rather shy around here up to the present and prefer rather to run back than try and reach their objectives. A German formation, turned back by our fighters this morning, dropped their bombs by mistake on their own troops. One Hurricane, which landed on soft ground should be difficult, if not impossible, to repair by the Wing. Two buildings acquired for use as Airmen's Recreation Rooms.'[1]

The 16th saw another funeral, this time of one of the Russians' air aces and a Soviet sergeant pilot. The wing sent a firing party and Wing Commander Isherwood along with several of the Wing Executive. The local brass band turned out and played Chopin's Funeral March. It was a very political occasion with speeches made at the graveside lasting from 1700 until 2215. Hubert Griffith described it in his diary as 'Impressive – in a different way'.

Back in the mess, Hubert Griffith reports that 'Mickey Rook had been testing his Hurricane and was asked if he'd made a good landing. Our Squadron CO's reply was, "Perfect, old boy! Put her down as light as a gnat's whisker!"'

Hubert goes on, 'Seeing that a twelve-gun Hurricane weighs nearly four and a half tons, the phrase had great verbal charm, if some exaggeration.

'Dozens of fresh eggs have appeared in the Mess, served, fried, in plates of three. Mickey Rook eats three, then is pressed by the Russian waitresses to take another plate of three, and complies. Then is pressed to take another three but declines. "I can eat a flight but not a squadron . . ."'[2]

There were no patrols that afternoon or evening owing to the weather.

The 17th was another red-letter day for 81 Squadron, and Wag in particular. The mountain of fresh eggs that the waitresses had seemed so keen to reduce courtesy of Mickey Rook showed no sign of disappearing any time soon. I'd enjoyed a wonderful lunch with Wag, Ibby and Johnny consisting of more smoked salmon, caviar, some wonderful ham and, yes, fried eggs. Thoughts of that awful egg powder that we were reduced to eating as a result of rationing back in England were long gone. The Russian wait-ress tried to foist more eggs on us but Wag, Johnny and I had eaten our fill. Ibby must have had hollow legs because he was given a plate of three eggs just as Mickey Rook had been. Still, Ibby could relax, as could Johnny; Wag and I were on readiness that evening and down for a bomber escort job.

Squadron Leader Tony Rook was to head things up, leading the squadron in eight aircraft – four from each flight. He would lead Red Section as Red one, and Wag was earmarked to lead Yellow Section, with Bushy leading Blue Section and Avro Anson Green Section. I was flying as Wag's wingman as Yellow two, with Ken Bishop as Yellow three, and Basil Rigby was Blue two. Squadron formation would be the familiar set-up they'd developed during the Battle of Britain in those halcyon days of summer 1940. God, things had been so different then. How'd we end up in Russia?

Red Section would lead in a Vic of three, Blue and Green Sections in trailing Vic formation behind Red two and Red three, with Yellow Section as 'weavers'; Yellow one would fly line astern of Red leader, with myself and Yellow three stepped above and below the formation looking out for bandits and protecting the formation rear.

Things were a little more relaxed with bomber escorts, so having made myself at home in the flight hut, I walked out to dispersal to get some fresh air and walk off some of my lunch. I watched as ground crews readied the waiting Hurricanes for their sorties; while some of the airmen wiped down and cleaned wind-screens, others plugged in the accumulator trolleys or inspected the aircraft for damage. Just outside the hut, a few airmen were manning a suction pump in an attempt to drain a small lake which had formed and was edging towards dispersals. For a moment, I stood and drank it all in – the clouds scudding across the endless sky, the aerodrome, the aircraft – RAF aircraft – here in Russia, high up inside the Arctic Circle. The temperature was noticeably colder than it had been but my Mae West, which I wore like a padded waistcoat, kept me warm, as did my other clothing – my battledress, thick white polo-neck jumper and heavy, fur-lined flying boots.

I pondered for a moment. My first gig in Russia. I was strangely apprehensive, but reminded myself it was all familiar. I knew the aircraft, I'd flown patrols before, just not here. 'C'mon, Eric,' I told myself, 'it's the same meat, different gravy.' I checked my watch and thought about heading back.

As I entered the flight hut, I heard the sound of the field telephone being put down.

'C'mon, Ginger, bandits reported, we're to scramble and patrol the area around the Kola inlet,' Wag told me as the pilots grabbed their gear and ran out to their waiting aircraft on dispersal. I missed the Battle of Britain, so the concept of being 'scrambled' was new to me. I felt galvanised, empowered, *amplified*, every sense hyper-alert, my nervous system seemingly energised as I climbed into the cockpit of 'my' Hurricane. Cockpit drills were automatic for me now, carried out subconsciously before I signalled to my ground crew, waving away the chocks and firing up that trusty Merlin engine. I watched the stabs of flame swiftly followed by the black puff of smoke that emanated from the six exhausts either side of the cowling ahead of me.

There wasn't time to sit and idle, waiting for the needle of the oil temperature gauge to move; I eased the throttle open and pointed my aircraft down the rudimentary runway, my machine bumping and rocking over the undulating ground before slipping gravity's chains and climbing skyward. I quickly got into formation. Meanwhile, across the sky from me, Wag, flying Z5208, looked across to his left and saw me and Ken Bishop to his right. He waved us into a line astern formation, and as he watched us throttle back and tuck in behind his tail, he in turn adjusted his throttle to move into position behind Red two of the leading section. We were all playing our parts to perfection as the squadron manoeuvred into battle formation.

We kept a lookout as the formation climbed to 5,000 ft before levelling out below billowing great clouds, the sun glinting off windscreens. I kept my head up, eyes constantly searching the sky for threats. With no enemy in sight, I even started to enjoy the sensation; I drank in the view as the sunlight glinted off lakes and other bodies of water on the tundra below, watching the way the clouds cast shadows on the ground.

This is what I loved about flying, what attracts most aviators. It's the freedom, the view, the sensation of being able to control a machine that operates in three dimensions. Even the sensation of G, that elemental force so benign on the ground that could be so deadly in the air, is enjoyable at times. It comes on in high-speed turns and other violent manoeuvres as hypotension, gravity pooling blood in the legs and feet and starving the brain and eyes of sufficient oxygen. You feel it as a so-called 'grey-out' [monochromatic vision], followed by tunnel vision. In the most extreme cases it results in g-induced loss of consciousness or g-LOC – also known as 'end point' in that it almost invariably has fatal consequences. Knowing how to spot the signs – and easing off when it gets too severe – are key. But it is just another aspect of flying that I loved; it's another feeling, something that made me feel *alive*, so I just rolled with it and enjoyed the sensation.

I noticed the absence of Russian flak bursts pointing towards bandits and wondered whether this would prove to be yet another patrol with no engagements; the past few days had seen lots of patrols but no contact with the enemy. The squadron flew on over the inlet, above the port of Murmansk and the town of Kola, then turned to port and headed south, maintaining a watch towards the border and Petsamo. We made a turn west, flying directly into the sun now, and I adjusted the intensity of the reticule in my gunsight, bringing the brightness up to full so it was easily visible.

Suddenly, I saw tracer flashing past, above and to the right of Wag's starboard wing. 'Shit,' I thought, 'where on earth did that come from?'

We soon discovered it had come from an Me109 that had appeared out of nowhere, but its pilot had messed up because he'd made the cardinal error of flying past Wag and ahead of him. Wag didn't hesitate; he kicked on the rudder bar and opened the throttle wide, closing in behind the German fighter. He gently pulled the control stick towards his stomach, and there it was: the Me109 was perfectly positioned in his sights. He flicked the button to 'fire' and gave it a five-second burst. He felt his aircraft jump from the recoil.

I watched and it was as if time had become elastic. Tracer has that effect too – loaded every tenth round, it has a strobing effect that is undeniably mesmeric. I looked through my windscreen as the tracer and incendiary rounds appeared to describe a line in slow motion, and hit underneath the Messerschmitt's port wing root. I saw white glycol vapour pouring from the damaged aircraft, swiftly followed by telltale black smoke. Its nose dipped slightly and it started losing altitude. I saw the canopy go back, and the pilot struggled for a moment, then climbed out and dropped like a stone. Within seconds his canopy opened and his descent slowed. If he got down alive, there was a good chance he'd be taken as a prisoner of war by the Russians.

Suddenly, there was another Me109, and it was ahead and slightly below me. It must have dived on us with the one Wag had just hit. I pushed forward gently on the stick and levelled up; the reticule on my gunsight sat right on the enemy aircraft ahead. My finger hovered over the fire button and a momentary thought came into my head: 'I'd better make this right because he won't half be cross if I miss!' 'What a stupid thing to think, Eric!' the silent voice in my head told me, but that was just the place my head was in at the time. I brushed the thoughts away and cleared my head as my finger pressed the button and I gave him a three-second burst. I followed the tracer and saw the shells hit and leave a series of holes along his fuselage but he disappeared into cloud and I lost him.

Did I just dream that? It all happened so quickly. Was it a kill? I don't think so; I *know* I hit him. Did I see him go down? No. I couldn't even claim it as a probable unless someone else saw it. I looked around me and the sky was clear. The absence of aircraft spooked me; it was as if I'd gone through a wormhole and into a parallel time and space. Where was the rest of the squadron? Where did the 109s go? It always surprised me that the sky could be a maelstrom of activity, full of aircraft one minute, and suddenly completely empty, where you were the only aircraft and the sky was clear to the limits of visibility in every direction.

I flew around for five minutes, but the sky around me remained empty so I turned and ran for home, and on the approach took a closer look at the village of Vaenga, which lay about a mile and a half outside the aerodrome. It was a Wild West shanty town straight out of central casting, a series of wood-built structures with boardwalks and lots of dirt. My interest was more than passing; we were due to go there the following day for an escorted visit to the village steam bath house. I was looking forward to getting out and seeing life outside the aerodrome, even if it was run down and close by. It was a change of view.

Wag meanwhile, having taken his shot, didn't see the pilot bale out. He didn't even see the aircraft go down. So far as he was concerned, he needed to get away from the target, in case his rounds hadn't hit and the pilot had designs on taking another shot at *him*. He pulled back hard on the stick and booted hard on the rudder, hauling his Hurricane away from danger in a high-speed climbing turn, twisting his head as he did so in search of other threats. His head was a haze of sensory overload – fragments of sunlit waters on the ground as he continued to climb in a violent spiral, the non-stop chatter over the RT that told him he wasn't the only one engaged in a dogfight, the weight-intensifying effects of the high G-forces pinning him to his seat and making his arms feel like lead.

He broke into cloud and, with no visual input, focused on the cockpit instruments to fly straight and level. Denied visual cues, the brain loses the ability to correctly assess your altitude relative to the horizon; it tells you you're climbing when you're descending, and vice versa, banking left when you're flying level or turning right. The cockpit instruments always read true, but even so, it takes time during training to override what your brain is telling you and rely instead on what *they* tell you.

The tracer fire that the Me109 had fired at Wag had really shaken him. He felt both shocked and indignant; that German pilot had meant him harm! It sounds stupid, I know, but it's one thing being the hunter, quite another when you're the one being hunted. It was a real wake-up call for him, and he took the opportunity while he was flying on instruments to calm down a little. He breathed in deeply through his oxygen mask, focused on flying straight and level while his brain processed the events of a few minutes earlier and made sense of them. They were bounced by those 109s, he knew that now. They must have dived on them through a gap in the clouds while the squadron was flying towards the sun. He was amazed, though – just as on his previous sortie, he'd come up close and personal with another inexperienced Luftwaffe pilot who not only failed to shoot him down but went on to present Wag with the sort of perfect target that fighter pilots dream of.

It dawned on him that there was no way that 109 had made it home. Not with the number of rounds he had put in it and their location. He still couldn't get his head around the pilot making it so easy on him; 'Fire at me, miss, then fly straight and level fifty feet above and ahead of me, so all I have to do is shift the nose up a few degrees and goodnight!' he thought. He checked his watch . . . damn, he'd been airborne for thirty-five minutes already. It'd be close on an hour when he got back.

It did him good to take a time out, and as he broke cloud again into clear sky, he was feeling a little more confident and relaxed again. He headed north to pick up the familiar shape of the Kola inlet and made his way back to Vaenga. The thought that he'd shot down a second 109 to go with the one he bagged on the 12th lifted him and he flew a few loops, rolls and inverted turns on the way back. Having a near-death experience does tend to bring out the *joie de vivre* in you like that. He selected flap and made a curved approach to ensure he touched down well up the airfield and his 4½-ton Hurricane sank on to the sandy, uneven surface of the 'runway'. He taxied on to dispersal, where he gave the engine a final burst from the throttle before shutting it down and climbing out. He removed his oxygen mask, helmet and gloves, breathing in great gulps of cold, fresh air. Nobby, his engine fitter, wandered over and, smiling, handed him a mug of hot tea. He was joined by his rigger and armourer and he grinned widely at them. They knew, without any words being exchanged, that he'd bagged another one. He handed his Hurricane over to the care of his ground crew, and somewhat jauntily made his way back to the flight hut.

I walked over to him as he entered. 'Bloody good work, mate,' I said, 'you always seem to be in the right place at the right time. I saw you pull up your nose and knock down that 109. Nice one!'

'Cheers, pal,' he acknowledged as Avro Anson slapped him hard on the back.

'Bloody hell, Wag,' Avro said, 'I really thought he'd got you at first, his bloody tracer was so damn close I don't know how he missed. Then you really let him have it and I saw loads of white smoke followed by the black stuff and he spun in. I saw pieces of his aircraft flying off and he went into a vertical dive. The pilot baled out but I saw the aircraft go down, mate, that's a definite.'

Wag's wasn't the squadron's only success on that sortie. At 1855 Tony Rook in BD792 had opened fire as an Me109 passed in front of him. He saw his shells hit it, and glycol started to pour from it. After chasing it for five minutes, slowing it to 150 mph and repeatedly opening up on it, his Hurricane ran out of ammunition, so Flight Sergeant Peter Sims in Z5228 and Avro Anson in Z5207 attacked it, and saw its engine catch fire. Then it spiralled down out of control and they watched it crash beside a lake.

A little later, at 1915, six Me109s dived on 'B' Flight, which was escorting some Russian bombers back following a raid across the front line, and Bushy, who was leading the flight in Z4017, took one of them on and gave it a short burst, following which it went into a steep dive and crashed into a hill. The other German fighters fled back to their own lines, and the Russian bombers and Hurricanes returned safely and everyone sat down for the debrief. Bushy's combat report is rather illuminating. His write-up goes:

On date mentioned [17 September 1941] I was leading 'B' Flight 81 Squadron after being ordered up at 18:30hrs. To cover the retreat of some Russian bombers. At 19:15hrs two Me109Es were sighted about to attack the bombers. On looking behind I noticed six more Me109s diving from above and behind and turned sharply to port to engage the outside 109 which was nearest. A dog fight ensued in which I was able to outturn the E.A. and deliver a two sec. burst from the starboard quarter. Thick black smoke came from the E.A. as it dived to earth, and getting in another short burst E.A. burst into flames and crashed into hill. A second E.A was diving upon me as I looked behind but after turning sharply to port, I lost E.A. and after cruising around for another five mins, I returned to base.[3]

Following the debrief, the wing's intelligence officer recorded that three Me109s were confirmed as destroyed. An Me110 was also shot down according to the 81 Squadron 540, which states, 'although it is not known who hit it, the Russian Observer Corps insist that it was shot down by the Squadron'.[4] 'So, after two full days of operational flying, the score stood at seven-to-one in the Wing's favour, apart from any enemy aircraft "probably destroyed", destroyed or damaged. Except for the loss of our one Hurricane and pilot, there had not been a single bullet-hole in any No 151 Wing machine.'[5]

Incidentally, it was no use claiming you'd shot six down when in reality you'd shot down one, two or even none at all, because there was a camera on each wing. They weren't there to catch us out, or to record what we'd done per se, but the images from them were pored over in great detail after each sortie, purely to see whether anything useful could be learned from the footage. As soon as we landed, the gun tapes went straight to the intelligence officer so he could have a look, see what information he could glean, after which he'd quiz us. It was a very primitive sort of set-up for the intel team there in Russia – they had a little hut, just like everyone else. They'd be looking for anything we could use – were the pilots we were up against green, newly commissioned, or old sweats? Had their aircraft been modified in any way? Was the ammo they were using standard stuff or enhanced? What were the registration numbers or decals on the sides of the 109s? Every detail, no matter how small, was logged, analysed and interpreted.

Of course, being the first British forces in Russia, we were targeted by William Joyce, better known as Lord Haw-Haw. The Germans knew we were there, so he'd come on the radio saying, 'We know the Royal Air Force is here in Murmansk. Well, you got in, but I'll see you never get out again.' It was all targeted specifically at us. He'd say our wives and girlfriends had gone off and were sleeping with other men. 'Did you know your wives are being seen to by other men while you're here, and they love it!' He tried anything and everything he could to try to break our morale, but it was water off a duck's back to us. Traitorous bastard; he got what he deserved in the end.

That night, the aurora borealis put on a show the likes of which I'd never seen before, nor since. It was, quite simply, stunning in its intensity and range, the colours drawn from some celestial paintbox of infinite hues. They danced like bent searchlights, continually shifting their beams, and the display left me open mouthed in wonder. It was as if nature was applauding the work we'd done since we'd arrived in fighting the German curse on Russia and doing our tiny bit towards ending the war. On the other hand, it might just have been a natural phenomenon caused by the collision of energetic charged particles with atoms in the high-altitude atmosphere! Perhaps it always looks as it did to us on that night. Whatever the case, I've never forgotten its beauty.

While we'd been busy in Russia making our presence felt among the Germans, Stalin had been pestering Churchill for more assistance in the form of 'a second front somewhere in the Balkans or France, capable of drawing away from the eastern front thirty to forty divisions, thirty thousand tons of aluminium by the beginning of October next, and a monthly minimum of aid amounting to four hundred aircraft and five hundred tanks'.[6] There's no pleasing some people, is there?

Churchill had made it clear to the Russian leader that the Hurricanes he'd already committed to northern Russia had seriously diminished his reserves, so Stalin tried a different tack. In a telegram to Churchill dated 15 September, he said that, in the absence of a second front, 'Great Britain could, without any risk, land in Archangel twenty or thirty divisions, or transport them across Iran to the southern regions of the USSR'.[7]

His request shows perhaps how skewed Stalin's perspective was. This must have appeared ludicrous to Churchill, rooted in the absurd, but in an effort to reassure Stalin, he dispatched Lord

Beaverbrook on a mission to Moscow to reiterate the message that aid to Russia was of prime importance with one proviso; some things were quite obviously impossible.

Group Captain Bird arrived at the base from Moscow on the 18th, bringing with him copies of two signals relating to 151 Wing's initial operations in Murmansk. Air Chief Marshal Sir Charles Portal, Chief of the British Air Staff, wrote,

British Air Squadrons have arrived in the U.S.S.R. and are now operating from Soviet territory against the common enemy. On this first and memorable occasion of our two Air Forces fighting side by side on Russian soil, I send you the warmest congratulation of all ranks of the Royal Air Force on the skilful and heroic resistance maintained by the Soviet Air Forces against the German invaders.

Permit me to express the confident hope that this may prove the beginning to ever wider and closer collaboration between our two Air Forces, each of which is already straining to the utmost to hasten the final defeat and collapse of the Nazi aggressors.[8]

Major General Kuznetsov, commander-in-chief of the Russian Fleet and Air Service [under whose supreme command the wing came], replied,

Dear Air Chief Marshal,
I am happy to confirm receipt of your telegram on the occasion of the first RAF operations at MURMANSK. These operations are the very real expression of the inflexible will of the two great freedom loving peoples who have mobilized their armed and economic might for a decisive and merciless fight against the German invaders.

I am sincerely happy at the fact that the lucky chance of beginning operations against the common enemy side by

side with the RAF on an important part of the Front has fallen to the Air Force of the Soviet Navy.

I take this opportunity of expressing to you, Air Chief Marshal of the British Royal Air Force, my sincere regards and respect. [9]

The full text of the two signals was copied and the exchanges put up on every noticeboard throughout the aerodrome at Vaenga. Reading them gave us all a renewed sense of unity and purpose, because we felt that the fact our operations had attracted the attention of both high commands here and back in England was an extraordinary achievement. There was an *esprit de corps* about the wing now, and this made us all feel important, I suppose, because what we'd done so far had been recognised at the very highest level.

Little did we know that the concern for our welfare went right to the top back home and Churchill himself exercised a personal interest in how we were faring, as evidenced by a personal memo that he drafted to Sir Charles Portal a few days later. Stamped 'PRIME MINISTER'S PERSONAL MINUTE Serial No. M.918/1', dated 22 September and signed in his hand, it reads: 'C.A.S, I asked a week ago for a report on the sorties made from Murmansk by our two Squadrons. We have hardly heard a word of their activities.'[10]

Sir Charles Portal's reply to Churchill, which he wrote and delivered the same day, is a classic exercise in arse-covering. Marked 'Secret', it reads,

Prime Minister,
Your Minute M. 918/1 dated 22nd September. You directed last week that you were to be provided with daily news of R.A.F operations at Murmansk anf [sic] *you were accordingly placed on the distribution list of the Daily Operational Summary from 151 Wing, Murmansk with*

THIS DAY

PRIME MINISTER'S
PERSONAL MINUTE

10, Downing Street,
Whitehall.

C.A.S.

SERIAL No. M.918/1

I asked a week ago for a report on the sorties
made from Murmansk by our two Squadrons. We have ~~not~~ hardly heard
a word of their activities.

22.9.41

This memo, written and signed by Winston Churchill himself, shows he took a
personal interest in Force Benedict throughout our time in Russia.

effect from 18th September. This meant that you would receive a Daily Summary for the 17th September and every subsequent day. After that we had no more until the 20th September, when we received summaries for three consecutive days. Since then they have arrived regularly. The failure was probably due to the electrical disturbances which were widespread last week.

Bad weather has restricted flying recently and analysis of the last five Daily Summaries show 6 patrols flown, 4 M.E. 109's destroyed and none of our aircraft lost.[11]

The Russians appeared to really go to town in promoting what we were doing off the back of those cables, which were published in both the London and the Soviet press. But it's a truism that with success comes publicity, and with our victories in the air, they wasted no time in using us for propaganda purposes. News reporters, camera crews and photographers invaded our ranks in swarms and we were photographed in every pose and location imaginable – standing on wings, getting into, out of and sitting in cockpits, taking off in formation, landing, and with great belts of ammunition being loaded into our aircraft. They had us shaking hands with Russian pilots and posing with our arms around the young and attractive female Russian interpreters. It was novel at first, but we got fed up with it very quickly.

We had our first bath since arriving at Vaenga on the 18th, and it was an interesting experience to say the least. Arrangements had been made for airmen to attend on four afternoons a week and for officers on two evenings, and I thought after that first visit even once a month might prove too frequent for some of the more, er . . . 'modest' fellows in the wing. Let me explain.

Shouldering our haversacks containing our wash kits and clean clothes, we boarded a three-tonner for the short drive along a bumpy road to one of the few brick-built buildings in the village of Vaenga itself. My appraisal from the air the previous day hadn't been too wide of the mark; there were no pavements, nothing much of anything really. A few wooden buildings stood looking much, as I'd thought, like a film set out of the Wild West, complete with dirt roads and footways.

We entered a locker room where we all stripped off and made our way into the steam bath, which was a room very similar to a modern sauna. There were four or five giant steps leading from the floor at the front almost to the ceiling at the back. Obviously, the higher up you went, the hotter the steam was, with the hottest temperature near the roof. You'd sit there for fifteen minutes or so, before retiring to the washroom. That's when it got *really* interesting. All of a sudden, a team of middle-aged Russian women appeared dressed in overalls, with peasant scarves around their heads, whose job it was to attack you front and back with birch twigs. I can't say it was an unpleasant sensation per se, but it was a bit disconcerting listening to them laughing uproariously while looking at our, er, 'physical attributes'! Once we'd withstood that, we moved into showers, some of which spouted freezing-cold water, while others gushed scalding hot. If you survived this, you returned to the lockers, dried yourself off and dressed in clean clothes feeling re-energised and clean. That done, we reboarded the three-tonners for the ride back to camp, and boy did we feel the cold then – it was a bit of a shock after the heat of the Turkish bath.

The Russians tended to keep strange hours. Hubert Griffith recounts in his diaries that Kuznetsov, who we must remember was Isherwood's immediate superior, had taken to sending for our CO for operational conferences at 2200 hours or later. He recounts, 'The other night, he [General Kuznetsov] happened to be in the middle of a steam bath so our own Winko went and had a steam bath with him and a conference at the same time.'[12]

14

Killing Time

After all that excitement, the biggest problem confronting us over the following days was the intractable issue of boredom. Over the next week, only a total of five defensive patrols were flown by both squadrons, owing mainly to the adverse weather conditions. Initially, the aerodrome was heavily waterlogged with the taxiing area at 134 Squadron's dispersal being 90 per cent under water. Keeping fighter pilots entertained in downtime is never straightforward, and even less so in a war zone.

Going into town wasn't really an option. There was a cinema in Vaenga, quite a large one capable of accommodating five hundred people or so, but the logistics of getting to it were rather more complex than you might think. As for the somewhat larger metropolis of Murmansk, forget it. The main reason was the fact that Murmansk was technically in the front line, which meant Russian passes were required, and they were, in any case, in short supply. Oh, and because we were in the front-line part of Russia, they also required photographs and signatures and a long-delayed process of registration. Nothing was straightforward in Russia.

Front-line regulations governed everything as the Germans weren't more than a few miles away, and the loosely held front line was dynamic, thus it was in a continuous state of flux so it moved roughly every day. Everyone we'd seen since we arrived, whether inside the base or outside, male or female, was in direct military employ. That included the deliciously different and often flirty waitresses who served us at mealtimes, and the labour force within the camp on a continuous hamster-wheel of back-breaking work – they all came under the umbrella of the Red Army. There were Russian sentries armed with rifles and bayonets on the gates of the camp, outside our very own Kremlin and living quarters, and throughout the forests of silver birch trees that surrounded the camp.

All British officers and senior NCOs were required to wear sidearms at all times, even when walking from building to building within the confines of the camp. This was partly for the purposes of self-protection if it ever came to it, but they were just as much a badge of office which, in this context, pretty much came down to the same thing, as anyone in an officer's uniform who wasn't armed was automatically regarded as an enemy prisoner escaping. Russian sentries tended to shoot first and didn't bother to ask questions afterwards, so, as I said, it paid to be armed. It all came down to self-protection in the end.

The morning of the 19th saw the first proper snowfall since our arrival, and we awoke to a world of silence. Over six inches of snow had fallen in the night, smothering the landscape in a noiseless white. Honestly, it was so quiet you could hear the sound of silence; nothing. Roads, such as they were, and walkways merged into one; trees bent under the weight of the snow, looking like old men in silhouette. As Artie Holmes wrote in his diary,

> *The Russians weren't as taken by surprise as we were. They see it happen every year . . . sledges had already taken over as transport. This was their normal life; to us, it was something novel and exciting. We were all schoolboys again. Snowmen, and snowball fights before breakfast, then down to dispersal on their sledges all tied in a line behind a four wheel drive jeep. We appreciated now the double windows throughout the Officers' Mess, for keeping bitter cold at bay, while central heating boilers kept the rooms pleasantly warm.*[1]

As the time went by, we discovered that the snowfalls were usually very heavy and very sudden, each one buttressed in daytime by clear blue skies, which would turn battleship grey and dump huge snowflakes on the ground that cut visibility down to a few yards at best. As soon as it was done, the clouds would disappear and the sun would shine again. The Russians dealt with the snowfall by bringing out huge rollers that made light work of flattening the latest fall, and eventually our 'runway' was covered with a foot or more of compacted solid ice. At least it evened out the bumps!

With the snow came the predictions from the weather experts, who forecast that the good flying days would work out to little more than about six a month. Given the depth of the snow and the way the weather had been since we arrived, that sounded like a pretty good estimate to me.

Hubert Griffith records in his diary that Wing Commander Isherwood, plus Tony Rook and Tony Miller, the two squadron commanders, had been invited to a party in the officers' club-house in Vaenga that evening by the neighbouring Russian squadron, which had been awarded the Order of the Red Banner. Group Captain Bird, plus two officer interpreters, also went. It must have been quite a night, because Griffith records on the following morning that

> *It seems to have been quite a bit of a party last night, with a concert, two suppers, (one before the concert, and one at half time), dancing and endless mixed drinking. The Russians have been at their tricks again, trying to deceive their innocent guests as to the alcoholic potency of vodka. The CO – usually the world's earliest riser – does not appear at breakfast, neither do the two squadron leaders. (They have all no doubt woken, cocked their eye at the weather – the pilot's first instinct on waking – and decided that as it is impossible operationally, they might as well lie in). Other members were still counted unserviceable after lunch.[2]*

The Russian bomber and ground crews on the base had separate accommodation to us and lived in a camp some distance from our own. Their technical officers, however, had taken to dropping into the RAF mess for their meals, although more often than not it wasn't the food that was the draw so much as the opportunity for them to be sociable and engage with their opposite numbers. They were a delightful bunch, good natured and friendly, but it'd been noticed that they did tend to have something of a problem when it came to pronouncing RAF ranks, particularly flight lieutenant and squadron leader. To overcome this rather difficult linguistic issue, they came up with a rather novel solution, addressing the wireless and engineering flight lieutenants as 'Meester Feesher' and 'Meester Gittins'.

The 25th turned out to be something of a big day in the wing's Russian adventure, although the way it started weather-wise didn't augur well for much of anything. It dawned a really filthy morning with light snow followed by freezing heavy rain that was having something of an identity crisis before turning into sleet. A strong northerly wind drove leaves from the trees, and the camp with its lakes of standing water, mud, bits of snow and bronchial-looking silver birch trees shed of their leaves looked desolate beyond belief. Still, it was home for now, so we made the best of it. There was no operational flying, but there was a flight later that afternoon that proved to be a turning point.

Major General Kuznetsov had, on a number of occasions, spent time at the aerodrome to receive instruction on flying the Hurricane. He had a young female interpreter who always came with him who had previously been a schoolmistress, and she'd written down all the cockpit drills and had tested him on every aspect of its operation exactly as if he were one of her school pupils. A spare-built man in his late thirties, with close-cropped greying hair, he was a very experienced pilot with thousands of flying hours in the bank; he also had considerable experience as a flying instructor, so I don't think an aircraft as forgiving as the

Hurricane was ever going to present him with any problems. I heard Hubert Griffith describe him as '. . . one of the most charming personalities I have ever met – very quiet and reserved but with an ever-present sense of humour and a way of saying little but to the point. He always did everything he could for us and if he wanted us to do anything, he put it to us in such a way that we felt we had suggested it.'

As morning gave way to afternoon, the weather lifted a little and Kuznetsov climbed on to the wing and into the cockpit of his Hurricane, Z5252. This one really was his; a 'spare', it had been devoid of RAF markings and had been painted over with Russian stars and the number '01' on the side. Conditions were far from perfect as he fired up the Merlin XX power plant and cycled her up, but they presented no difficulties to the general. Before an audience including our own CO, who must have had his fingers and everything else crossed that nothing untoward happened, Kuznetsov made a perfect take-off, flew a couple of circuits and made a couple of beautiful landings.

His flight opened the door for the wing to make the transition and start to fulfil the other part of its mission and begin operating as an Operational Training Unit. While those of us on 81 Squadron would continue providing fighter escorts to the Russians' PE2 bombers and undertaking patrols, for the most part, 134 Squadron would look after the training of the Russian pilots, and the ground staff would ensure their Russian counterparts could look after and maintain the aircraft to RAF standards. There'd already been considerable cooperation and interaction between ground crews, so the objective now was to strengthen that bond and ensure that the Russians could fly and service their Hurricanes fully independently. Once they could do that, we could think about going home.

The 26th dawned with a thick layer of cloud covering the aerodrome, so there was no flying in the morning. The grey, dull pallor of the day matched my own mood that morning. I'd woken with a sharp pain in my lower abdomen, and after moaning to Johnny about it over breakfast, I presented myself at the wing 'hospital' and was immediately admitted with suspected appendicitis.

Later that afternoon, the heavy cloud that had rested over Vaenga like a shroud began to break up and 81 Squadron was briefed that, later that evening, they would be escorting Soviet bombers that were targeting front-line troop concentrations in and around Petsamo. 'A' Flight of 81 Squadron was due to escort the dive bombers, with 'B' Flight detailed to look after the heavies.

Hubert Griffith watched the squadron take off at 1800 that evening and was sufficiently moved by the 'magnificent sight' to write about it in his diary. First he saw 'A' Flight depart in formation, swiftly followed by the Russian Petlyakov Pe-2 dive bombers, then 'B' Flight followed shortly thereafter by a formation of Pe2FT heavy bombers, until the sky above the vast sandy aerodrome was full of aircraft taking station.

The formation flew west towards Petsamo at around 10,000 ft and dropped their load without incident. It was only as the lead aircraft began to bank gently in a wide sweep that took them heading back due east towards Vaenga that 'B' Flight was bounced by six Me109Fs, which opened up from a distance. Several of the 81 Squadron pilots saw cannon shells going past them and Wag, who saw an enemy aircraft hurtling straight down on him, took evasive action, breaking away from the threat. He saw another 109 down below him that had just broken off an attack on another Hurricane, so he dived down on to it, narrowly missing *another* 109 being chased by a Hurricane that flashed underneath his nose, but the momentary diversion was all the bandit he was chasing needed; this one wasn't so green, and the pilot turned his aircraft towards Wag's, narrowing the angle of attack and forcing them to break away as they closed on one another. A dogfight ensued in which Wag managed to gain the advantage and get his gunsight ahead of the German, firing a six-second burst, narrowing the angle in the turn. As soon as he was directly behind his target, he fired another burst and watched as the 109 turned turtle, then dived straight towards the ground, trailing thick black smoke behind it.

As he broke off from the fight, he looked behind and saw another 109 bearing down on him, and Wag found himself in his second violent dogfight in as many minutes. Flying the Hurricane to the very limits of its performance, he sought every advantage he could to out-turn the Messerschmitt, and eventually the German pilot realised he was at a disadvantage and turned away. In that split second, Wag saw his chance and took it, hitting the fire button as soon as he had the 109 in his sights . . . and nothing happened. He'd used all of his ammunition attacking and downing the first aircraft, and was now as vulnerable as a toupee-wearer trying to impress an attractive girl in a force-ten gale! The German pilot immediately saw his mistake and turned towards him. He later recalled,

> *I knew that the German was not out of ammo. I was climbing like mad I did the only thing I could. I sort of threw my aeroplane at him and he sheared away. We were down at 5,000 feet. Then I put my Hurricane upside down, and went straight to the ground and I flew back kissing the ground. I don't think I have ever been so shaken in all my life. I could see this yellow nosed thing behind me. If you fly low there is no way they can shoot you down because they cannot possibly look at you without hitting the ground. Though I say it myself, that was sheer flying skill that got out of that one. I was shaken, very shaken. I was so relieved when he pulled up, but my God, I thought to myself, 'I'm only 21 but I'm getting old'.*[3]

On the plus side, though, he'd almost certainly bagged yet another 109 and was buoyed by the thought that, not only had he escaped almost certain death, he might just have shot down his third fighter in as many sorties. Wag was making quite a name for himself.

While Wag was engaged in his fight for survival, other pilots in 'A' Flight had been involved in their own battles. Artie Holmes and Scotty Edmiston both took evasive action when the Me109s first bounced them, and Artie described what happened: 'The Messerschmitts came from behind, and at least five thousand feet above. They were streaking steeply down when I first saw them, sending out vapour trails from their wingtips in the freezing air. I bellowed a warning to Red Leader, but Mickey [Rook] did not seem to get my call and "A" Flight cruised serenely on. There was no choice but to hope he would see them.'

Still transmitting a warning, Artie swung round in a tight left-hand circle to attack head-on.

Bushy was sticking to my tail. There were six Messerschmitts only three or four miles back now, diving at about thirty degrees and at terrific speed. When I had made half my turn and was heading towards the leader at ninety degrees, he and his companion opened fire on the bombers. He had seen me and wanted to get in a quick burst before I intercepted but he was well out of range and the tracer from his twin 20mm cannons made a glowing chain of fire as the shells chased each other across the fading evening sky. The bombers and their escort flew on unharmed.

My quarter attack placed me in an ideal position but their leader was diving far too fast for accurate shooting. I needed at least four ring-sights of deflection, reducing to two as the angle-off diminished, to keep my bead right on to Mickey Rook's Hurricane.

To Hell! Mickey was safe enough at this deflection. I pressed the firing button and kept it pressed. The twelve guns blasted out blue flame in front of my wings. The airframe lurched momentarily with their recoil, as though an invisible hand had applied a brake and I was going to fall out of the sky.

I had no tracer. I was firing alternate armour piercing and de Wilde explosive bullets, so I could not see where they were going. With such a snap shot I was far from hopeful. But it was a deterrent, for the other Messerschmitts broke away without firing, and to my surprise did not return for a second attack.

Meanwhile, the leader pulled out of his dive and was flying at tremendous speed over the top of the steadily plodding bombers. Possibly even now they did not know they had been attacked. Then the 109 rolled on to his back and from the inverted position, his nose fell into a vertical dive. The manoeuvre looked part triumphant, like a victory roll, and part evasive. But he kept going vertically down, spiralling slightly and at increasing speed. I had to take my eyes off him to look for other Huns who might be jumping me. But I knew if he pulled out of that dive before he hit the ground, he'd do well.

At debriefing, two Russian air gunners said they saw my Messerschmitt go in so I must have hit him. My kill was not confirmed however until the following day when word came from German-occupied Finland by underground radio that what was left of the Messerschmitt had been found with no survivor.

I was sad he never managed to bale out. That German pilot, whoever he was, was a resolute fellow. But I was glad to get an Me109F and the Russian bomber boys were over the moon. It boosted their morale no end, for they had been having heavy losses with their own fighters escorting, and this was the first German they had seen shot down.[4]

Scotty, who was flying in Z5227, saw another 109 on the tail of another Hurricane and also gave chase, opening up and hitting that one below the cockpit. His combat report details the circumstances:

At 18:05hrs I took off as Green 2 acting as escort to four Russian bombers over the enemy lines. When 50 miles west of base, at 18:25hrs I noticed Green 1 suddenly break away. I turned violently to the left and observed two enemy aircraft diving down on me. I took evasive action, aileron turning towards the ground, I pulled out near the top of the clouds and climbed to about 6000ft. I then observed two aircraft below me one of which was Black 1, the other was an Me109. I dived down on the enemy aircraft and fired a short burst. I observed the tracer bullets entering the aircraft below the cockpit hood, he then turned gently to the left rolling over slightly and disappeared into the clouds. I then joined Black 1 and returned to base having expended 30 rounds from each of twelve guns.[5]

Hubert Griffith wrote in his diary,

They are all back in just over an hour, after a brilliant action on the part of 'B' Flight – perhaps the best thing the Wing has done yet. 'B' Flight was jumped by six Me109s from cloud. When this happens the Flight that has been jumped is usually pretty lucky if it gets away without loss to itself or its charges.

    'B' Flight did better than this, however: they turned into the Messerschmitts, more or less each for each, getting in bursts as the opportunity offered after the first evasion of the 'jump'. They shot down three of them – all confirmed – and got back to base without a single bullet hole in any of their machines.

    The Soviet bombers carried out their mission unmolested and the Russian General telephoned a message of thanks.

The weather completely wrong-footed those pundits who'd forecast a paucity of good flying days by dawning bright and sunny on the morning of September 27th. There were few clouds in the bright blue sky, and they were at high altitude, making it a perfect day for flying when 81 Squadron took off at about 1125 to escort four Russian bombers. Yet again, the squadron was bounced, on this occasion by four Me109Es. Flight Sergeant Vic Reed got one, which went down in flames. Then Scotty Edmiston, who was flying as Blue three in 'B' Flight, made an attack on one from above and behind, diving on to it and opening up on it with forty rounds from each of his Hurricane's twelve guns. The 109's canopy broke away and the aircraft then turned and went into a spiralling dive from which it never recovered, crashing into the ground in flames.[6]

Those two confirmed kills made it 13–1 in the wing's favour, although, so far, they were all down to pilots from 81 Squadron. Several, such as Wag and Scotty, had more than one to their credit (three to Wag, two to Scotty), but there was a good spread with seven pilots shooting down one or more. 134 Squadron, who were based at the other end of the aerodrome, hadn't flown anything like the same number of patrols or bomber escorts but it wasn't through lack of trying; they spent as much time on readiness as us, but we always seemed to have luck on our side. It must have been intensely frustrating for Neil Cameron, Dicky Wollaston, Tim Elkington, Peter Knapton and all the others.

At around 1230, the Germans sent a Junkers Ju88 reconnaissance aircraft on a mission to photograph the airfield; given the punishment that we'd been doling out to them, it was thought that the aircraft had been sent to gather intel preparatory to their launching a raid on the aerodrome. In any case, 134 Squadron was on readiness, and as soon as the aircraft was spotted, they were scrambled to intercept it.

134 Squadron's dispersal area had suffered a perennial problem with standing water, and despite it being regularly pumped clear, the ground remained waterlogged and marshy. Compounding the issue was the fact that the ground outside the dispersal bays in which the aircraft were kept on readiness was on a slope. All of this meant that the pilots had to use a great deal more engine power to get through it. This increased the likelihood of the engine's torque combined with the slope tipping the aircraft on to its nose, and early on there had been a number of incidents of broken propellers, so a Heath Robinson approach was adopted. This saw two ground crew members – usually the aircraft's fitter and rigger – draping themselves over the tail end of the fuselage to add weight while the aircraft were taxiing through the puddles. The procedure had been followed for over a week without incident and, although it wasn't universally popular, it was an essential job and the airmen did it without complaint.

We'll never know what really occurred, but in his haste to get airborne and at the Ju88, Vic Berg opened the throttle the moment the chocks were away and roared out on to the airfield, not realising Aircraftmen John Ridley and Glanville Thomas, his ground crew, were now pinned to the tail by the force of the slipstream.

The Hurricane reached flying speed and when Vic Berg pulled back on the stick to get airborne, the additional weight of the two men dragged the tail down, pulling the nose vertical. Initially, the Merlin XX engine provided sufficient power, but when the Hurricane reached a height of sixty feet or so, it couldn't maintain positive climb and the aircraft stalled, spiralling back down to the ground nose first. As the propeller hit the earth, the aircraft cartwheeled and the unfortunate fitter and rigger were flung high into the air, landing some 150 yards from the wrecked plane. John Ridley and Glanville Thomas were both killed instantly; they were both just twenty years old. The aircraft didn't catch fire but as it broke up, the engine, wings and rear of the fuselage were flung in all directions. Vic was pulled, unconscious, from the cockpit, which was the only part of the Hurricane to remain intact.

Although he was seriously injured with a perforated fracture of his right thigh, lacerations and a serious case of concussion, considering the wreckage and the huge debris field, the miracle is that he survived at all. When he regained consciousness, he had no recollection of the incident, so couldn't say how the accident had happened. He was eventually evacuated to the UK by cruisers via Archangel. Poor Vic; when he eventually returned to the UK, X-rays showed that his thigh had been badly set, so it had to be broken and reset. His injuries meant he was unable to fly for over two years. All that, and he never once fired his guns in anger in Russia.

That incident was a bitter pill to swallow for 134 Squadron, although it was the only incident of its kind for the duration of the wing's stay in Russia. It did have one positive effect for Neil Cameron, who, you might recall, had only been a lowly flight sergeant until just before the wing left Leconfield. Vic Berg had been the flight commander of 'A' Flight, 134 Squadron, and Neil was appointed in his place, still as a pilot officer. Another plus was that several ground crew were Mentioned in Dispatches for coolness under fire during the raid. They were exceptional, our ground crews; they really gave us an edge.

John Ridley and Glanville Thomas were both buried the following day, in plots next to Nudger Smith in the Cemetery of Soviet Heroes. Members of the Red Air Force again turned out to assist at their funeral and joined with the RAF in firing the last salute over their graves. Most of the pilots from both squadrons attended with as many airmen as we could transport. Nudger, John and Glanville lie there today; on the top of a hill on the Murmansk coast, their three tombstones standing in a cemetery alongside the graves of Soviet airmen.

That afternoon, the Finns, who were fighting alongside the Germans, broadcast over the radio that they had taken the strategically important town of Kandalaksha, about 150 miles south of Murmansk. Its railway junction linked Murmansk with the networks of Moscow, Leningrad and Archangel, so all supplies and reinforcements for the front had to be routed through Kandalaksha. If the Finns' claim was correct, it cut the wing off from all rail-borne supply sources.

While the weather on the following day was clear, the situation regarding Kandalaksha wasn't. The Russians denied the Finnish claim [they would] but the Finns' claim was then broadcast [as a rumour only] by British radio at lunchtime on the 28th. Four bomber escorts were carried out by 151 Wing but there was no contact with the Luftwaffe, and no casualties. I remained bedbound in hospital with a grumbling appendix, although I was feeling significantly better. Two events outside of the 'normal' routine of wing life in Russia occurred on this day which are notable enough for me to record them here.

The first concerned one Corporal Flockhart, an assistant carpenter on the wing, who was marched smartly into the wing commander's office to appear before him for a rather unusual, er . . . 'offence'. Now carpentry, even during wartime and conducted 15 miles away from the front lines, is hardly a death-or-glory occupation, but then Flockhart wasn't your usual carpenter either. Before he'd become a dab hand at working with wood for the RAF, young Flockhart had been aircrew, flying as an air gunner on Whitley bombers, and it was this that had, indirectly, led to him being up before the CO. Hubert Griffith recorded that Flockhart had 'drifted off, with no official sanction, and taken part in an operational raid over the Lines as air-gunner in a Russian bomber'.[7]

How he managed to achieve this feat was a story in itself. During the war, Flockhart had served in the Merchant Navy and had made contacts at Archangel when his ship docked there during one of his early voyages. When 151 Wing had arrived there, he somehow renewed his contacts, and they, in turn, introduced him to Russian aircrew at Vaenga, who arranged for him to join them on a bombing raid.

His unique 'offence' wasn't catered for in the rulebook, and although it was against English disciplinary orders, it was one of the few offences that hadn't been included when they were drawing up the King's Regulations. Knowing that Isherwood was a strict disciplinarian, Hubert Griffith wondered how the CO would treat this strange offence, although, in the event, he records that the wing commander's discourse in the orderly room was 'sharp and to the point'. In his clipped New Zealand accent, he said, 'Personally, I admire your spirit. Personally, I think it a bloody good show. But all the same, if you *had* got shot down you'd have put me in the soup, see? Now get out!'

The story passed into legend almost as soon as it got out and word of Flockhart's Russian adventure spread like wildfire. Everyone who heard it wondered in astonishment how he'd managed to pull it off, especially given the language barrier. In the end, people assumed that the Russians had smuggled him out because nobody in their right mind would venture out of camp on their own, would they? Regardless of the how and why, the story put a smile on everyone's face and little Flockhart, the assistant carpenter, became a legend within the wing.

The other notable event that day came about with the advent of the cold weather, which descended over northern Russia at the end of September, and again involved the wing commander, who had consulted Squadron Leader Jackson, the wing's senior medical officer, and decided that it was a good time to commence the daily evening issue of rum to the wing's personnel. Simple enough, right? You'd think so, wouldn't you? But then you remember how many personnel were in the wing, and Hubert Griffith's assertion that arranging the distribution of the rum involved as much work as 'a large-scale movement order on the part of the Wing staff' doesn't seem so unreasonable. He wrote:

*For days past, my notebook has been jotted with notes
about drawing the rum, diluting the rum, getting exact
noggins made to measure out the regulation half-gills of
rum neither more or less, detailing sergeants to supervise
the dishing out of the rum etc, etc [. . .] the paramount aim
of all this supervision is, of course, that no airman shall, by
doing a deal with another airman who 'don't drink the
stuff,' be able to get two tots per evening, or alternatively
drink his tot neat. The Navy have a traditional method of
diluting it and dishing it out. We have to improvise our own
arrangements.*[8]

Perhaps if he'd known just how unimportant the rum ration was
to the men, he wouldn't have gone to so much trouble. Because
while it was undoubtedly welcome to some, it wasn't universally
popular. Peter Knapton said of it, 'The daily issue of rum was an
ill-judged attempt to keep us warm. Unfortunately, it was not
administered so strictly as in the Navy and one corporal, having
disposed of three of four rations, passed out on the way to his
billet. Luckily, he was found before he froze to death.'[9]

You have to bear in mind that we went to the mess almost every
night and gin was only four shillings and six pence a bottle. There
was simply nowhere else for us to go, and nothing much for us to
do, so it became our refuge.

I got out of hospital the following day and 134 Squadron did
some flying, undertaking a bomber escort. Although there were no
engagements with the Luftwaffe, they did encounter some anti-
aircraft fire. Now, 134 Squadron normally flew with one aircraft
weaving above the formation, and one below. The aim of this
manoeuvre was to keep a lookout for enemy fighters. It was universally unpopular with the pilots, for whom it was a tiring business.
Peter Knapton, like many of them, regarded it as defensive and
inflexible compared to the more aggressive, fluid four formation.
After they'd landed from this particular sortie, he said,

One of the squadron commanders angrily turned to Flight Sergeant Paddy McCann and shouted,

'Why didn't you weave when they were firing at us, McCann?'

McCann, who had that typical rather dry Belfast wit, replied:

'Well sur, I would have looked rather bloody silly if I'd weaved into it, wouldn't I?'

That sortie did a lot for relations between ourselves and our Russian partners. One of the pilots on that mission recounted to the wing adjutant,

As we headed for home after the Soviet bomber-boys had done their stuff, we thought for fun that we'd show them some of our formation flying. Their bombers were flying back in fairly wide formation, so a couple of our Hurricanes closed in on each of them, and began flying back absolutely wing-tip to wing-tip with them. The Soviet pilots saw that something was up, so they thought that they'd show us a bit of their formation flying! So all their bombers closed in on one another – and there were the whole lot of us, tucked in tight together. We were close enough that I could see their rear gunners laughing as they leaned out of their turrets and gave us the thumbs up sign![10]

Spirits were obviously high within the wing because when Johnny and I went to the mess that night, our boys were shooting the lights out with their revolvers. There was a lot of celebrating going on owing to the number of German aircraft we'd shot down, and they'd had a fair bit to drink when we got there, so, as there's not much to do in a situation like that except join in, that's just what we did!

The final day of the month saw the wing receive a signal of congratulation from the Secretary of State for Air, Sir Archibald Sinclair, which was pinned to the noticeboard in the Kremlin. It read, 'The destruction by your squadrons of 12 German aircraft for the loss of only one of your own [we'd actually shot down thirteen but were awaiting confirmation on the thirteenth at that stage] is a brilliant achievement; it is a source of particular pleasure and satisfaction to us here that you are working so closely and so successfully with the Russian Air Force. Good luck to you, 151 Wing.'

So ended our first month in Russia; a month that saw the pilots of 81 Squadron rack up 184 hours of flying, including the flying times of the Hurricanes flown off the *Argus* and those brought up from Archangel. One of our aircraft had been handed over to General Kuznetsov, so the squadron finished the month with seventeen machines. For me personally, the month finished pretty much as I'd started it; thinking of home, of Phyllis, who I missed desperately, and my mum and dad back home in England. We'd had not a single item of mail, neither personal nor official, since the wing's formation in Leconfield almost nine weeks earlier, and this was becoming a morale issue for every man, so the wing commander reported the issue to the Air Ministry, which responded saying, 'Mail will be despatched in convoy loading in England now . . .' This was as close as we were going to get to an admission that someone had made rather a mess of things or that they'd simply forgotten. In the meantime, all I could do was remember my loved ones back home and hope they were all OK.

15

Whiteout

The weather changed suddenly at the end of September 1941. Daylight was in very short supply. As October dawned, a lazy, blood-red sun wouldn't get out of bed before 1100, would nod hello and then disappear below the horizon again – by 1300 it would be gone for the day and evening had arrived. The Northern Lights, which I'd seen only once previously, became something of a regular occurrence, but the paucity of light would radically reduce our flying operations because there were no aids at Vaenga for us to home in on after dark.

There was no flying at all in the early part of the month because the weather was so miserable. The dull, heavily overcast days meant we spent all our time on the ground. It rained heavily on 3 October and then the Russians announced that the aerodrome's water supply would be offline until 1700 hours. Nobody gave that a second thought until the announcement was amended and it emerged that the water supply was actually going to be disconnected for *five whole days*, news which put a completely different spin on things. Because of the coming onset of a winter that was expected to be cold even by Russian standards, they had to bury and lag their mains deep underground to protect them against freezing. I suppose they'd been too busy defending the airfield previously to worry about things like lagging pipes. It was just another obstacle for us to overcome, so plans had to be hastily drawn up to conserve and ration existing supplies, which now had to be stored. Responsibility for that fell to poor old Hubert Griffith, who, as wing adjutant, always seemed to be the busiest man in the wing.

Once we'd calculated what water was available, it worked out to just over a pint per day for every man in the wing, which wasn't anywhere near enough for washing, cooking, cleaning and everything else. The officers did a little better because their batmen were directed to catch the rainwater in buckets as it cascaded down off the Kremlin roof. Hubert recorded his sentiments in typically dry style in his diary: 'A return to primitive life with a vengeance! – but on the whole rather fun. By way of contrast – one of the everlasting contrasts that make life here so fascinating – Champagne and pancakes for supper.'

It was at supper that evening that the wing commander announced that the usual Russian Air Force tariff of 1,000 roubles per enemy aircraft destroyed would be paid by the Russian authorities to any British pilots who had confirmed victories. This now amounted to some 12,000 roubles, which was roughly £240 at the agreed exchange rate [roughly £10,000 in today's money adjusted for inflation], and he asked for suggestions as to what to do with the money. One of the lads called out, 'We can't take it, it would spoil our amateur status!', which drew laughter from everyone in the room, but it was eventually agreed that the money paid by the Russians would be collected by the wing and donated in its entirety to the RAF Benevolent Fund in London.

It snowed frequently from the 4th, and when it fell, it was heavy – often, we'd get three or four inches at a time, which invariably landed on top of previous snowfalls. The air wasn't at all damp; it was very dry, so the snow itself was thick, deep and crisp. In his diary, Hubert Griffith described the snow in Murmansk thus: 'In moments of bright sunlight, the clear air here in the north, the absence of soot, factory smoke etc, the snow takes on a brilliant, incandescent whiteness that is unearthly.' When it fell, it fell thick and fast, and visibility dropped to almost nothing. In these storms, the temperature often dropped as low as 27°F – below freezing. Our breath would freeze on our eyebrows and eyelashes in these temperatures and aircraft had to be lavishly treated with antifreeze to prevent cockpit hoods and panels being frozen into place.

It made life difficult whenever we got airborne, as the first few pilots discovered on one early sortie after the snow had settled. Take off wasn't a problem, but landing was exceptionally difficult when the runway and surrounding area was a sea of white. As Nat Gould recalls, 'It was almost impossible to judge landing on the rough surface at Vaenga once the snow started. In the end, the Russians put a chap out to wave flags to give the pilots a better clue as to where, and how far down the runway to touch down. Judgment from height was non-existent in the white-out.'

However, if we thought things were bad for us, the Germans had it much, much worse. That winter of 1941 was Russia's coldest for over a hundred years and saw temperatures plummeting in the area north-west of Moscow to an astonishing –63°F. At those temperatures, if boiling water is poured from a kettle, it freezes before it hits the ground. Those temperatures – and Russia's sheer, incomprehensible size – had a huge impact on the German advance, and by October the initial blitzkrieg that Hitler's forces had unleashed on such a broad front across Russia was beginning to stall. Things certainly hadn't reached their worst – not yet – and huge numbers of Soviet troops and equipment had been lost, but there were definite signs that the next stage of Operation Barbarossa wasn't going to go quite as smoothly as it had started.

One of Russia's biggest saviours was its vastness, and the number of people available and under arms. Hitler's forces seized unimaginably great tracts of territory, but however much was captured, there was always more remaining; however many of Stalin's armies were destroyed, still more were waiting to take their place; it was a Sisyphean task. The deeper into Russia the Germans advanced, the greater the supply problems they faced. The toll on machinery too was unrelenting; as German soldiers grew tired, so did their vehicles. Tracks wore out, cables frayed, springs broke.[1] Towards the end of September, some 20 per cent of the original invasion force had been killed or wounded, along with two-thirds of its armour and vehicles.[2] The winter's bitterly cold weather took its toll on the mobility of the Nazi forces, who were utterly unprepared. Vehicles succumbed to the sheer intensity of the cold, as did many German soldiers, who, hampered by a supply chain that floundered under the difficulties of shifting food and equipment across hundreds of miles in weather that deteriorated daily,[3] froze to death still dressed in their summer uniforms.

A young SS officer wrote: 'It is icy cold . . . To start the [vehicle] engines, they must be warmed by lighting fires under the oil pan. The fuel is partially frozen, the motor oil is thick and we lack anti-freeze . . . The remaining limited strength of the troops diminishes further due to the continuous exposure to the cold.'[4]

Paralysed by cold, German soldiers were unable to accurately aim their rifle fire; bolt mechanisms jammed, strikers and striker springs shattered like glass in the bitter winter weather. Machine guns became encrusted with ice, and fluid in artillery recoil mechanisms solidified, crippling the piece. Mines were no longer viable, and mortar shells worse than useless as they detonated harmlessly in deep snow with a hollow thud. Only one German tank in ten survived the autumn rainy season, and those still available could not move through the snow because of their narrow tracks.[5]

And although the weather locally affected us to a degree, it affected the beleaguered General Eduard Dietl even more. As he had predicted, the terrain hindered the advance of his *Gebirgsjäger* troops, despite them having been reinforced with two additional regiments, including the 9th SS *'Totenkopf'* [Death's Head] Infantry Regiment.[6] For the advancing army, the topography of the tundra belt led to an overdependence on poorly constructed roads for mobility. This, in turn, meant overly long and tenuous lines of communication and supply problems.

193

Dietl's *Gebirgsjäger* had stalled at the high ground along the 'Long Lake' in the Gulf of Kola, along whose shore the port of Murmansk sits, but strategically and tactically he was holding a busted flush. The Luftwaffe's Stuka dive bombers employed to neutralise the threat posed by the rocky terrain that the Siberian troops took shelter in proved totally ineffective, making the Russian forces almost impossible to eliminate. Throwing more troops at the problem failed to solve it either; Hitler transferred the 388th and 9th SS Regiments[7] to Dietl to support the operation, but they were unable to gain a foothold. Although brutal, ruthless fighters, the SS troops were untrained in mountain warfare and suffered heavy casualties. Stalin's forces, meanwhile, were heavily entrenched and they greatly outnumbered their attackers.

British and Soviet naval forces had made repeated attacks on Dietl's cargo ships, causing even greater supply-chain problems for him – any vital stores and equipment that did get through had to be manhandled across nightmarish terrain and up impossibly steep slopes. It was hugely manpower intensive, requiring Dietl to deploy some two-thirds of his troops to deal with supply problems, leaving them stretched dangerously thin in the combat area. The Russians had no such worries and were in a strong position to launch counter-attacks, given that they were in very familiar territory, and were supported by local supply bases. They could bring reinforcements and supplies by road right up to the battle front.

The German forces had failed to put the Murmansk railway out of action and Operation Platinfuchs [Platinum Fox], the code name given to capture Murmansk, stalled just 20 miles away from its objective. By the start of October, after repeated attempts to advance past the Litsa river, the German offensive was broken off. We were no longer in any danger of German forces overrunning the base at Vaenga.

194

The Soviet aircrew at the base had an unusual method of warming up the machine guns on their aircraft. The usual drill for us was to fire them into the lake once we got airborne to make sure they were working, but the Russians did things differently! Loud bursts would be heard from the other side of the aerodrome, followed by the scream of bullets passing over our heads to end up in the hills behind our dispersal. For them, it was much easier to sit in the cockpit with the aircraft in their dispersal bays and just hit the 'fire' button. The Brownings on our Hurricanes were electrically heated; we never had a single stoppage throughout the wing's tour at Murmansk.

However, one of the biggest issues for us as a result of the extreme cold was the snapping of the shaft drive that ran to the generators on our Merlin engines. These shafts were no thicker than a pencil, with an eggcup-shaped end, and teeth around the inside rim of the cup. The steel was skimmed thinner at one end than the other, a design feature that ensured it would break there under abnormal load to avoid shearing more costly components in the generator. The extreme cold we experienced kept causing these shafts to snap, and we eventually exhausted our entire supply of spares. These were available only from Rolls-Royce back in England, so we were faced with quite a problem. Cue the Russian engineers yet again! They came to our rescue just as they had when Gittins discovered some vital tools were missing at Keg-Ostrov. Within twenty-four hours, they'd jigged up machines to manufacture the shafts from scratch, right down to the eggcup-shaped end with the internal teeth. Gittins also came up with an engine modification that cured the problem, so the temperature changes never affected us again.

The 5th saw a party of about twenty of us making our first excursion to Murmansk, in transport laid on by the Russians. It was, once again, a break from the normal camp routine, particularly when it came to dress. Most of us had been dressing for warmth and there were lots of idiosyncrasies and individual interpretations of that, including fur hats bought from Russian pilots in exchange for cigarettes or other goodies, with the result that the wing in general bore more than a passing resemblance to a bunch of tramps. It must have been quite amusing for the officers to see their batmen laying out best uniforms for them to wear and polishing buttons again.

We endured a punishing drive at dusk over potholed and typically bumpy snow-covered Russian 'roads' to Murmansk, and we were all curious to see this strategically important place that was so vital to the Allied war effort we'd been sent to defend at all costs; that Nudger, and Airmen Ridley and Thomas, *died* for.

The city of Murmansk itself is a creation of the 1914 war, when Russia circumvented the closure of the Baltic and Black Seas by building an ice-free port through which British supplies could be forwarded by direct railway line to Leningrad. It's naturally protected and out of gunfire range from the sea, where the Gulf Stream laps the entrance to the Kola inlet on which Murmansk is situated. The northerly winds that blow here are much colder than the prevailing temperature of the water, with the result that, in winter, there is a perpetual curtain of fog hanging over it. This provides another natural layer of protection, defending the port and its city against German bombers.

We could see from a distance on our approach that its wooden buildings appeared neat and the huge new brick-built tenement blocks seemed to have some architectural features. As we got closer, however, the illusion vanished. As in Archangel, the wooden buildings were in a hopeless state of disrepair.

The authorities weren't indifferent to the safety of the masses. Probably one of the finest air-raid shelters in the world was excavated at Murmansk by convicts who were employed by the hundreds to tunnel into the massive granite hills surrounding the town. Perhaps thousands of years hence, these structures will be discovered by future civilisations who will wonder about their purpose in the frozen north. The winding entrance led to three enormous halls into which thousands were packed whenever the Luftwaffe sent bombers to drop their loads upon the city.

Murmansk's hub was a large and well-built *'Dom Kultura'* [House of Culture], with a wide flight of stone steps leading up to it via a paved terrace featuring a bronze statue. Once inside, there was a large theatre that would accommodate a thousand or so people, a smallish cinema seating 300, a large foyer with a beautifully laid parquet floor and grand piano, various club-rooms and a library. Everything was well kept, the communal areas clean and tidy, but the toilets defied description. There seems to be a theme where sanitation in Russia is concerned, at least so far as we'd experienced it. Culturally, Murmansk seemed well developed, but where its sanitation was concerned, it was still in the Dark Ages.

Murmansk is where we came across Russian civilians for the first time, although 'civilians' was a bit of a relative term in Russia; at least half of the women we came across were in uniform – boots, khaki tunics and shirts, and a very workmanlike revolver slung round the waist. They were perfectly willing to dance with us – *that* was an interesting and pretty unique experience, to say the least, and we all made sure our hands didn't wander inappropriately.

Tim Elkington has very favourable recollections of our time there. As befits a fighter pilot, they of course concern the girls.

Well, the only ones who might stir the imagination were mostly those we met early on – our three translators. Anna was the blonde with the sweet singing voice and streamlined figure who worked with Gittins, our engineer officer. Bella was the 'Merlin Girl' on account of her spinner-like bosoms. Fat in face with a good voice for modern music, she worked on translating technical publications. Mira was the dark gypsy girl who was so far from her loved one in Moscow. She instructed the Russians in aircraft handling. Sadly, I am told that all their lives ended in misfortune.

I'm not sure if it was that Anna – she wore a .38 on her hip – but, as I walked off the floor with her after a pleasant evening dancing in Murmansk, she was intercepted by a man who I presumed was her husband and who also wore a .38. No argument from me there. But I still have her handkerchief!

16

A Rude Awakening

The weather that had blighted our flying programme for the first few days of October changed completely on the morning of the 6th, and we looked up at clouds drifting lazily at high altitude. There was nothing threatening or dark about them, and visibility was good all round.

Following Vic's tragic accident, we often wondered whether the Ju88 that had prompted his dash to get airborne had got its photos. On the afternoon of the 6th, we learned it had. The clear weather saw a number of 134 Squadron's pilots getting some practice flying in over the airfield when suddenly the Russian guns a mile or so away opened up, and all hell was let loose.

Clearly we'd got under the Luftwaffe's skin since our arrival, and they had resolved to try to do something about it. On its way to us from its base at Banak in Norway was a force comprising fourteen Junkers Ju88 bombers, and an escort of six Messerschmitt Me109Es that had been delayed but was on its way to meet them. The Ju88 was one of the mainstays of the Luftwaffe's bomber fleet, a formidable, fast and effective aircraft that could carry a 5,500lb load. It was well armed, with six movable machine guns, could be used in the dive bombing or conventional bombing role, and had been deployed and proven over London during the Battle of Britain.

Six Hurricanes of 'A' Flight, 134 Squadron spotted the Ju88s at 10,000 feet and radioed what they'd seen through to base. The wing commander came straight through on the ops phone to order both squadrons to scramble. 'Don't worry about who's with who, just get the bloody kites off the ground,' he bellowed.[1]

As the Luftwaffe force bore down on our airfield, twenty-four Hurricanes, taking off from all angles, tore skywards to meet them, and the sky was full of aircraft. It's a wonder there were no collisions. Remember when you were at school and a couple of boys started fighting? Suddenly, it seemed that the whole school would descend on them to watch, and there were boys *every-where*. Everyone was mixed up, and often other boys would get drawn into the fight. That's what it was like in the skies over Vaenga as our Hurricanes arrived, with guns blazing, on the Luftwaffe's formation.[2]

Then the bombs started to fall on the aerodrome. Any plan, any organisation that the Luftwaffe may have had in mind, evaporated like mist on a hot summer's day because the 88s, already split up by the ack-ack fire, were now busy trying to deal with the Hurricanes climbing up to attack them. Squadron Leader Tony Miller led the charge and locked straight on to the third in a formation of six Ju88s with a two-second burst, which hit its target, taking out one of its engines. He then intercepted another aircraft with a beam attack along with Pilot Officer Rex Furneaux of 134 Squadron, and they both opened up on it. It immediately burst into flames and they watched it crash into the ground. Pilot Officer David Ramsey, who was flying as Red two, went after another aircraft in the formation as Tony Miller launched his first attack and fired on it with a three-second burst, seeing thick black smoke pouring from one of its engines. Ramsey then attacked another aircraft, giving it a quarter-to-stern burst of fire at close range, chasing it down to ground level. Another 134 Squadron aircraft also attacked the same Ju88.[3]

Ken Bishop, flying as White two, attacked a Ju88 from below, at about three hundred yards, and saw smoke billowing out from the starboard engine. Then two more Hurricanes attacked it and it was last seen going to ground. Tim Elkington climbed to 8,000 ft and locked on to the tail of an 88, firing two long bursts at it which both found their target. He watched the tail start to break away. Black one, Flight Sergeant Barnes, then closed in on it and fired long bursts from above and astern.[4]

Neil Cameron, flying as Red one, wasn't idle, either. He attacked the lead 88, firing a five-second burst from below, and was rewarded by seeing the aircraft's starboard engine emitting thick smoke. He then broke away and attacked a second aircraft, and breaking away from that attack, spotted a third directly ahead of him, which he fired on. Turning to port, he saw that aircraft going slowly at a steep angle, both engines appearing to have been hit.[5]

Back on the ground, Bushy, Scotty Edmiston and Artie Holmes had been on stand-by and, seeing the bombs falling, decided they'd be better off in the air. As Artie was making his take-off run, a bomb exploded just behind him. He said, 'My tail was off the ground and I was gaining speed fast when there came an almighty crump behind me. The blast of a bomb that missed me by feet lifted my tail as if it were a toy plane and I thought I would stand on my nose and then somersault. But the engine kept dragging the nose forward, and I hauled the stick hard back and somehow the tail came down and I had control again.'[6]

Scotty Edmiston, whose birthday it was, wasn't quite so lucky; a bomb landed in front of him, the blast ripping through his engine and stopping it dead. Enraged, he jumped out of his aircraft and stood on its wing, shouting to his ground crew to bring him a starter battery. At that moment, another bomb exploded in close proximity and its blast blew him clean off the wing and into a deep snowdrift. Luckily, he was completely unhurt, but he played no further part in the battle.

Another bomb exploded near wing engineering officer Gittins' dugout on the east side of the aerodrome, the blast of which lifted him and three of his airmen from the ground in front of the dugout's entrance, and blew them inside. That was incredibly fortuitous as it transpired – another five bombs landed in quick succession in the same vicinity, but the four men were well protected from the blasts inside the dugout. The only injury was to Gittins, who suffered minor abrasions to his legs when he landed after the first blast.

The day really belonged to 134 Squadron because Tony Miller and his boys broke their previous run of bad luck by shooting down two Ju88s, along with three probables and six damaged. One was destroyed by Tim Elkington and Sergeant Binny Barnes, the other by Tony Rook and Rex Furneaux. Rex Furneaux also shared a probable with Pilot Officer Ramsay of 81 Squadron, and Ramsey shared another with Tony Miller. Two other 81 Squadron pilots had probable claims – Pilot Officers McGregor and Walker. Two Ju88s are believed to have crash-landed behind enemy lines and two survivors from one of the aircraft that was destroyed baled out and were captured on our airfield. They were questioned by 151 Wing's German-speaking intelligence officer and spoke frankly and openly to him, being grateful, I think, for the opportunity to speak to him rather than be handed over to our Russian friends for more 'rigorous' interrogation. It transpired that they had known for over a month that we were at Murmansk and they had been brought over from Norway specifically to bomb us.

This raid has an interesting end note which nicely highlights the confused nature of aerial combat. While chasing a couple of Ju88s, Mickey Rook, who was flying as Blue one, became separated from the rest of 81 Squadron and, returning to base at 8,000 ft, saw six aircraft in pairs flying line astern. Believing them to be Hurricanes from 134 Squadron, he joined them in a left-hand climbing turn, although he wasn't close enough to see their markings. He even waggled his wings in greeting. It was only when they reached the cloud base that the leader of the centre section of aircraft peeled off and flew straight at Mickey, who spotted its yellow-painted nose cone and finally realised his mistake – they weren't Hurricanes, they were the escort for the fourteen Ju88s arriving late to the party. Instinctively, he opened fire on the 109 from 250 closing to 50 yards with his twelve guns and watched the front of the aircraft explode in a huge fireball, blowing it completely to pieces. Then the German fighter aircraft turned and crashed to earth.

What followed was complete chaos as the five remaining Messerschmitts all got in each other's way as they tried to get their guns on him and shoot Mickey out of the sky. They fastened on to his tail and, in a life-or-death battle for survival, Mickey spent the next few minutes desperately trying to shake them off. He flew all over the sky in tight, twisting turns, using every manoeuvre in the book in an effort to break away. Finally, he dived down to low level and hugged the valley floor to make his escape, much as Wag Haw had done a couple of weeks earlier. He remembered flashing past a destroyer lying in Murmansk Sound at mast height before noticing he'd finally managed to shake them off. When he landed, he was so shaken up he couldn't get out for several minutes and sat, sweating, in his cockpit.

Hubert Griffith recorded in his diary, 'It is an accepted fact that even the most brilliant of fighter-pilot victories are a combination of luck as well as brilliance. On the whole, Mickey Rook, the eater of a Flight of eggs as well as the consort of a flight of Me 109s, is rather lucky to be alive.'

He goes on, 'Casualties, considering the size of the raid, have been almost comically slight . . . one flight mechanic has got a chip out of his shin, and is being taken to hospital to be x-rayed, another flight mechanic has either been knocked over on his head, or had a clod of earth hit him on the head, and his head is lightly abrased. Our overworked Engineer Officer has likewise been blown clean across his own repair workshop but is otherwise unscathed.'

When all was said and done, we were incredibly lucky that day; another three aircraft for certain, three probables and six damaged, plus two German aircrew captured. The widely spaced buildings on the aerodrome were undamaged, as were the aircraft shelters. Our aircraft themselves told the story. After he'd landed,

Artie's ground crew discovered the bomb blast had shredded the tip of one blade from his Hurricane's propeller with two jagged holes farther down. The other two blades were holed and riddled with bomb fragments. Bushy's aircraft had holes in his bullet-proof windscreen from one of the bombs, with shrapnel holes all along its fuselage. Scotty Edmiston's machine had shrapnel holes in the nose, windscreen and all along the fuselage from the bomb that had taken out his engine (and very nearly him too, but he was completely unscathed).

17

Russian Conversion

L ooking back now, I can see that Dietl's failure to capture the port of Murmansk played a large part in Germany's failure to break Soviet Russia after the invasion earlier in the summer. Following the Beaverbrook–Harriman Anglo-American mission to Moscow in October 1941, which agreed a series of munitions deliveries to Russia, the Germans were confronted with Anglo-American aid arriving through the port on an ever-increasing scale. Hitler knew how vital its capture was, because its fall would have meant there was no other way to get the supplies that were so vital to its continued defence into Russia.

The shopping list agreed with Stalin by Lord Beaverbrook and Averell Harriman on their mission to Moscow was of staggering proportions. As well as military hardware including over 1,000 tanks, 3,000 further RAF Hurricanes and other arms and munitions, there were to be extensive quantities of other vital supplies. Britain and the US had offered[1] some 20,000 tons per month of petroleum products, half a million tons of food, oil and war materials per month and vast quantities of medical supplies, including 10 million pieces of surgical equipment and half a million pairs of surgical gloves. The British and US governments also agreed to supply aluminium, copper, tin, brass, nickel, cobalt, steel, industrial diamonds, machine tools, rubber, wool, jute and lead in substantial quantities on a monthly basis.

The Anglo-American mission to Moscow and the supplies agreed under the Lend-Lease agreement saw the birth of the Arctic convoys, which would follow in the path of that first voyage which had brought our wing to Russia, so we can only imagine the frenetic activity going on behind the scenes to have them begin so quickly. Churchill had been putting pressure on his Chiefs of Staff Committee to ensure the first convoys sailed immediately. As we were repulsing the Luftwaffe's air raid on our base on 6 October, Churchill sent Stalin a personal telegram, which stated, 'We intend to run a continuous cycle of convoys leaving every ten days. The following are on their way and arrive at Archangel on October 12th: 20 heavy tanks, 193 fighters (pre-October quota).'

He goes on to list all the supplies that will be sent by this route in the next few weeks, including a further

140 heavy tanks, 100 Hurricanes, 200 Bren carriers, 200 anti-tank rifles and ammunition, 50 2-pounder guns and ammunition. The following will sail on October 22nd: 200 fighters, 120 heavy tanks. The above shows that the total October quota of aircraft and 280 tanks will arrive in Russia by November 6th. Total of tanks shipped will therefore be 315 which is 19 short of our full quota. This number will be made up in November. Above programme does not take into account goods from the United States. In arranging this regular cycle of convoys we are counting on Archangel to handle the main bulk of deliveries. I presume this part of the job is in hand.[2]

Churchill took a deep personal interest in the Russian air programme, studying its progress on an almost daily basis, and reiterated Britain's continued and all-out support for Russia's fight in every signal and personal telegram he sent to Stalin.

It was around this time that we started to train the seven Russian pilots who would be learning to fly and operate the Hurricanes. We'd shown them how to operate the aircraft but getting them familiar with flying it was a bigger problem owing to the language barrier. The interpreters that were sent from

Moscow to facilitate this did help things somewhat, although there was one called Irena who we were convinced worked for the NKVD [*Narodnyy Komissariat Vnutrennikh Del,* Stalin's secret police].

Not all of the interpreters were a worry. Tim Elkington remembers one in particular – Vladimir Krivoshchekov, a nineteen-year-old naval lieutenant who had been assigned to the wing commander for the duration of 151 Wing's stay in Murmansk. Says Tim,

> *We didn't make friends easily then. Sure, there were the people one drank with and flew with, but life was short in those days so you tended to keep your distance. Vladimir and I got on really well though, right from the off. His English was immaculate – he'd learned it at the Institute of Foreign Languages and we got on famously. Throughout your life, you meet people that you have an instant connection with and Vladimir and I had that.*

The Russian pilots selected to fly were among the best in the Soviet Union. Their role would be to act as instructors, teaching others how to operate the thousands of Hurricanes that we'd be sending to them during the war. Training sessions took place on a one-to-one basis, and the technique involved us perching on the wing of the Hurricane with the interpreter on one side and the trainee pilot in the cockpit. It was messy, but there was no other way of doing it, so with a three-way conversation, we'd get them familiar with all the controls and idiosyncrasies of the aircraft.

Bill Lowes, one of our RAF ground technicians, had his work cut out for him on the communications side. He says, 'We had to alter their headsets, because the Russians used carbon throat mikes and we used electro-magnetic mics that were incorporated into the oxygen masks.'

Most of the training was done by 134 Squadron, and it began when Kapitan Raputsokov was introduced to Tony Miller in the operations room in the 'Kremlin'.

Kapitan Raputsokov was a thickset, cobby sort of chap with a quiet sense of humour. He obviously had a lot of flying experience because his job was to fly round to various units checking out all types of aircraft. Raputsokov told me that he had flown Hurricanes, and by the universally understood gesture of 'thumbs up' indicated that he thought them 'horosho' – the goods!

That evening we were entertained by the Russian airmen at the first of many convivial parties staged between us – and believe me, it was some party! Raputsokov sat next to me solid as a rock upon whom waves of alcohol were breaking without any effect whatsoever. Later that evening when Bacchus took over, he quietly and politely escorted me through concert halls and dining rooms guiding my wavering footsteps until I was firmly ensconced in the transit van taking us back to base.

In the circumstances, and especially as he was a very good type, I decided to make him an honorary member of the Squadron – a rare distinction! Major General Kuznetsov agreed right away when I asked whether Raputsokov could be semi-officially attached to 134 Squadron saying that Raputsokov was going to be the first instructor on the Hurricanes anyway.[4]

Artie Holmes recounts his memories of that same party in his diaries. He writes,

Flt Lt Hodson, our adviser on all things Russian, gave us a fatherly talk on the vagaries of vodka. But to no avail. The Russians have their own way of drinking a toast. They put one inch of neat vodka in a tumbler, click their heels, raise

*the glass to you with the greeting 'Za zda-ró-vye', swallow
the vodka in one, and replenish the glass. If you sip your
vodka, or even only half-drink it, you are a cissie and they
are offended and walk away.*

*Despite the stern warnings of our well-meaning and
well-informed Hodson, casualties became very heavy
indeed, the delayed action of real Russian vodka being
almost lethal. Those who managed to slip away early
crawled back through the snow to our own Mess with
nothing worse than a blinding headache, and a hobnailed
liver. But many were carried back bodily by the gleeful, and
none too gentle Russians. One of our admin officers in a
paralytic coma swallowed his tongue, and would have died
had our MO, Squadron Leader Jackson not fortunately
been at hand to save him from choking by fishing it out
with forceps.*

*This was not the end of the social scene, although we
readily conceded that at this point it was without doubt,
one-nil to the Russians. The weather, we were assured,
would stay bad so we invited them next to our Mess. The
visitors arrived in full regalia in a motor coach which had
an entrance each side at the front. It soon became apparent
they had been warned that our Scotch whisky would be
quite safe to drink provided they diluted it with plenty of
water. At their request, water jugs were placed on all our
ante-room tables. With each double whisky that they were
handed, they slurped the glass half full of water. It looked
like being rather a dull evening until some joker had the
bright idea of refilling all the water jugs with gin. When the
Russians started topping up their whisky with gin, the
party immediately livened up. By the end of the evening,
when they were leaving, we had a great game pushing them
into their bus at one side, and catching them as they fell
right through and out the other. This game went on for*

quite some time, the funniest part being that our guests
seemed to be enjoying it every bit as much as we were. We
decided this levelled the score.[5]

When they were all sober, we got down to business. Artie Holmes was allocated one Kapitan Markavitch to train, whom he describes in his diary as 'an extremely experienced pilot, keen to learn'.[6] Markavitch had been given a set of Hurricane handling notes, which had already been translated, and, having discussed the controls, instruments and handling characteristics, he'd immediately progressed to start up, taxi, brake and switch off again. Artie wrote in his diary,

On his fourth day, he had a last check on the cockpit drill
for takeoff, the climbing, approach and stalling speeds, and
the engine boosts. Then he plugged in his R/T jack, called
Control for permission to take off, and was away. I was
proud to see this handsome Russian flying my Hurricane.
He circled the aerodrome twice, made a superb landing,
and taxied over to me to give a delighted thumbs up before
turning and making for the Russian hangar. There the RAF
roundel would be obliterated and a Russian star painted in.
Suddenly, I was a pilot without an aeroplane.

Unfortunately, Kapitan Raputsokov, who had made such an impression on Tony Miller at that first party, never got to fly with 134 Squadron; he never even managed to fly a Hurricane. Sadly, he was killed a few days after that memorable party, trying to fly back a crippled Russian bomber that had been hit by flak while on a raid. The bomber crashed near Vaenga with the loss of everyone on board. His body was brought back to Vaenga and a number of our officers attended his funeral.

We flew four patrols on the 8th, escorting Russian bombers, but there were no engagements with enemy forces. Hampered by just three hours of light each day, the worsening conditions and the increasing pace of the Russian pilots beginning to solo, those were the last flights made by 81 Squadron pilots in Russia.

One of the seven pilots under instruction was Russian fighter ace Kapitan Boris Feoktistovich Safonov of the Russian Naval Aviation's 72nd Air Regiment. This squadron was one of a group of squadrons – bomber and fighter – already based at Vaenga when we arrived, and Safonov had already been credited with twelve victories and held the Russian equivalent to our VC, 'Hero of the Soviet Union'. He was a large, solid, serious man whom we all rather liked. He could often be seen in dispersal waving his hands aloft, arms at different angles, demonstrating how he'd got his latest kill. Like almost all the Russian pilots in training, he was older than us with considerably more flying hours, so humility was in rather short supply initially, and he, like the others, thought there was little we could teach him. These Soviet pilots were never slow to tell us how good they were. Most of their experience was gleaned flying the Ilyushin I-16, a stubby-winged monoplane which they liked to emphasise was difficult to fly.

We did stress that the Hurricane was without vices and any old fool could fly them, so they were suitably chastened after bending a few through heavy landings. Even Safonov, who, without exception, they all looked up to, managed to damage his flaps after one particular landing, so when he started to listen to what we were telling him, everyone else followed suit.

Safonov headed up the training programme for the Russians, assisted by his colleague Kapitan Kuharienko, a short wiry man with a permanent grin etched across his face. The two men couldn't have been more different, and had temperaments that matched their flying styles. Safonov was a considered, careful man, methodical in his approach to learning and meticulous in his preparations. Kuharienko, on the other hand, was very much a 'suck it and see' type of fellow who flew by the seat of his pants.

When Safonov took off on his first solo, he climbed to 1,500 ft before he turned. His landings were the same – he did two or three circuits-and-landings with his undercarriage down before he even thought about attempting anything else. Kuharienko, on the other hand, simply jumped into his aircraft, took off with the rudder bias in the wrong position and flew a series of violent and sickening swerves before beating up the aerodrome and flying a series of flick-rolls. He was laughing like a drain when he landed, evidently believing the whole thing to be a great joke.

Another of the Russian instructors was Yacobenko, an ex-cavalry officer who remarked that he'd got bored with riding one horse when he realised he could drive so many hundred of them all at once when he was in the cockpit of a fighter aircraft. He had this gesture that he used to make after muttering 'fascist crafts!' [Fascist aircraft] with incredible venom. He'd pretend to spit on the ground, grind in what he'd 'spat out' with his heel, draw his finger across his throat and then dance around and stamp on the floor. The whole pantomime was adopted by 134 Squadron as their squadron war-dance.

Most of the training on the RAF side was done by the diminutive Flight Lieutenant Jack Ross, DFC, and he and Kuharienko formed a close bond. Safonov liked to joke that 'they are great friends because they are both practically dwarfs and have the same problem in not being able to see out of the cockpit!' Hubert Griffith was a great fan of Ross, describing him in his diary as 'one of the most unfailingly amusing of all our pilots who ever trod Soviet soil'.

I think our performance since we'd arrived in Russia really went before us as far as the Russian pilots were concerned. When you think how few flights, patrols and escorts we'd managed owing to weather and other restrictions, we'd really set the bar high and they respected us for that. Plus, they were really impressed with the twelve-gun Hurricane, which we'd shown to be a lethal fighter. As a wing, we'd shot down fifteen of the Luftwaffe's aircraft for the loss of just one of our own, plus four probables and seven damaged. In all likelihood, the real figures were higher than that, but we'd set a standard the Russians respected and wanted to emulate. That helped us immensely, although the nights in the mess helped too. Nothing fosters and lubricates international relations like alcohol!

The Russian pilots were all intrigued by the darts board in our flight hut at dispersal. They'd never seen one before and we learned that, after watching us play, they were convinced we did it to improve our aim in air combat. After that, they would line up to play, although, as in most things they did, there were no half-measures and they launched the darts as if they were firing harpoons. They'd end up buried so deep in the board we'd need pliers to get them out.

I'm not sure whether they were foolish or just without fear but after the winter really started to bite, they would come into the flight hut and put a tin of petrol on top of the stove to 'warm it up for the vehicles'. You've never seen a group of men run so fast in all your life!

This over-exuberance and desire to test everything to extremes showed itself in everything they did. It was as if there was no Russian word for 'understatement'. If they saw the word 'maximum', they interpreted it literally. One pilot read about the Hurricane's maximum range, but it didn't occur to him that endurance was directly related to fuel consumption and, therefore, to throttle use, in much the same way that the range today's car manufacturers cite for their vehicles is based on ideal conditions and driving at the most economical speed. He proceeded to fly flat out in an attempt to reach the aircraft's maximum range, but he did so at full throttle, with the inevitable result that he ran out of fuel and wrote off that Hurricane.

They were a fascinating people, the Russians. Their grit and determination, tenacity – call it what you will – was astonishing. Flight Lieutenant Gittins set an exam for all of the Russian technicians who had been studying under him and – how can I put this? – even by the standards of the time, he was one of the most bigoted men I'd ever encountered. He set the exam, and he went all out to make it as fiendishly difficult and weighted against the Russians as he could. Bear in mind that they'd had only a few weeks to get to know the Hurricane, and that they were working through the medium of an interpreter, yet one of the candidates got 98 per cent in the exam, and the average mark for all those who passed was 80 per cent. Even Gittins had to concede that was impressive. He'd never seen anything approaching those results back in England. I heard the CO talking about them one day, and he said, 'They learn as fast as hell and they're flat out to do anything they can for us.'

Once the training regime gathered momentum and all the Russian pilots had soloed, there was no stopping them. Their 'training' lasted five days and after three flights they were officially signed off and ready for operations. They were eager enough, and they certainly weren't going to be held back by weather, no matter how bad. I remember one pilot took off in a snowstorm so bad you literally couldn't see a hand in front of your face. It was madness. Three attempts he made to get back down, and each time he went around I was convinced that was it, we'd never see him again. Somehow, he made it, though. He had balls, I'll give him that; there wasn't a single pilot in our wing who'd have even thought of flying in conditions like that. Safonov was the same – he seemed to be without fear. He was either very, very good, or he was crazy. To this day, I'm still not sure which.

I often wondered what happened to him, and twelve years later,

I found out. After the war, Peter Knapton had been posted to Moscow as assistant air attaché. He told me,

In 1953, I was visiting Tolstoy's old family house at Yasnaya Polyana and to get there, I had to pass through the town of Tula, about 60 miles south of Moscow. Standing in the centre of the square was a statue of an airman in a leather flying jacket and helmet. I stopped the car and had a look at the inscription. It was to the memory of Boris Safonov, killed in action in May 1942. He had 20 kills to his name when he died. I wondered whether at the time he was in one of our Hurricanes.

The Russian naval air station at Severomorsk – the name now given to what had been Vaenga – is named after Safonov and the local museum has a rich vein of material on his exploits. It is also richly equipped with memorabilia of our short stay in the region.

Gradually, as October passed, we handed over more and more of our kit to the Russians. The agreement was that we were to take nothing home but our personal belongings; everything else was to be left for them – vehicles disappeared, followed by parachutes, flying helmets, oxygen masks, goggles, headphones and Mae Wests. It was like a fire sale with no money changing hands. Everything must go! As the Russian pilots became more experienced in flying the Hurricane, so we stepped back and they began to assume more of the responsibilities.

By the 10th, we were on the verge of at least half of 81 Squadron being entirely non-operational as the Russians were all but ready for us to hand our aircraft over to them. We were hoping we weren't going to be in Russia throughout the winter; for starters, we hadn't been issued with suitable clothing so we began to get restless. Later that day, news came in that we should be prepared to leave for home on the 25th. That really lifted us all; finally, the end was in sight.

Killing time at dispersal on a sunny day while listening to the wind-up gramophone. To the far right sits Mickey Rook while Scotty Edmiston sits on the log to his left. The Hurricane, Z5227 is Scotty's.

Russian workers toil to excavate 134 Squadron's dispersal area while Russian soldiers look on and ground crew prepare a Hurricane for flight.

The aerodrome was often heavily waterlogged, with the taxiing area at 134 Squadron's dispersal being 90% underwater.

Hector Keil, Sergeant Kirvan and Bart Campbell after another stressful mission escorting Soviet bombers to their target.

Propeller spinning, an 81 Squadron Hurricane emerges from its shelter to begin a sortie while a Russian bomber passes overhead.

Some of the 134 Squadron pilots, four of whom would die within six months of the Wing's return to England. From left to right, Paddy McCann (KIA Alamein), Sergeant Pilot Douglas, Neil Cameron, Peter Knapton, Dicky Knight (at rear) and Dicky Wollaston (KIA Alamein), Jack Ross (Killed Eglington, Jan 1942), Tim Elkington, Bella (interpreter), Bunny Barnes (KIA Alamein).

RAF technician Aircraftsman Freeman gives instruction to Soviet pilot V. Maksimovich on flying the Hurricane.

Officers of 151 Wing indulge in physical exercise in the chill of an Arctic morning at Vaenga. We had to get ever more inventive in killing time once we'd handed over our aircraft and equipment to the Russian pilots.

Impromptu games of football were a frequent aside in the weeks leading up to our departure from Russia.

Hector Kiel uses a draughts board to collect snow for a pot of tea. We took to wearing all our kit, including the Mae Wests, when off duty, in an effort to stay warm in the sub-zero temperatures that defined October and November 1941.

The CO, Wing Commander Ramsbottom-Isherwood with *Droochok*, the three-month-old reindeer calf presented to the Wing by General Kouznetsova.

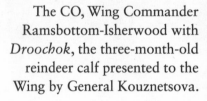

Journalist, diarist, and Battle of Britain hero Ray 'Artie' Holmes (far right) stands next to Scottie Edmiston. Also visible are Mickey Rook (3rd from left) and Basil Bush to his right.

A Red Air Force propaganda poster from 1941 extolling the prowess of its pilots following their training by the RAF. It reads 'Glory and honour to the falcons of Stalin against the horror of fascist vultures'.

Zakhar Sorokin. Sorokin rammed a Luftwaffe aircraft near Murmansk in November 1941 and had to have both legs amputated. Despite this, Sorokin returned to duty and continued to fly until the end of the war.

134 Squadron pilots outside the 'Tartan Dive' bar, London, February 1942. From left to right: Dicky Wollaston, Rex Furneaux, unknown, unknown, Borneo Price (Canadian, replacement pilot), Hector Keil, Peter Knapton, Binnie Barnes, Bart Campbell and Neil Cameron.

Russia conferred one of its highest awards, the Order of Lenin, on (from left to right) Flight Lieutenant Wag Haw, the two Squadron Leaders Tony Miller and Tony Rook, Wing-Commander Ramsbottom-Isherwood. In March 1942, they were invited to the Soviet embassy in London where Soviet ambassador Ivan Maisky presented the medals.

Ramsbottom-Isherwood's medals. They comprise his DFC (1942), AFC (1940), 1939–45 Star, Air Crew Europe Star, Burma Star, Defence Medal and War Medal, and Order of Lenin. Also shown are the book which accompanied his Order of Lenin and his original Murmansk Aerodrome pass.

In 2006, I went back to Murmansk to lay a wreath at the Commonwealth War Graves Cemetery.

In 2011, I was given the opportunity of a lifetime and flew a Spitfire for the first time in 70 years.

At last, in 2013, the British Government gave us, and the survivors of the Arctic Convoys, the recognition we'd been fighting for. We received the Arctic Star at 10 Downing Street and I am pictured here with Vic Bashford on my right, and Tim Elkington on my left. Next to Tim stands Peter Knapton.

18

Endgame

Two days after we were told to be ready to leave on the 25th, 81 Squadron reached a milestone: on the 12th, 'B' Flight handed over all of its aircraft and became non-operational. It was followed ten days later by 'A' Flight.

The 12th was Mickey Rook's birthday, so a party was held for him that night. With none of us required for flying by this stage, the drink flowed and we really started to relax. That is, we did . . . right up until Wing Commander Isherwood breezed in. We knew something was amiss from the purposeful way he arrived; his whole demeanour was different. As a rule, he'd have made a great poker player because his face never gave anything away, but on this occasion it was as if his whole body was telegraphing his feelings. The room fell silent as he read out a cable he'd just received from the Air Ministry. In summary, it said, '151 Wing to prepare to move south through Russia to the Middle East.'

As he said the words, all the energy left the room. It was as if someone had taken a fully inflated party balloon and stuck a pin in it. Many of the pilots staggered to their billets that night very, very drunk indeed. We felt let down, betrayed, angry and frustrated. We'd been misled initially as to where we were going, had endured the snow, the cold, the deprivation, the appalling toilets, the rich food, no mail from home since Leconfield, and now this. Home was in our sights now, but it seemed more remote than ever. We were counting on moving back to England on completion of the job, not several thousand miles farther away from it. We had visions of travelling through Russia to fight on another front where we'd probably end up until the end of the war. I felt utterly desolate and depressed. I missed Phyllis desperately. This really was the most sickening news.

Somehow, we had to pick ourselves up from this and carry on. But while we fretted about our prospective move south, unbeknown to us, Isherwood was working furiously behind the scenes on our behalf to destroy the Air Ministry's case. A further signal arrived on the 14th hinting at the unspecified move 'south', causing Hubert Griffith to wonder, 'What exactly does south mean?' According to him, Isherwood '. . . contemplated sending the Air Ministry a cryptic message, "Ref your movement order of 12.10.41, see Psalm 146, verse 3." The Verse in question is the celebrated "put not thy trust in Princes."'[1]

What he actually did was send the Air Ministry a message requesting further details to buy more time, while simultaneously talking to the Russians to get information that would support his quest to get us home. They told him it would take at least two months, although four was a more likely assessment. Using that information, wing staff calculated they'd need a *minimum* of 40 tons of rations to make a journey that would cover some two thousand miles through central and southern Russia. Those in authority back home would have had no understanding whatsoever of the difficulties of travelling by rail over such long distances through the Russian heartland; if they had, they'd never have come up with such a ridiculous plan.

As if things weren't bad enough, the Air Ministry sent a further signal the following day saying, 'Embassy and whole of Military and Air Mission leaving Moscow tonight for Kuibyshev. Please inform Archangel.' Given that the message's priority was marked 'emergency', giving it precedence over all other signals, it didn't exactly instil confidence in the Wing Executive that all was well in Moscow. As the Russian news regarding the position of the front line around Moscow had been vague, I can only imagine how they felt. When Griffith realised that 'Kuibyshev' was the new name for the ancient town of Samara, some five hundred miles east of Moscow, there was only one conclusion to be inferred; given the speed at which the embassy appeared to be evacuating, they must have assumed that Moscow was close to falling.

Although the weather had closed in and it really felt like winter had arrived, the Luftwaffe managed to carry out a night bomber raid on Vaenga on the 16th that was notable for the fact that almost all of the 1,000lb bombs dropped failed to explode. We learned from our Russian friends that they'd been made by Polish POWs who had sabotaged the detonators. Now, back home, unexploded ordnance was treated with the sort of respect and reverence you'd generally reserve for high-ranking royalty, so the crater would be cordoned off and traffic diverted in case the slightest vibration triggered an explosion. The highly trained, expert bomb disposal team would then arrive with their armoury of stethoscopes and sensitive equipment to begin the unenviable and dangerous task of dismantling and making safe the monster before them.

In this case, a three-ton truck arrived, and out of the back jumped six or seven soldiers with shovels; they started digging as soon as they hit the ground. Whenever they reached an unexploded bomb, they'd fasten a chain around it and winch it on to their lorry. Then, they'd drive it down to a lake about a mile away from the base, winch the bomb off and lower it on to the ice, at which point they'd take cover on the far side of the lake and detonate the bomb with machine-gun fire.

We were utterly astonished at this, so I asked the Russian officer in charge why they did it this way. He looked at me quizzically, as if what they were doing was the most natural thing in the world. 'They are lucky to be doing this,' he said. 'If they were fighting the Germans on the front line, they could be killed at any minute. Doing this, they take only the one small risk that the bomb might explode and kill them.' There was a strange kind of logic to this, I decided, as they worked throughout the morning recovering all of the unexploded bombs and detonating them on the lake. By the time they'd finished, not a single soldier was injured. We decided if this was the way they were going to fight their war against the Germans, they would win it.

We flew three patrols in 134 Squadron's aircraft on the 17th, escorting Russian bombers, although given the weather, the Germans weren't in any mood for fighting so there was no contact with the enemy. Since we'd arrived in Russia and provided escort to their bombers, not a single one of their aircraft had been lost to enemy activity. The Soviet pilots paid us a short but impressive compliment, saying that, when we escorted them, they never even looked up in the air. They had such faith in us, they said, they could fly straight to their targets, knowing they were safe in our hands.

Those three patrols turned out to be 151 Wing's final flights in Russia; just two days later, every remaining Hurricane, dinghy, vehicle and item of equipment save for our own personal kit was handed over to the Russians. Tim Elkington asked the Russian who was taking his aircraft to sign his logbook, noting alongside Sergeant Romanov's statement that 'The undersigned, namely Sergeant Peter Daniel Romanov, is now the proud possessor of a very fine "fighter craft".'

After just six weeks in the Soviet Union, the wing had ceased to be operational. A signal was sent to the Air Ministry on 20 October saying simply, 'All aircraft handed over to Soviet Pilots'. It was a memorable day for more than just that reason, though – it was cold enough that the ink froze in some of the office and bedroom inkwells!

The CO was still working hard on our behalf to kill any prospect of a trip south, and around this time engaged the assistance of Admiral Sir Richard Bevan, the Senior British Naval Officer in the region. Finally, on the 23rd, he put together every argument he had come up with in a signal to the Air Ministry, to convince them of the foolishness of their idea. The signal, sent at 1200, reads:

Following information obtained in conference with the Senior Base Naval Officer North Russia and Soviet staff. Journey south, or to Archangel of large party by Murmansk – Kandalaksha railway impossible owing to nearness of front line and consequent congestion by troops and supplies for front line, plus repeated cutting of railway by bombing. No, repeat no roads. Russians unable to provide sea transport to Archangel. S. B. N.O. unable to arrange Naval transport to Archangel. Russians using all railways to move supplies and troops to defence of Moscow and southern war area. Inevitable delays would occur at junctions. Estimates of the duration of the journey vary from six weeks to three months. Rations now available would probably prove insufficient. Unable to rely on Russians providing. Average temperature last week was minus ten degrees Centigrade. No, repeat no winter equipment available. Above information shows conclusively that journey south is impossible and evacuation to UK advisable.

As stated above, no repeat no means of transport to Archangel available here and S. B. N.O. advises no, repeat no accommodation for personnel on convoy now at Archangel. Suggest therefore that only practical solution is for home authority to send fast troopship direct to Murmansk-Vaenga for embarkation of Wing at night. Fighter protection can be arranged if necessary. Enemy bombing of Murmansk and district only very slight and totally ineffective up to now.

S. B. N.O. North Russia concurs. Request you repeat to BRITLISTAF.[2]

There is clear evidence that Churchill was looking to deviate from the original plan in a response to one of his personal minutes that I came across at the National Archives. Churchill was angry and disappointed at the limited scope of the operation and the refusal to extend the RAF's Hurricane operations to the Russian front. A memo he wrote to Sir Charles Portal, his Chief of the Air Staff makes his frustration plain. 'The most serious mistake we have made about the Russians was in not sending eight fighter squadrons, which would have gained great fame, destroyed many German aircraft and given immense encouragement all along the front,'[3] he wrote on 24 October. Sir Charles Portal's reply, written on the same day, is extremely detailed. It reads,

Prime Minister,
In reply to your minute M.1013/1 of the 24th October, I agree that the story of the Murmansk squadrons is not a very satisfactory one. You will remember that originally we had two objectives in sending a small air force to Murmansk:
(a) the encouragement that would be afforded to the Russian people by the knowledge that the Royal Air Force had joined with the Soviet Air Force;
(b) the protection of the port of Murmansk so that British light naval forces could use it.
Neither of these objectives was achieved. The Russians refused to permit any publicity, and so far as I know the British naval forces have scarcely used the port.*
2. It is true that a proposal was at one time made that the two squadrons should be transferred complete from the Russian left flank. This however, involved going back on our original offer to give the Russians the 40 Hurricanes, or

---

* It appears that the rules on publicity, something the Russians had previously embraced with open arms, had changed.

*what were left of them, when the weather closed down at
Murmansk, and it was considered politically inexpedient to
go back on this offer.*

*The next development was that we decided to keep the
squadrons in action beyond the originally agreed date, i.e.
end of September, and after handing over, to send the
personnel overland to Persia and the Middle East.*

*This plan, which was agreed by the Russians, has now
been frustrated by the congestion and confusion on the
Russian railways. According to our people at Murmansk,
the Russians say that the journey might take anything up
to three months, and as our units were not equipped for
the Russian winter, have only limited supplies and have
already handed over their equipment, I think the best thing
to do is bring them home by ship from Murmansk before
the weather gets any worse. Alternatively, we might send
them to Archangel where supplies of winter equipment
should by now have arrived, but if the port freezes up they
will be stranded with nothing useful to do and no means
of withdrawal, except across Russia, or by the Murmansk
railway, which is already suffering constant interruptions.*

*I realise the political difficulty of withdrawing the Wing
from Russia, but I think you will agree that there might be
equally serious trouble if we allowed 500 airmen to become
stranded in Arctic Russia for the winter, or if we sent them
into the heart of Russia with no lines of communication
and no means of looking after them.*

*3. In dealing with the criticisms of the smallness of the
force sent to Russia, I suggest we should bear in mind that
at the time it was decided to send them, we had no idea
how successful the Russian resistance to the German
invasion would prove. We were by no means clear of the
menace of invasion this year, and we were doing our
utmost to build up our forces in the Middle East. Two*

*squadrons were an adequate force for the defence of
Murmansk, and operations on any other front would have
involved maintaining a line of communications that cross
the Russian l. of c., and many administrative difficulties
which would probably have prevented the efficient
operation of the units that was possible from Murmansk.*

*4. I should be grateful for your instructions on
paragraph 2 above.*[4]

For all of us, while this was going on in the background, apathy
and boredom reigned supreme. It had been bad enough when we
weren't flying, but with nothing to do, no aircraft to fly and no
vehicles to drive, there are only so many times you can play cards,
read or chat to one another without going mad. At least Sir
Charles Portal recognised the obstacles facing Isherwood in maintaining morale and keeping us occupied. His concerns were
conveyed in a signal to Isherwood on the 28th that was at pains to
point out that he was working on a solution. It reads,

*Private and personal for Wing Commander Ramsbottom
Isherwood from CAS. Begins,*
*I much regret the delay that has occurred in giving a
decision about the disposal of 151 Wing. We fully realise the
dullness and discomfort in which you must all be living now
that you have completed handing over aircraft to Russians
and the anxiety that you must be feeling personally about
welfare of personnel under your command. Delay is being
caused by necessity for avoiding anything which might be
misinterpreted by Russians, either locally or at centre of
government. You can rest assured that we are doing our very
best to obtain a decision as soon as possible.*[5]

Artie Holmes' diary records the frustration and sense of deser-
tion felt by us all at this time:

There seems to be a remote chance now that we may not after all be going to the Middle East. There is still no sign though, that we will instead return home.

26 October. This awful uncertainty persists. No aircraft now. Nothing to do but debate our fate. Maybe they'll send us to Moscow to operate there. Maybe the convoy route back across the Arctic has become too dangerous and they don't want to lose us! Maybe after all the publicity about the Wing in Murmansk they are afraid our return home would look like an evacuation and the Hun will be saying he's kicked us out. There are whispers that the Wingco is sending rude messages back to Air Ministry, becoming ruder each day. We now go on long walks in the snow [which was more than twelve inches deep now] *to pass the time. We were enjoying the skiing but that is finished because we have broken all the skis. Today, we started a five rouble sweep on the date for leaving Murmansk for – anywhere!*

8th November. Still killing time. The boredom is killing us. Now seems possible we will stay here for the winter, and start operating again next spring. Some suggest we may even go through Vladivostok to the Far East.

Tonight, the first mail since we left home has arrived. Twelve bags of it! First for three months. I had 23 letters. They took a day to read, and three days to answer. My replies went by submarine, for posting in England.[6]

To celebrate the arrival of the mail, a double rum ration was issued in the evening , which helped to relieve a certain amount of boredom. It's amazing the difference twelve bags of mail can make to 550 men, but you could sense an immediate lift when it was delivered to us, although, for many, our delight at hearing from loved ones and feeling physically closer to them was muted by the uncertainty over when we'd see them again. Once that first lot of mail arrived, though, the floodgates opened, and on the 12th a further consignment arrived consisting of seventeen bags of parcels and letters, including correspondence dispatched in England up to 7 October.

In an effort to lift everyone's spirits, we sergeant pilots decided to stage a variety show in our mess. Never underestimate the abilities of airmen to conjure something out of nothing – somehow, we managed to construct a stage, with curtains and scenery. We even managed to acquire a piano from somewhere, so Wag was in his element; he could charm any tune you like from the keys. We wrote the script ourselves, and loads of people came up with lyrics for a song we had composed. It covered our frustrations, and included rude references to personalities within the wing, from Isherwood down. Nobody escaped, and the sharper the barb, the louder the applause. It ran to over a dozen verses, although it was being added to constantly, even as it was performed. Called 'Hardships', it was sung by Avro Anson, Ibby Waud and myself, with Wag on the ivories. Even the Russians stepped up, with accompaniment on trumpet and drums. One of the more memorable versions is produced below, but there are several other versions in circulation.

'BINDERS HO' OR 'THE SGT PILOTS DIRGE'
Words by Butch Reed
Music by Nobby Clarke

Off to Russia we did go,
To that land of ice and snow –
Hardships, you bastards, you don't know what hardships are.
The aerodrome was bleak and bare
And all the Russkies did was stare –
Hardships etc
The roads were so damned awful

They just shattered our joints,
Dispersal huts could not be found
Cause they were so far underground –
Hardships etc

The shithouse had a wooden frame,
But no one had a deadly aim –
Hardships etc
The food was full of goo and grease, and always there was
    rice,
And very soon we turned it down, not even looking twice
And a glass of Russian tea
Tasted just like maiden's pee –
Hardships etc

Washing would have been quite nice
If we hadn't had to break the ice –
Hardships etc
We drank the water out of tubs,
The Russkies never heard of pubs –
Hardships etc
And just after we arrived that fucking awful breeze
Brought down snow in blizzards till it came up to our
    knees
Our bedrooms were just like a cell
As cold as cold as bloody Hell –
Hardships etc

The women were such a bind
You couldn't get a fucking grind –
Hardships etc
French letters we had by the score
But you couldn't find a Russian whore –
Hardships etc

The girls all treated us like rams,
Were scared out of their wits,
They wouldn't let us touch the spot,
The rotten lot of shits.
We tried to woo them with this song,
But the Russian girls knew right from wrong –
Hardships etc
The lines were thirty miles away,
And we were over twice a day –
Hardships etc
The aerodrome was boggy sand,
You shat when you came into land –
Hardships etc
When our work was finished, no more flying there to do,
They said 'damned good show boys, now the Middle East
    for you'
Please don't wonder if we grieve,
Cause we've had no fucking leave –
Hardships etc

While we were kicking our heels and trying to come up with ever more inventive ways of killing time, the Russian instructors and the pilots they'd trained on the Hurricanes were really showing their mettle. On 26 October, one of the Russian pilots shot down a Luftwaffe Bf110 while he was flying an ex-151 Wing Hurricane, and on the last day of the month the first Soviet-assembled Hurricane shot down a Ju88 over the Rybachiy Peninsula. By this stage, over one hundred additional Hurricanes had arrived in the country with the first convoys.

One of the most interesting stories to come out of the Russian squadrons flying the wing's aircraft happened a few days earlier, on the 25th, and really demonstrates that blind determination exhibited by the pilots we encountered. It involved Lieutenant Zakhar Sorokin, who'd been flying a patrol over the Kola Peninsula, with Dmitri Sokolov flying as his wingman. They sighted four Me110s and Sorokin engaged one, shooting it down in a ball of flame. During the engagement, the Me110's pilot had got off a burst of fire, and Sorokin realised he'd taken a round through his leg. Undeterred, he engaged another of the aircraft but realised as he lined it up in his gunsight that he'd used up all his ammunition in the previous attack. There was nothing else for it, so he rammed the enemy aircraft, and watched it go into a dive. With his own aircraft stricken, he managed to make a crash landing on a frozen lake. As he came down, his wingman followed him, and Sorokin was surprised to see his friend fire a warning burst as he did so.

As he climbed out of his aircraft and stepped out on to the frozen tundra, he saw a dog running towards him. He was momentarily confused before realising that if there was a dog, there were likely to be Germans near by. Sure enough, when he looked into the distance, he saw the Me110 which he'd shot down . . . and it was then he realised that its two-man crew were heading in his direction. He heard the crack of rounds as they whistled past him and realised that the Germans had their pistols out and were shooting at him. The closest threat was the dog, which he shot and killed with his revolver. He managed to shoot one of the Germans, who dropped to the ground, dead, but by then he'd run out of ammunition, and he and the remaining German were in close proximity to one another. While he'd been focused on the man he'd just shot, he saw that the other pilot had drawn a knife. A short hand-to-hand fight took place in which Sorokin was stabbed in the cheek, knocking out several of his teeth. After a further scuffle, he managed to bring his Very pistol up and shot his German assailant dead.

In great pain from his wounds, he then set off on foot in the direction in which he'd last seen his friend Sokolov flying. It took him almost seven days of walking across frozen tundra in freezing temperatures, yet somehow Sorokin survived. He stumbled into a small village, which was the first sign of civilisation he'd seen since being shot down, and from there, he was rescued by his comrades. His feet were so badly frostbitten that he ended up having both legs amputated beneath the knee, yet even this didn't deter him. He was fitted with prosthetics and eventually returned to front-line flying, shooting down a further nine German aircraft to take his personal tally to fourteen. He was later awarded the OBE by King George VI, who remarked, 'With men like you we do not need anyone else.'[7]

One of the most extraordinary occurrences of the whole Russian adventure occurred on 5 November when General Kouznetsova, having already presented the CO with numerous gifts during our stay, capped them all by arriving at conference with a three-month-old baby reindeer to present to him. This led to one of the more bizarre notices of our tour being placed up with the daily routine orders by our wing adjutant, which read: 'A reindeer has been taken on Wing-strength as from today's date. Volunteer (preferably with experience) to report to Orderly Room for duties of grooming, feeding and exercising same.'

Unfortunately, and much to the general's disgust, the reindeer – named 'Droochok' [Little Friend] by our CO – died within two weeks. This despite the best efforts of the wing's two doctors (granted, neither had any veterinary experience). The whole tragedy was so much harder to bear as a similar gift had also been made to Admiral Bevan, RN, commanding our naval contingent at Polyano. The BBC announced that the Naval Reindeer, which had been conveyed on board our submarine HMS *Tigris*, had arrived safely back in Blighty and been placed in Whipsnade Zoo.

No man could have done more to ensure the success of the mission than General Kuznetsov, a fine fellow and one well liked by everyone who met him.

A few days later, the wing received a signal that Royal Naval transports would shortly be arriving in Murmansk to take us home. You can imagine the sense of relief that swept through the aerodrome when we were told.

Stalin sent a rather terse message to us which was read out by Wing Commander Isherwood. It stated merely that he 'appreciated' what we had done. Talk about damning with faint praise. But that was a minor blip and nothing could dampen my spirits now that I could see light at the end of the tunnel. Finally, home was in sight; we might even get there before Christmas. Now we knew we were finally going home, our days felt as if they had purpose again, even if we were living in almost perpetual darkness now. And although we weren't overrun by things to occupy ourselves with, matters improved markedly when the Royal Navy stepped up with some great films for us to watch in the local cinema. George Formby in *It's in the Air*; Errol Flynn in *Robin Hood*; Gracie Fields in *Shipyard Sally*; and *Snow White and the Seven Dwarves*.[8]

A form of demob spirit overcame us pilots at this point, and we started to get ever more boisterous and adventurous in our pursuits. We invented a new winter sport by harnessing the immense power of a Ford V8-engined shooting brake to a sleigh, attached via a length of rope. Sitting on the sleigh, we'd then be hauled across the aerodrome at great speed, although every time you hit a bump you'd be hurled a few feet into the air. It was brilliant fun, and we thought it might even make for an Olympic event except for one small flaw – every time the car took a sudden turn, the sleigh and its occupants would be thrown over great distances. *That* didn't hurt, but the landing often did! One of our number split his head open in the process, so the CO had words and our newly devised sport had to be radically rethought and scaled back in terms of speed and ballistics . . .

And of course, we couldn't say farewell to Russia without a party, which was thrown and organised by the wing itself. Flight Lieutenant Griffith recorded the details in his diary:

The long, echoing first floor of our Kremlin – the only space in it large enough to accommodate half-a-hundred Russians to whom we'd sent written invitations, was laid

*out to look like a party – with tables stretching down it
covered with white table-cloths, extra electric lights
installed for the occasion, some green stuff plucked from
neighbouring birch forests draped round the lamps, and the
tables groaning under bottles of English spirits and Russian
edibles – an amateurish affair when compared with the
hospitality of the Berkeley in London or the Metropole in
Moscow – but serving its turn with the frozen rim of the
Arctic Circle and enjoyed by all. As a party – like the small
expedition as a whole – it was a classic.*

Meanwhile, as the Arctic winter gripping the Soviet Union wors-
ened, the Russians fought to maintain a passage through the White
Sea in order that the Arctic convoys might use the port of Archangel.
They'd undertaken to do so throughout the winter, but they were
fighting a losing battle. The winter of 1941 arrived earlier, bit
harder and was colder than anybody had forecast. The Russians
threw everything they had into keeping the passage open, even
using an icebreaker around the clock in a desperate attempt to cut
a channel through the ice on the River Dvina into the harbour.
Aided by two icebreakers, it took six weeks for British Arctic
Convoy PQ-4 to cut through 150 miles of ice in the White Sea,
which served as the gateway from the port into the open Barents
Sea, but it was an impossible task, and the project was abandoned.
This made Murmansk even more important, as it was Russia's only
open port with access to the Atlantic Ocean until June 1942, when
the warmer weather would clear the way for ships to use Archangel.

Our own departure from Russia began in much the same way as
our adventure had begun, with the wing departing from the Soviet
Union in various parties, using different ships, setting off on
different dates and from different places. First to leave on 16

November was a party of seven officers and sixty men. Tim Elkington was in charge of the group, which included Bushy, and Artie Holmes. Tim says,

> *I had to lead them all through deep snow, in virtual night, down ten miles or so of treacherous track to Rosta oiling jetty. I knew when we'd reached our destination, at 17:00hrs because all our kit became black with oil. Our only casualty was one airman with a broken arm. We waited there six hours for the fleet minesweepers we had to board for the voyage to Archangel – HMS Hussar, Gossamer & Speedy, but they had docked at a different jetty. Eventually bed, without food for 14 hours, at 2 am.*

Artie Holmes picks up the story, as recorded in his diary:

> *I was on Speedy with Bushy and eighteen men. We were told we'd sail round the peninsula and join a convoy preparing to leave from Archangel. The rest of the Wing were going home in two destroyers and a cruiser from Murmansk.*
>
> *Halfway to Archangel, our trio of minesweepers received orders to turn north to meet an incoming convoy and escort them back through the Russian minefields into Archangel. We met the convoy at latitude 76 on 22 November in an Arctic gale.*

His description of the first part of the journey leaves little to the imagination:

> *To be in a minesweeper in such seas is nobody's idea of comfort. Your chair slithered across the saloon deck while you sat in it. The plates would not stay on the table unless they were secured in box-like compartments. It was*

*impossible to play a gramophone record. Drawers flew
open, emptied their contents on the floor then, when the
ship rolled the other way, slammed shut again. The revving
of the screw when the stern came clear of the water
threatened to shake the entire craft to pieces. And the
smack as the keel flopped down on the waves again must,
you fear, snap the vessel in two. That four days gale seemed
like four years.*[9]

They met ice 20 miles from the mouth of the River Dvina, which
was frozen solid, so they stopped at the beginning of the ice field
and dropped anchor. Tim and his party then climbed down a ladder
and walked across the ice to board a Russian icebreaker which,
through brute force, was going to take them the 20 miles to the
convoy by crushing the ice as it went. There was no accommodation
for them on the ship so, while some slept on the bare floor, others
took turns at the few dining chairs and slept, head on arms, across
the table. The heat inside was intolerable, the dry air over time causing the panels to warp, giving easy egress for cockroaches, which left
them with nasty bites and bumps. Prisoners in jail eat better than
they had there; cabbage soup, black bread and tea without milk. It
got better only when they finally arrived. His diary goes on,

*The river, a mile wide, where our convoy is moored, presents
a remarkable spectacle. It has now become a regular
highway for traffic from one side to the other. Troops march
across. Horses, probably with spiked hooves, pull sledges as
big as lorries, laden with provisions, equipment and people.
At night, powerful searchlights are switched on to the wail
of high-powered generators, and the activity continues.
Parties of engineers are laying twenty miles of railway line
up the frozen river for cargo to be unloaded direct from the
ships on to trains to save the time of icebreakers smashing a
route for them up to the landing stage.*

*Our berths are already allocated for us when we reach
the convoy. The organisation has been immaculate.*

Meanwhile, the cruiser HMS *Kenya* arrived at anchorage in the
Kola inlet early in the morning of 21 November, followed by the
destroyers HMS *Bedouin* and *Intrepid* a day later. The remaining
personnel of 151 Wing would be evacuated by these three ships,
and, accompanied by HMS *Berwick*, *Onslow* and *Offa*, taken to
Rosyth while escorting Arctic Convoy QP3. The largest party,
which among a great many others included Neil Cameron, Ibby,
Wag, Peter Knapton, Johnny and me, embarked on HMS *Kenya*.
The Russian dockers at Polyana seemed to have relieved themselves on the dockside wherever they felt like it and I remember us
having to tread very gingerly towards the embarkation steps.

What we didn't know was there was an ice problem in the Kola
inlet, so QP4 would be slightly delayed. I was beginning to feel
that after all we'd been through, Russia wasn't going to give us up
without a fight! The Royal Navy doesn't like to sit around idly
and, after realising that it'd be two or three days before we could
depart, the rear admiral decided to take maximum advantage of
the time available. He suggested to Vice-Admiral Golovko, the
commander-in-chief of the Northern Russian Fleet, that perhaps
one of his destroyers might like to accompany us, *Bedouin* and
Intrepid on an operational sweep along the northern coast of
Norway. Golovko jumped at the opportunity and offered up two
of his destroyers – *Gremyaschi* and *Gromki*.

Peter Knapton says, 'It's obvious from Naval reports at the time
that Rear Admiral Bevan, who was the senior British Naval Officer
in the Murmansk area, had already forged a close, friendly relationship with his Russian colleagues and I think that the favourable
atmosphere was key in allowing the only recorded, combined
British and Russian naval operation of the war to go ahead
smoothly.'

At the time, in his diary, he wrote,

Endgame

The three Royal Navy ships rendezvoused with the two Russian destroyers at 16:00hrs on the 24th November and set off at maximum speed in line astern with HMS Kenya leading; the order of battle was Kenya, Bedouin, Gremyaschi, Gromki and Intrepid. The objective was to search for and destroy enemy shipping and to bombard military objectives consisting of batteries, harbour works and a fort at Vardø on the Finnish coast.

We were at 'action stations' from the off. There are no passengers on a Royal Navy ship so all of us RAF personnel were given tasks. I was put in a gun turret with some Royal Marines. The night was clear and the sea millpond-calm as we headed out along the Norwegian coast as far as Nordkyn. Unfortunately, we didn't see any German ships so we sailed towards Vardø to carry out the second objective. The Navy cooks knocked up a fantastic sausages and mash which was served on the way and which settled my stomach nicely for what was to follow.

I had never seen, let alone been in, a six-inch gun turret during a naval action so I had no idea what to expect but the noise when the guns opened fire was almost tactile. I felt it throughout my body, it echoed in my chest and shook me to the core. Inside that turret, it felt like the room where God practiced shouting. The blinding flash from the guns was on a similar scale. It was a real demonstration of 'son et lumière'. I had no frame of reference for this but it felt like I'd simultaneously lost two of my senses as my hearing faded to a ringing noise, and I felt blinded by the light.

Shells were being fed up constantly via a conveyor belt that came up from below and through a hole in the floor. Bear in mind, we'd had no contact with the Royal Navy before this mission but I found the discipline and control that I saw on display were enormously impressive. This superb operation was largely down to a Royal Marine sergeant-major who ruled the turret with a rod of iron.

Almost 17 tons of munitions were fired by the British ships in just ten minutes, targeting fort, harbour and battery installations. After being thanked by the Commodore over the tannoy, we then returned to Murmansk. Then, on the 27th November, we rendezvoused with QP3. Finally, we were on our way home.

19

Going Home

While almost all of the airmen and sergeant pilots were on board HMS *Kenya*, the wing's officers were spread over a number of cargo ships. Artie Holmes, who was a keen diarist with a real eye for colour, kept a detailed account of the journey back. I can't really do better than to let his writing describe the trip that saw us return to England:

> *Bushy and myself were allocated to the Harrison Liner* Harpalion, *and the first mate had kindly vacated his cabin on the bridge for us. We were next door to the master, Captain Thomas, who was a rugged, gentle, genial Welsh giant. We felt that under his command no ship dare sink.*
>
> *Our quarters were most comfortable. Twin bunks with blankets and sheets against one wall, and a separate bathroom and shower. We and a Naval Commander who has a cabin further along the bridge share the Captain's saloon.*
>
> *Captain Thomas tells us our ship has taken on a cargo of manganese ore at Archangel. This he assures us, will have us swinging like a pendulum if we strike heavy seas. He was right.*
>
> *25th November – Outside our ship's hull is locked solid in six feet of ice. Our decks are deep in snow. Icicles festoon our rigging. Every water supply on the ship is frozen solid. Yet even in these truly Arctic conditions we get hints of home. Captain Thomas talks about Cardiff, and the nearby village where he lives. A clock on his saloon mantelpiece*

has the maker's name Kelvin and Baird Ltd, Glasgow, on its face. Beside it a large glass ashtray proclaims the excellence of 'Lockside Ales' – probably won in a Glasgow pub, when our skipper called as a young midshipman.

Beneath the mantelpiece is the most homely thing of all, a brightly flickering genuine coal fire in a wrought iron gate, with coffee-coloured tile surround and an oaken overmantel that would have graced any English dining room.

This then was our last billet before England. Not bad, provided we could break free of the grip of this ice, stay afloat for three weeks defying the rigours of mid-winter Arctic gales, and dodge bombs from above and torpedoes below.

26th November. Early this morning, the icebreaker Lenin *gnawed her way through the ice and came alongside* Harpalion *to break us loose from our captive cradle. She worked around us until slabs of ice the size of tennis courts floated free, threatening to stave in the side of our ship when they drifted back against our hull. At ten minutes past noon, our engines without warning throbbed into life and* Harpalion *trembled, sharing our excitement.*

'We're bloody well off' shouted Bushy, thumping one fur-gloved fist on the bridge rail and wiping an icicle off the end of his nose with the other. We weren't of course, but it was a start. Lenin *was making a channel linking all the boats in the convoy. As they were freed, their skippers started manoeuvring their ships up and down the channel before it froze solid again.*

With *Lenin* in the lead charging up on to the ice, waiting while it crashed through, then backing for another onslaught, the line of merchantmen started their 20-mile crawl to the open sea. The convoy's departure did nothing to deter the Russians from

crossing the river – the broken ice froze so quickly once a ship had
passed that it would easily bear a man's weight before the next
one arrived . . .

*One poor chap, a bit too keen to cross, slipped on some
slabs of ice which had not properly joined up, and he
toppled into the water. Our crew threw ropes down, and
soldiers on the ice fished him out and tied the ropes round
him, but when he was hoisted on to our deck his body came
up as stiff and as straight as a log, frozen solid. They
lowered the corpse back down again without even
attempting to revive him.*

*Soon we were all heading slowly in single file towards the
estuary. 24 hours later, averaging a mile per hour, we were
with our naval escort. Our icebreakers took back a newly
arrived convoy. The Russians, even working at a
temperature of 46°F below freezing, were, we
acknowledged, hot-stuff organisers.*

*As the merchant ships manoeuvred to take station with
their naval escort, a most impressive spectacle met our eyes.
From over the Kola peninsula, silently climbing into the sky
came a squadron of Hurricanes. They were in beautiful
battle formation, and heading for our convoy. Our Russian
counterparts, as a goodwill gesture and a farewell tribute,
were giving us a protective convoy patrol away from their
country.*

*Bushy and I could imagine Safonov's broad grin of
silver-coated teeth as he led his fighter pilots towards us in
their new Angleeski Hurricanes. All twelve waggled their
wings in salute as they crossed the convoy before breaking
up into two flights of six to make separate patrols, one
encircling the convoy and the other flying up and down the
coast ready to intercept any raiders approaching from the
battle zone. They stayed with us until we were well out of*

sight of land and their fuel was running low. Then Safonov must have called up the other flight to rejoin him for they came speeding in from the coast and the twelve reformed as a squadron. Immediately, they went into 504's 'Hendon formaggers' – the formation we used in the Battle of Britain when we flew as a box in six pairs, and which we had taught the Russians.

Through the powerful binoculars Captain Thomas passed to me, I could plainly pick out my aeroplane 'B' leading the second flight, and visualised Kapitan Markavitch sitting proudly at the controls. They made a long, low, sweeping salute over the middle of the convoy, climbed steeply and broke into feathers, reformed as two flights and set course back for their base. Nobody ever said 'Goodbye, and thank you', quite so courteously or so touchingly. We waved from the bridge: 'Dosvedanya.'

Harpalion was the slowest ship, wallowing under the weight of its manganese ore cargo, and the others had to hold back to our speed. After 24 hours we have averaged seven-and-a-half knots. Captain Thomas told us our escort was being increased, and Bushy and I were quite amazed shortly afterwards to see plumes of smoke over the horizon ahead gradually materialise into two destroyers and a cruiser. Captain Thomas brought us a signal he had just received from the Commodore of the convoy saying 400 officers and men of 151 Wing were in the cruiser and seventy more in each destroyer. The skipper says if we maintain seven-and-a-half knots throughout the voyage, we'll reach Kirkwall, at Scapa Flow in fourteen days. Better than we had hoped.

29th November. The view never changes – just our little huddle of ships plodding manfully through mile upon mile of black heaving ocean under a leaden sky. Now we are so far north that being mid-winter, it is continual night.

Going Home

The North Star no longer points to the North Pole, for we are almost there already, and the only way to follow it would be vertically upwards. I fished out my pocket compass to see how it sought magnetic north in these latitudes, but the ship's degaussing cable wound round our ship to neutralise magnetic mines screened my compass completely and the needle just spun aimlessly. Our old friend the Plough is still with us, and Orion's belt and his sword are just peeping over the southern horizon.

Although the skies are now clear, we are meeting very heavy weather indeed. Harpalion is plodding manfully along in the teeth of a fierce nor-easter gale. Despite her bulk, and her heavy cargo, she is bucking like a bronco. Waves wash over her bows and eddy between her hatch covers, frothing and swirling around the winches and derricks. Just as the little minesweepers did, her stern lifts clear of the water for her enormous twin screws to race, fit to fly off their shafts. The ship shudders violently each time as the engines race, and groans as they slow to normal revs again.

Our forward speed has dropped to three-and-a-half knots in the gale. We covered only 81 miles in the last 24 hours. At this rate, we'll be lucky to be home by Christmas – if at all.

Today, the cruiser flashed this signal across to us; 'All personnel are to be warned that the Air Ministry consider it essential not, repeat not, to disclose in the UK that 151 Wing or its component squadrons are being withdrawn from Russia.'

This is obviously to stop Lord Haw Haw from gloating over the radio that the Huns have kicked us out.

Today the naval Lieutenant Commander who has been saying this weather is not bad and has been boasting about the really bad weather he has experienced while serving on trawlers has remained in his cabin, refusing all offers of food from the stewards. I don't think we'll get any more talk like that from him.

The weather is actually getting worse. Twice while writing this in my diary I was thrown over the back of my chair. Each time I slithered on my back with the chair across the saloon floor and out through the open door, finishing in a heap at the foot of the stairs. All doors, including cabins, have to be hooked open at all times in case a torpedo hits the ship, warps the hull and wedges the door fast shut making escape impossible. Playing cards won't stay on the table, food won't stay on the plate. Sleep is impossible with the noise of the crashing waves, the howling wind and the creaking hull.

Suitcases and loose items like shoes chase each other with the rugs around the floor. Coats swing to almost ninety degrees from the walls and fly off the hooks and join the shambles. Books topple over the ledges specifically designed to hold them on the shelves. Drawers shoot out of the dressing table. We leave everything on the floor until the sea gets calmer.

Our sitting room fire had to be doused in case the hot coals fell out on to the floor. The downdraught in the chimney three times showered the room with soot. A sooty saloon, with no fire and a temperature well below freezing, is a cheerless place. For the next two days Bushy and I stayed in our cabin where at least we had a radiator.

1st December. One quickly becomes time-disoriented in perpetual darkness. You feel like a prisoner in a sealed cell. It is strange having to consult your watch to remind you whether your next meal is lunch, or tea, or if there will be another meal before bed.

This evening, we had our first submarine scare. If we are torpedoed, it will be impossible to launch boats in these seas. We have been in dangerous waters for some days now since we have been sailing around the top of Norway some 300 miles distant. Suddenly about 7pm as I was writing this diary upon my knee, there was a deafening roar. It felt as if our ship had been ripped open from stem to stern. I waited to see whether she would list to port or starboard, ready to climb up the side with the air bubble. Bushy came rushing in yelling, 'What the hell was that?'

We ran out onto the bridge. The crew was collecting at action stations. The skipper told us there was a German sub around – which seemed pretty obvious – and that the explosion was a depth charge a destroyer had put down. At that moment, there was another crump and a volcano of water erupted in the middle of the convoy. If the sub was there he must have been lying in wait for us right in our path.

As we hurried indoors for our life jackets and warmest clothing a third depth charge exploded. We snatched up small personal items and stuffed them into our pockets and ran out on to the bridge again. Four more explosions seemed to come from almost under our bows, but Harpalion's Chief Officer assured us they were two or three miles away. That's not far when you're about a thousand miles from port. The convoy was now zigzagging violently, each ship taking its own evasive action. The sea looked angry, icy and uninviting.

Five more depth charges exploded in rapid succession.

The suspense, waiting for our ship to be suddenly split in two and blown up in a mountain of flame, was chilling. After half an hour, when nothing happened, and we were frozen to the marrow, we went into the mate's cabin. The three ship's officers there were all members of 'The Raft Club' for torpedoed sailors. We had no desire to join it. Of all topics, they chose to talk about sinkings at sea.

Force Benedict

They described how sudden it all was; what a small percentage of crew survived when a ship went down; how it was sheer luck if you were saved – like being sucked down a funnel or blown out, or being caught in an air bubble inside an overturned lifeboat; how a torpedo in the right spot could down a ship our size in twenty seconds; how the first thing that happened was that the lights fused and the pumps failed; then the ship rolled to such an angle that it was impossible to launch boats from either side. The steam radiators would burst and scald you; the open doors would slam shut with the blast and trap you like a rat in your cabin.

After an hour of pretending we were not frightened, the chief steward brought us all cocoa and informed us that we were back on normal course again. Captain Thomas judged it almost certain that the sub had been sunk. The depth charges had stopped when the soundings stopped. My thoughts turned to the brave men in the sub, German or not. If we had been scared in the comfort of our cabin, how must they have fared under fifty feet of water in a tin box that is suddenly split apart. But it was them or us. This was what war was all about.

Bushy and I went back to our cabin, fished out the bottle of Gordon's Gin that Captain Thomas had sold us and drank the squadron toast 'Here's to the next man to die'. We began to feel better. Captain Thomas looked in last thing and dampened our spirits by advising us to sleep in our clothes, with our life jackets and a torch handy, and be sure the door was wedged hard open.

I had one of my best nights yet. It was probably the reaction after what did not happen, and resignation there was nothing we could do if it did. We slept in our clothes for the next fortnight. There was unlimited hot water, so we took turns to read for an hour in the bath during the day

244

with water up to our chin. Only trouble about this was that the swirling bath water tended to make you seasick.

3rd December. More excitement. We are being shadowed either by German submarines, or a German raider, or both. Bushy grabbed my arm. 'Quick, the Commodore's signalling to Harpalion. *What's he saying?' He fished in his pocket for a pencil and an envelope, and as I shouted out the letters being flashed across the water, he jotted them down.*

'All ships disperse, and proceed independently to destination', was the order that came across. The Captain had read it at the same time and he immediately gave full speed ahead on the telegraph. In the midday gloom the convoy was already breaking its tidy formations and spreading out. Ships were scurrying towards distant horizons. In a few minutes, the dispersal was complete. Everyone had gone. We were on our own in the Arctic, ready to meet – what!

5th December. With our engines flat out we should have been making between 240 and 260 miles a day, but headwinds have kept our mileage down to between 140 and 150. I doubt this ship has a sound rivet left. Sleep at nights, with the throbbing engines, the howling winds, and our luggage careering around our cabin, is quite impossible. The loneliness is oppressive and depressing. Nothing but water. Never offer me a cruise for my summer holiday.

We are now 500 miles short of Iceland. It is another 500 miles from Iceland to Scapa. Even the last leg can be dangerous. We're still 1,000 miles short of the UK after nearly three weeks at sea.

6th December. Having spent my birthday in Iceland on the 20th August, I am back to spend my mother's birthday here on 6th December. On the way into the fjord, we missed by yards a British mine which had broken away from its mooring in a nearby minefield. The sight of any land after

*so long at sea under such conditions would have been
sweet. But Seyðisfjörður, with its narrow waterway
between craggy precipitous cliffs rising sheer to 3,000ft, and
the rosy tint of the rising sun turning the snow-capped
peaks mother of pearl was a picture I'll always remember.
   9th December. Left Iceland for Scapa Flow.
   12th December. 6pm. Dropped anchor at Kirkwall. No
one allowed ashore. Were able to send telegrams home
saying we had arrived, but not where. To our surprise, a
Customs Officer came aboard to check for smugglers. From
Murmansk, indeed! On top of my kitbag, which was
packed to go ashore, was a small parcel containing four 36
exposure 35mm films I had taken in Russia. It was
addressed to my brother, a photographic chemist, for
processing. The Customs Officer asked what the parcel
contained and when I told him, he promptly confiscated the
films. I stressed how important they were to the Air
Ministry as a valuable record of an historic event. He still
insisted upon taking them, but promised the films would be
returned after censoring, providing they were not harmful
to the war effort. I said goodbye to my photos.*

With the men of 81 and 134 Squadrons having travelled via different routes and on different boats, we reached the UK in fits and starts. Those of us travelling on HMS *Kenya* fared best – sailing as the advance party, the eleven officers and 220 airmen on board with me docked at Rosyth at 1500 on 6 December. By 1730, everyone had disembarked.

The following day, the 7th, was the day that the Japanese launched their early morning attack on the US base at Pearl Harbor, an event that served as the catalyst for America to finally enter the war later that same day. On the 12th, *Harpalion* sailed to the Firth of Forth and Artie and Bushy disembarked at Leith on 13 December. They were the last of the wing to arrive back.

246

20

Band of Brothers

We were unquestionably lucky, the 550-odd men of 81 and 134 Squadrons plus the wing's HQ staff. The Arctic convoys turned out to be a complete lottery in terms of their chances of getting through unscathed, yet we were lucky enough that we made both outbound and return journeys without a single loss. By contrast, in July 1942, convoy PQ 17 suffered the worst losses of any convoy in the Second World War, losing twenty-four of thirty-five merchantmen. Between 1941 and 1945, the Arctic convoys lost 3,000 men and 100 ships taking vital supplies to Russia.

151 Wing was disbanded upon its return to the UK and we were all sent off on two weeks' leave. Those of us in 81 Squadron returned to RAF Turnhouse in early January to learn that we'd be converting to Spitfires, and were immediately posted to RAF Ouston, a modern aerodrome with two good intersecting runways about six miles along Hadrian's Wall from Newcastle-upon-Tyne. One over-enthusiastic airman painted a hammer and sickle on the nose of each aircraft but the station commander failed to see the funny side and they were smartly removed. 134 Squadron meanwhile reassembled at Catterick, where they also converted to the Spitfire Mk V, before being posted, in January 1942, to Eglinton, near Londonderry in Northern Ireland.

For a small handful of us, the interlude in Russia was to be the high point of our war. Some would see no further action; a significant number of pilots would never know the outcome of the war, or peace, dying both in accidents and on operational service overseas. Others still would go on to fight in a number of significant battles, in other theatres that have become seared into the fabric of the UK's history.

Although our families and close friends knew where we'd been – and more importantly, that we were now back – there was no official announcement made to confirm our return as Churchill had insisted on complete secrecy. The press knew we were back, but had been told not to report the fact. Censorship played a huge role in wars back then and it was easy for the Ministry of War and the Ministry of Information to control what was reported, when and by whom, because of the limited methods of communication and the technology available. There was a great deal of positive PR value to be had from our time in Russia, and by February 1942 the clamour was growing louder; both the press and the Ministries of War and Information wanted to report our success, so Sir Charles Portal argued the case.

On 11 February, he wrote a memo to Churchill:

Prime Minister,
Soon after No. 151 Wing returned from Russia in the early part of December, you expressed the view that there should be no publicity about its arrival home. The Russian Military Authorities also wanted it kept quiet, and it was arranged that a ban should be put on any reference to its return to this country.

These officers and men have now been in this country for about two months. It is fairly widely known that they are back. There is a strong demand from the Press for the lifting of the ban; we can give no publicity to the awards to Wing Commander Isherwood and to Squadron Leader Rook. There is no longer any security objection from our standpoint but of course we should have to consult the Russians before publication.

In these circumstances, do you agree that I should ask the

Russian Military Authorities whether they have any
objection to our raising the ban?[1]

Evidently, there were no problems, because in March 1942, 151 Wing's return and stories of our successes in Russia were widely reported in all of the UK's national papers. For their part, the Russians had sent photographs and film material to the Air Ministry for distribution to press and cinema news networks. Both the Air Ministry and the Ministry of Information seized the opportunity of using the wing's success as a major propaganda exercise on the Home Front. Clementine Churchill headed up a huge campaign for aid and support to Russia in her role as chairman of the Red Cross Aid to Russia Fund. Isherwood too was heavily involved in a campaign to get the public behind support for Russia and appeared in a film to argue the case.

The biggest announcement following our return was that of the award of the Order of Lenin by the Russians to Wing Commander Ramsbottom-Isherwood, the two squadron leaders, Tony Rook and Tony Miller, and Wag Haw [by now a pilot officer, having received a commission on his return], who, with three confirmed kills, was 151 Wing's top fighter pilot. They were the only four British servicemen so honoured in the whole of the Second World War. On a fine spring day in late March 1942, the four were invited to the Soviet embassy in Kensington, where the Soviet ambassador, Ivan Maisky, presented them with their medals. Representing Winston Churchill was his wife Clementine, a move that highlighted the importance of the event for Anglo-Soviet relations.

Wag, who would go on to receive the DFC and DFM[2] and reach the rank of squadron leader, found himself something of a poster boy for the mission as far as the media were concerned. He and his then girlfriend May found themselves on the front pages of national newspapers following the award of his Order of

Lenin. The local press urged readers to see him in action on the Russian front in *British Movietone News* at the Embassy Cinema. 151 Wing also received widespread coverage in Russian newspapers and on the big screen. The Ministry of War and the Ministry of Information between then maximised every opportunity for publicity, sending Wag and a number of other pilots on visits to factories making tanks and other equipment for Russia through the Lend-Lease scheme.

The award of the Order of Lenin to four members of the wing ensured its place in Russian military history, and its short stay in Russia also saw a change to the two squadrons' badges to ensure their Russian interlude would be forever remembered. The badge for 81 Squadron was embellished with a red star in the centre, and the badge for 134 Squadron received a red-coloured gauntlet.

Around the same time, Artie Holmes finally received by registered post the four films that he'd had confiscated by the customs officer when the *Harpalion* docked at Kirkwall. They'd all been fine-grain-developed by Kodak and were accompanied by a complete set of prints. They were sent with the compliments of the Air Ministry together with a flattering note praising the quality of the photographs. The note also mentioned that about twenty giant enlargements from his negatives had been included in a 'War in Russia' section at London's Imperial War Museum.

Our individual stories in the aftermath of our return are as varied and random as each and every one of us. Sergeant Neil Cameron, who showed amazing chutzpah and foresight in arranging his own commission ahead of the official announcement, went on to extraordinary success. In 1976, he was appointed Air Aide-de-Camp to the Queen, and a year later, having been promoted to Marshal of the Royal Air Force, he became Chief of the Defence Staff – the head of all three of the UK's armed services. He retired in August 1979 and was elevated to the Lords as Baron Cameron of Balhousie. He died, aged just sixty-four, in January 1985. Tim Elkington says of him,

He was a wonderful, forceful character and even from the very beginning as a young Sergeant Pilot, you could see he had something in him that meant he was destined for greatness. I hadn't seen him since about 1943 and then I recall being up at the MoD main building in London in 1977 and as I was walking out, I heard someone shout, 'Krupps!' and I knew immediately it was him. He'd given me the nickname [Krupp was a German armaments manufacturer] *during the war because I carried a Colt semi-auto pistol in a shoulder holster, and to me, that was great leadership – after all those years, to remember me from afar like that – great leadership, a great man.*

Wag Haw retired from the RAF in 1951 after a successful career that saw him commanding 611 Squadron at Biggin Hill in 1943, moving in November that year to 129 Squadron. In April 1944 129 Squadron converted to Mustangs and, after covering the D-Day landings, Haw led the squadron in July and August in an offensive against flying bombs. Finally, as leader of a wing of long-range Mustang fighters, he escorted Allied bombers on daylight raids. He was awarded a DFM for his action in Murmansk. On 17 October 1944, he was awarded the DFC and his citation stated, 'Squadron Leader Haw is now on his third tour of operations and has throughout shown great courage and eagerness to engage the enemy. He is an exceptional squadron commander and a very keen leader.'[3]

The Russians never allowed Wag to forget that he was a 'Hero of the Soviet Union' and he was feted regularly over the years at special functions in both London and Moscow. The Order of Lenin carried with it a pension, which he received regularly, and whenever he returned to Russia, the red carpet was laid out for him and he was treated as a VIP; he was never allowed to spend his own money. After he retired, Haw and his first wife were the landlords of the Blacksmith's Arms, a public house in Sussex. He later referred to it as 'a six-year working holiday. We came out of there with the same amount of money in the bank as we did when we went into it but we had a hell of a six years. I shall never forget it.'⁴ He died on 27 November 1993 and was survived by his second wife, Audrey.

Peter Knapton also received a commission following his time in Russia. Following his return, he completed the RAF Russian language course in 1942, and later saw active service in El Alamein, India and Burma. He was awarded the DFC for an action while in Burma in 1944. His citation reads:

> *This officer has been engaged on operations since May 1941 in England, Russia, The Middle East and India, and has completed 236 operational hours. During recent intense air operations on the Arakan front, Flying Officer Knapton was leading a flight escorting supply droppers when they were attacked by two formations of enemy aircraft. Although heavily outnumbered, and in spite of the fact that two of his flight were shot down, he remained supporting the Dakota DC2s and succeeded in destroying an Oscar. He continues to show great enthusiasm and keenness and is a great asset to the squadron both on the ground and in the air.*

After the war, Peter remained in the RAF. He returned to Russia in 1952 as assistant air attaché at the British embassy in Moscow and, while there, met and married Rosalind, an Australian national working at that country's embassy. After promotion to air attaché, he was posted to Cyprus (1960–64), Tehran (1964–66) and Bangkok (1969–74). He retired from the RAF in 1975 having also been awarded an OBE, and was then recruited by MI5, the Security Service. Rosalind passed away in 1994. He lives in London.

Nat Gould was commissioned as a pilot officer in March 1942. In 1943 he returned to Australia and transferred to the Royal Australian Navy as a flight lieutenant, where he fought in the air over the Pacific against the Japanese, and took part in the Battle of Milne Bay at Papua New Guinea. As a Navy pilot, he flew Fireflies, Spitfires and Sea Furies. Later, he fought in the Korean War. In 1957, Nat married Sirenne. He retired from the Navy with the rank of commander in 1965 and became marketing manager for Hawker de Havilland's military aircraft in Australia. He also looked after Westland Helicopters and a variety of US and other aerospace companies. He later became a director of BAE Australia and retired from all commercial activities in 1990. Nat and Sirenne had no children, and happily, they are still together and enjoying good health. They live in Sydney.

Raymond 'Artie' Holmes, who wrote so colourfully of his time in Russia, served as an instructor upon his return until 1944. He then returned to operational duties, flying high-altitude Spitfires with 541 Squadron, a photographic reconnaissance unit, at Benson. In the dying days of the war, he was appointed as a King's Messenger, carrying personal papers and correspondence for Winston Churchill when he was preparing for the Potsdam Conference. He writes of one particular occasion when he was asked for in person by the 'Big Man' while he was in Biarritz, having flown in with the prime minister's diplomatic bag:

A car called and the driver announced that Mr Churchill would like to meet Flight Lieutenant Holmes. I thought it had to be a leg-pull, but the driver was deadly serious, so I jumped in the front of the brake with him. A few minutes' drive took us to a small but beautifully laid-out country house with white-rendered walls, black half-timbering and a slate roof with tiny corner spires. The driver led me in without formality. He showed me into a downstairs bedroom. Low windows looked out onto crimson early flowering rhododendrons.

In an enormous double bed, propped up with pillows, and surrounded by newspapers and documents, sat Mr Churchill. He beamed at me over heavy horn-rimmed glasses and extended a strong hand that looked lonely without a cigar.

'Holmes', he said, 'Battle of Britain, they tell me.'

'Yes, sir'.

'Glad to know you. Take a seat. Make yourself comfortable. Don't worry about me, I'm not ill. I do all my correspondence in bed and get up about noon. Had any breakfast?'

I thanked him and said I had.

He asked me about 541 and our job at [RAF] Benson, and said he'd be needing us again when he went to Berlin for the Potsdam conference. I was relieved he did not mention the Battle of Britain again. He said I was free for 48 hours if I wanted to make plans, and warned me if I went swimming to keep strictly to the small stretch of the beach that had been cleared of mines.[5]

Luck seemed to follow Artie as it did nobody else and, in the immediate aftermath of Germany's surrender, he'd flown his Spitfire to Berlin, maintaining the link between London and Churchill, who was there continuing to prepare for the Potsdam Conference. This role conferred on Artie and his colleagues diplomatic immunity.

He and a fellow King's Messenger from 541 Squadron hitched a lift into the city, hopped off at the Brandenburg Gate, and just waltzed into the Chancellery. The Russians had already been in and wrecked it, kicking oil paintings from their frames and slashing sofas. Hitler's medal room was ankle deep in medals and ribbons which had been swept from cupboards and shelves, so Artie scooped up what he could and filled a box with them. In Hitler's reception lounge, he saw a brass candelabrum hanging from the wall. It was the only one to survive an RAF bombing raid, although one of its arms had been blown off. He took out his knife and cut the wires so he could take it home along with the medals and an assortment of camera equipment he'd acquired.

Landing back at Kidlington in Oxfordshire two days later, he was told Customs would have to be informed so they could search his Spitfire. Artie told them he was a King's Messenger with diplomatic immunity and requested that an armed guard be placed on the aircraft, so three RAF Regiment corporals with fixed bayonets on their rifles were duly dispatched to prevent anyone interfering with it while Artie went off to enjoy breakfast in the mess.

Back home after the war, Artie wired the brass candelabrum up on his hall wall. A few years later, he was reading a book which dealt with the events leading up to Hitler's suicide and, in it, he saw a photo depicting the Führer with a group of visitors in the Chancellery in 1937. Above Hitler's head in the photo was his brass candelabrum. Artie writes in his memoir, 'Hitler would have been furious had he known that his lamp was to lose one of its arms when the RAF bombed his beloved Chancellery, and even more furious that the surviving two arms would finish up adorning the wall of an RAF pilot.'

Artie left the RAF in November 1945, having been Mentioned in Dispatches, and returned to journalism in Liverpool. After his extraordinary action during the Battle of Britain, he was feted by the press as a war hero who'd saved Buckingham Palace from being severely damaged by German bombing. Sixty-five years on, archaeologists unearthed parts of Artie's Hurricane in a live TV documentary broadcast on the UK's Channel Five. It was successfully excavated from the site near Buckingham Palace Road in central London. He was shown the fighter's control column, which he had last held sixty-four years earlier; appropriately, the firing button was still set to 'fire'. The aircraft's engine was recovered, and it is now displayed at the Imperial War Museum.

Artie died, aged ninety, in June 2005 following a two-year battle with cancer.

Tim Elkington had a long and varied career in the RAF, including tours in India in 1943, and after the war with Avro Shackleton squadrons in Northern Ireland, and Cyprus. He was promoted to wing commander in 1961, retiring from the RAF at the end of 1975. After leaving the RAF, Tim set up an art and picture-framing business. He lives with his wife Pat, whom he married in 1948, in the picturesque Cotswold village of Little Rissington. They have four children, John, Gray, Caroline and Tessa, and a host of grandchildren. Tim stayed in touch with Vladimir Krivoshchekov, Wing Commander Isherwood's translator while they were in Murmansk.

Says Tim, 'Vladimir was a lovely man and he did well for himself by any standards, especially given the Soviet political system. He was based in New York with the UN Military Staff Committee after the war, and then worked with Radio Moscow until 1953. He spent most of his life as a freelance journalist. He married twice, had five children and he came to stay with Pat and I several times. He died in 2001; he was a good friend who I miss still.'

Henry Broquet, the young engine fitter who in 1941 had worked closely with the Russians on a fuel catalyst to help the Hurricanes' Merlin engines cope with the lower octane rating of Russian fuel, left the RAF after the war and worked on developing the solution further for the commercial market. He established the company Broquet International to market and sell his fuel catalyst, which was adopted by heavy industry. Further development work saw it achieve a marked improvement in the performance of cars and motorcycles, and the company that Henry founded is still trading today with a global reach that covers over twenty-five countries. His efforts in developing the catalyst that was used by 151 Wing in 1941 were recognised by the Russians in 1987, when they awarded him the Peace Prize. Henry died just two years later.

The diminutive Flight Lieutenant Jack Ross, DFC, of mantelpiece fame, sadly died just a few months after we returned from Russia. Tim Elkington, who was flying alongside him in Ireland in early 1942, says, 'He just disappeared one day while we were on patrol flying from Eglinton in Northern Ireland. We were on patrol together, he was right alongside me on my port wing, and then suddenly, he wasn't there any more – he literally just disappeared. We can only assume his engine failed and he crashed into the Irish Sea.'

The flight were practising low-level dogfighting, and it's thought that one of Ross's Hurricane's wings clipped a wave while he was performing a manoeuvre and his aircraft was literally swallowed by the sea. Neil Cameron touches on the incident in his book *In the Midst of Things* when he says,

> *We searched for him for hours but the Irish Sea in early January is not exactly a friendly place and eventually we had to give up. His was a great personal loss to me and though I had got used to losing friends, I felt his death very severely. He was a little man, indeed a very little man in stature, but very large in spirit and courage. I wrote to his parents along these lines. I found it difficult in wartime to know exactly how to frame some letters to parents who had lost loved ones, but this one was not difficult because I felt so strongly about it.*[6]

My good friend Johnny Mulroy, with whom I'd gone through training and shared so much, died in the battle for El Alamein in 1942. That battle claimed several other young men who'd been on our Russian adventure; as well as Johnny, Paddy McCann, Dicky Wollaston, Binny Barnes and Flight Sergeant Griffiths all lost their lives flying over Africa in the war.

Wing Commander Henry Neville Gynes Ramsbottom-Isherwood was awarded a Distinguished Flying Cross for leadership following his Russian adventure. It's an unusual award for leadership; a more appropriate decoration might have been a DSO (Distinguished Service Order), but it may have reflected the fact that although he had been told by the Air Ministry not to fly while in Russia, he is thought to have taken to the air on a number of occasions; I imagine the lure was just too great not to for someone as driven as he was.

After a number of staff postings, he later flew in the Far East and at the end of the war, he was appointed as the commanding officer of RAF Martlesham Heath, in Suffolk. On 24 April 1950, he took off in a Gloster Meteor IV jet fighter, for a test flight. The Meteor was just coming into service, and as one of the RAF's most experienced test pilots, Isherwood was keen to get his hands on one. He ran into blinding snowstorms and icy conditions, and decided to divert to RAF Manston in Kent. He never made it; after flying over West Malling at around two hundred feet, his aircraft crashed near Tonbridge and disintegrated, killing him outright. He was forty-four years old. It's thought that extreme icing was the likeliest cause of the accident.

There's an additional piece of the jigsaw that I'd like to share, and it concerns Wing Commander Isherwood's medals.

Isherwood and his wife had only one child together and she was just ten years old when her father died. Now frail, she is looked after by friends. It was while her house was being cleared that a plastic bag was discovered at the back of an old wardrobe; in it were her father's long-forgotten medals, among them the AFC and DFC, and that rare and elusive Order of Lenin – gold, with red enamel and a central portrait of Lenin in platinum. She had little interest in them, which is how they found their way to

Sotheby's in 2009, for auction by Messrs Morton and Eden. The auction attracted a huge amount of interest and after some very lively bidding, they were sold to an anonymous telephone bidder for a total of £46,000.

The story might end there except there's a strange twist in the tail of this tale. When the auctioneers were researching the medals, they realised that the Order of Lenin held by Isherwood for all these years wasn't actually his; it belonged to Wag Haw, and the medal that Wag Haw had belonged to Isherwood. The auctioneers discovered this when they checked the Order Book that accompanied the award when it was made, by Ivan Maisky, the Soviet ambassador, in 1942. That Order Book identified Isherwood's medal as being No. 7381; the medal at auction had 7384 engraved on its rear face. Wag Haw's Order Book had recorded *his* medal as 7384.

Somewhere along the line, the medals were returned to the Russians to be updated, but they were then handed back to the pilots in the wrong order, and no one seemed to have noticed. Thus, the medal offered for sale was almost certainly the one that should have been in the possession of Wag Haw. All would have been well, except that the one Wag had – Isherwood's medal – was 'disposed of' many years ago, along with his DFM, DFC and other medals.

They were bought at least ten years ago by businessman and philanthropist Lord Ashcroft, who, over the past three decades, has collected more than 180 Victoria Crosses (VCs), and a significant number of other gallantry awards, the largest collection of such decorations in the world.

Wag's daughter-in-law Susan Haw told me, 'The medals never really meant anything to Wag. They certainly weren't why he joined the RAF; he just loved the thrill of flying Spitfires. He lived life to the full and he lived for flying, so the medals always seemed secondary to him. One day, he met someone who was interested in his story and Wag said he could have them. I think he might have had a few too many drinks at the time!'

Wing Commander Isherwood's medals, along with his miniatures, were bought at auction by an agent bidding in the room on behalf of a Russian collector. It's not known whether they remain in the UK, or have subsequently been exported.

For my own part, my flying career came to something of a tragic end following an accident early in 1942 while I was converting to the Spitfire at Ouston. I loved the Spitfire but it took some getting used to after the Hurricane, which was a very forgiving aircraft. The Spitfire made you raise your game, because if you got it wrong, it would bite you back. It was faster and more manoeuvrable than the Hurricane and it was just the most beautiful aircraft to fly. You felt it was a part of you and you were a part of it. It was so responsive, and it was about as accomplished as things got, both as an aircraft, and as a gun platform. I loved that aircraft.

I remember the day well. I'd been up for a routine flight and was coming in to land on the runway at Ouston. It was early evening, around 1700, and I'd just touched down but was still carrying a lot of speed. Remember, with tail draggers, the nose points imperiously up at the sky, so your forward vision is nil once you're on the ground, but it's not a problem when you're landing on a runway because it's the one place on an airfield you can guarantee will always be free of obstacles. At least, it *should* be.

Ouston was a work in progress, as were a great many RAF stations at the time. The RAF was expanding, and new buildings needed to be erected, so civilian labourers were employed to do the work. The RAF used to lay on transport to pick them up from a point near the control tower, and take them home at the end of each shift. Well, on this particular day, four labourers decided that the walk around the perimeter was too long, so why not just cut across the middle of the aerodrome? Which is what they did. And they happened to be crossing the runway just as I landed. There was absolutely nothing I could do and, to this day, it's all a bit of a blur.

I remember seeing something in my peripheral vision as I raced along the runway, scrubbing off speed, and I swung the aircraft to the side at the last moment. In doing so, I managed to avoid three of the men, but the propeller hit one poor soul full on. He died instantly, and the collision caused the Spitfire to tip on to its nose; then my port wing tip touched down. Because of the speed I was still carrying, the kinetic energy had to go somewhere, so the aircraft cartwheeled two or three times, then came to a rest. I was knocked unconscious in the crash, and pulled from the wreckage, following which I spent three weeks in hospital. While in hospital a very quick 'bedside inquiry' took place as a result of which the great and good decided the accident was a result of 'pilot error'. That was pretty much the end of my flying career, although I did see further service as supernumerary crew on Dakotas in Burma and India in the last years of the war.

Phyllis and I picked up our relationship when I got back from Russia, and in 1943 I was given a forty-eight-hour pass to marry her. We lived a lifetime in a day back then. It sounds silly now, I know, but when the war was on, you really wanted to live your life. Living under constant threat of death really helped cement our relationship. War makes you grow up very quickly, but it certainly served us well. We celebrated our sixtieth wedding anniversary in 2008 with a message of congratulation from the Queen!

I was demobbed in 1946 with the rank of warrant officer and after the war we settled in the lovely village of Chaddesley Corbett in Worcestershire. I worked as an electrical engineer and spent the whole of my career working in coal mines; by the time I retired in 1982, I must have been down every pit in England and Wales. Phyllis and I had one son, Andrew, who inherited my love of aeroplanes and became an aeronautical engineer. He married his high-school sweetheart, Mary, and in 1978 they moved to America to build a life there. My grandchildren, Abigail and David, and great-grandchildren, Colby, Caleb and Lilly Faith, were all born in America and now make Virginia their home. Phyllis worked as a magistrate in Birmingham for thirty-two years; she died in 2005 aged eighty-one and I still miss her every day.

21

Epilogue

I've often wondered how important Force Benedict was, pondered on its effectiveness. Considered on its own, it appears insignificant in terms of the Second World War as a whole. So it should perhaps be regarded in the context of Britain's overall aid to the Soviet Union and the several thousand Hurricanes that Russia received during the war. The mission undertaken by 151 Wing therefore was no symbolic flag-waving gesture, no display of hollow politics, but a precursor paving the way for the transporting of the enormous quantity of supplies that were waiting to come on stream even as 151 Wing set sail from Liverpool in August 1941. As an advance party for all that was to come, it had to display the utmost professionalism and achieve the highest standards of performance in every area; a mission that I think we more than succeeded in fulfilling.

All that said, who knows what would have happened if Churchill's wish for a second front had come to fruition and a way had been found to move us all southwards to fight on a second front? I don't think many of us gave the issue much thought after our return from Russia in December 1941; after all the uncertainty of whether we were going to be sent south or not, I think we were just glad to be back home. It was interesting to learn all these years later that for all Churchill's concern for us and how we were faring his first instinct was to commit us to further battles on Stalin's behalf.

The weakest link in the chain was always going to be Stalin's Russia; as a nation, our downfall was in our 'choice' of ally. In essence, Churchill had no option but to show support for the

Soviet Union; he knew that an Anglo-Soviet alliance was his only hope of defeating Hitler. At the time, Britain stood alone in its fight against the Führer; the US may only have been a few months from joining the war, but politically it was light years away and its involvement far from assured. If anyone doubts the precarious-ness and the risks inherent in 151 Wing's mission, this sums it up perfectly . . .

> *Co-operation was very much a one-way street where Russia was concerned and almost all British and US attempts to collaborate operationally with Stalin's people foundered on the rocks of their ally's secretiveness, incompetence, ill-will and paucity of means. The Royal Navy's requests for the aid of Soviet warships and aircraft to cover British convoys approaching Murmansk and Archangel yielded meagre responses. In August 1942, an RAF Catalina delivered to north-west Russia two SIS agents whom the Soviets had agreed to parachute into Norway. Their hosts instead detained the two men incommunicado for two months before dropping them, still in summer clothing, inside Finland rather than Norway, where they were swiftly arrested, tortured and shot. Thereafter, the British recognised that co-operation with the Russians was an exclusively one-way proposition; that the consequences of placing Allied personnel at the mercy of Russian goodwill were often fatal.*[1]

Things were no better ashore for the crews of later convoys, who would often find Russian hospitality sorely lacking. As a nation, we were under no illusions that our assistance merited the grati-tude of our Soviet allies, though; their war was markedly different to ours, their losses incalculably larger – total deaths within the Soviet Union at the end of the Second World War are estimated at 25 million, around 16 per cent of the population in 1939. As

Epilogue

one Russian soldier put it after the war, when speaking of the sacrifices of the British and American Arctic convoys to Murmansk and Archangel, 'God knows we paid them back in full – in Russian lives.'[2]

Doubtless the Soviet government was anxious to receive the badly needed supplies that the Arctic convoys were bringing, and it's my belief that they allowed their senior officers a large degree of autonomy and freedom of action to achieve that, as evidenced by Vice-Admiral Golovko readily acceding to Rear Admiral Bevan's request for a Russian destroyer to assist in bombarding Vardø. However, that said, it's also clear that once the Soviets realised that the tide was turning in their favour in terms of them resisting the German advance, the NKVD would have been instructed to reduce foreign contact to a minimum. Only that would explain the antipathy and unfriendliness that Allied troops experienced from Russia as the war progressed; it certainly wasn't down to the attitude or the tireless efforts of British or American forces.

Although the reception we got from the Russian pilots that we dealt with was resolutely friendly, at an official level we were barely trusted or tolerated; that much was evident from the fact that we were accompanied on the few occasions we ventured into Archangel, Vaenga or Murmansk. Commissars and the NKVD saw all foreigners as a threat to the Soviet system of communism, as if our democratic outlook was diluting the political ideology Stalin was so keen to foster. How fragile they must have thought it.

We sometimes wondered, after we'd left Russia, how effective their pilots were once they started to fly the two-hundred-odd Hurricanes we were sending them each month. Not very, was the assessment of one civil servant who went to Murmansk in 1942. George Cormack worked for Hugh Dalton, the Minister of Economic Warfare, who was in charge of the SOE. Cormack had fought with the BEF against the Bolsheviks in 1918 in Murmansk, so he knew the area when he returned there in late 1942 under the aegis of the Ministry of War Transport.

His personal diary records that,

After 151 Wing returned home, all the lessons that the Russians had learned in terms of aerial defence were roundly forgotten. While the Wing shot down 15 aircraft, the Russians put up a poor show afterwards and it was galling to watch German bombers coming over in perfect 'V' formation, selecting their targets and dropping their bombs apparently indifferent to the Russian pilots' Hurricanes flying around. The only real protection came from the guns of British and American merchant vessels and torpedo boats which might happen to be in the harbour. They at least, kept the Germans at a respectful height.[3]

That might explain why a mission almost identical to ours, but on a significantly larger scale, was planned for late 1942. Following a personal request from Stalin, Churchill tasked Sir Charles Portal with organising a new wing to return to Murmansk.[4] Portal then asked his deputy, Sholto Douglas, to look into how he might make it happen, and Douglas, after much negotiation, managed to get Air Vice Marshal Trafford Lee-Mallory of 11 Group to release a wing consisting of two squadrons of ground-attack Hurricanes, four squadrons of Spitfires, their pilots and ground crews – some two thousand personnel in all. Under the code name 'Operation Jupiter' they were brought under the umbrella of 153 Wing, which had been newly stood up on 5 July 1942, with the intention of resuming RAF operations on the Russian front. Ramsbottom-Isherwood was given a substantive promotion to group captain and appointed to lead the wing, with Tony Rook as one of his squadron commanders. Arrangements were put in place for the new wing to return to Vaenga, but on 20 July the operation was called off and 153 Wing was stood down.[5] Given the losses that were occurring on the Arctic convoys, it is highly likely that Churchill ordered Portal to pull the mission when he realised that the possible loss of 2,000 RAF personnel was too high a price to pay. If the aircraft were lost en route, they could be replaced; replacement crews would be much more difficult to find.

With any sweeping generalisation, there are always exceptions, and it's evident from the account of one particular Soviet pilot who flew Hurricanes that he and his fellow pilots were more than a match for any German bombers that strayed over the front line. Nikolay Gerasimovich Golodnikov had seven kills to his name by the end of the war and learned to fly the Hurricane in 1942. He says,

Our Squadron commander was Alexander Adreevich Kovalenko. I was his wingman. Murmansk was under attack and six of us scrambled. We heard on the radio, 'First Group [Squadron] of 109's'. I transmitted to Kovalenko 'I see the 109s!' He replied 'Good work. Boys, let's go get them!'

Then from the ground vectoring station we heard, 'First Group [Squadron] on 87s! Switch over to the 87s!' Again, he replied, 'Boys, let's go get the 87s!'

We spotted them on the approach to Murmansk. There were about 20 of them, perhaps more. We attacked them from below at high speed. I watched as Kovalenko placed his Hurricane almost vertical and fired up at the Stuka from about 50 metres with 12 machine guns. Then, as Kovalenko fell away, I also peeled off and observed how the tail of the Junkers went in one direction, and the rest of the aeroplane in another. Kovalenko had sliced through the Junkers right in front of my eyes.

Then the ground radio intercept station informed us that the Germans were screaming, 'We're surrounded by Soviet

fighters! They are killing us!' Along with another six Hurricanes who went after the Messerschmitts, we shot down eight aircraft that day.[6]

Many of us from 151 Wing kept in touch throughout the years, if only intermittently. The catalyst for a more structured and organised system was undoubtedly Peter Fearn, who back in the early 1990s was an executive working for CarbonFlo, the manufacturers of Henry Broquet's fuel catalyst. He worked tirelessly to trace all of the surviving members of the wing for the fiftieth anniversary of our mission, and it was he who established and ran the RAF Russia Association. I've been back to Russia a number of times in the last few years, but every trip I've undertaken has its origins in the work that Peter Fearn did. The first trip was in 1993, when he made contact with Air Commodore Phil Wilkinson, who at the time was our man in Moscow. Phil made all the arrangements from that end, and a small group of us flew out to stay with him.

I was fortunate enough to return the following year when Her Majesty Queen Elizabeth made a state visit following a request from the then president, Boris Yeltsin. This was the first time any monarch had visited the country since the Revolution in 1917, so Sergeant Pilot Freddie Crewe and myself felt enormously privileged to be invited to join her on the flight to St Petersburg, where we placed a wreath on the city's cenotaph. Peter Knapton, Freddie Crewe and myself also accompanied the then prime minister, John Major, and his CDS, Sir Peter Inge, on a trip to Russia in May 1995.

One of my most memorable trips was in May 2006, when along with my son Andrew, I had the chance during a trip to Murmansk to meet the son of our former Russian 'comrade-in-arms' Boris Safonov. Young Igor Safonov was just four years old at the time of the wing's arrival in Vaenga in 1941. He had vague recollections of the time, but through an interpreter he asked me what his dad was like, what sort of pilot he was, and requested all sorts of intimate details about him. I found it so incredibly sad that he'd never *known* his dad; he had no memories of him, no idea what he smelt like, what his voice was like . . . nothing.

Before we met, I took the time to lay a wreath in the Vaenga cemetery, where my former comrades lie still.

The year 2010 saw the sixty-fifth anniversary of the end of the Second World War and the Russian authorities once again sought out British and Commonwealth veterans of the Arctic campaign (there were four Australian pilots on the wing, and two Canadians, as well as one Rhodesian) and presented commemorative medals. Those of us from the RAF who are still alive were on the list, and a small number of us, including Peter Knapton, Vic Bashford and Leslie Burt attended special ceremonies at the Russian embassy and also on board HMS *Belfast,* itself a veteran of Arctic convoy duty, and with a refurbished mainmast thanks to Russian sponsorship to defray the bulk of the costs. Russian recognition of the role that Britain played in the Arctic campaign continues to impress – I recently received notification that we are to be awarded the Ushakov Medal by the Russians. Their concern for us, and continued recognition and support throughout the years, stands in stark relief to the lack of recognition shown to us by our own government.

Our role has been too easily overlooked, even by the Ministry of Defence. Back in 2005, repeated attempts to gain recognition for the Arctic convoys with their own campaign medal had finally borne fruit . . . of a kind. It was announced that participants in the convoys would be eligible for a badge, the Arctic Emblem, to be worn on the lapel. This was announced by then prime minister Tony Blair at a Downing Street reception in honour of convoy veterans, and was a welcome step forward. But Mr Blair's staff, guided by the Ministry of Defence, had forgotten that from the very beginning in that Arctic theatre of war there had been close on six hundred of us from the Royal Air Force. The situation was corrected just in time, and a couple of the fellows were there in Downing Street.

The role played by 151 Wing during the Second World War effectively made us the Arctic convoys' *raison d'être* and the trail-blazers for all successive voyages along the Arctic Corridor. The sense of resentment we felt towards successive British governments that failed to recognise what we'd done was shared by the numer-ous veterans of the Royal and Merchant Navies, who endured the hardships, risks and horrors of the Arctic convoys and who led the campaign for some official recognition of that. The resentment felt by all these men was, to a degree, assuaged by the eventual decision in 2013 to award a specific medal for service in the Arctic. But a single medal cannot wipe out the hurt of the seventy years in which they were, to all intents and purposes, ignored.

Of the original 550 men who went to Russia with 151 Wing, those of us still surviving are of an ever-dwindling number and, as I write, there are just eight of us left alive in Britain – Tim Elkington; Peter Knapton; Vic Bashford; Dick Davey, Albert Shrubsole, Bernard Watts and Leslie Burt [two aircraftman] and myself. Those of us able to – Tim, Peter, Vic and myself – all attended Downing Street in March 2013 to be awarded the long-overdue Arctic Star by David Cameron. Nat Gould received his medal in Australia.

It's not all solemn memorial services and long-waited-for awards, though. Even at my advanced age, I can still find myself bathing in the golden rays of good fortune, and it's funny how sometimes they're born of echoes of the past. I'm thinking of an incident that happened in January 2012 – the Germans never managed to shoot me down during the war, but I was certainly shot down at the Potteries Museum and Art Gallery near Stoke-on-Trent when I visited it then. They had a Spitfire on display there and, as you might imagine, I was delighted. I went to sit in it, but a member of staff rushed over to me and told me I couldn't as 'It's too dangerous!'

I had to laugh at that; too dangerous? When I think of how many times a day we took to the air in Spitfires and Hurricanes during the war to fight the bloody Germans – now *that* really was a health and safety concern, but there was nobody telling us to stay away in case we got hurt then! They were probably just trying to be extra careful at the museum, which was very nice of them. I just wish the Luftwaffe had been so caring.

Anyway, that particular incident came back to bite them because it was widely reported in the press at the time. The result of that was that I was most surprised and delighted to be invited to actually *fly* one. Matt Jones, of the Boultbee Flight Academy, saw the press coverage surrounding the incident at the Potteries Museum, and he invited Tim Elkington and me to each have a flight in a dual-control Spitfire over Goodwood Aerodrome in West Sussex. That particular Spitfire, PV202, was built as a single-seater in 1944 and flown in combat in northern France. It was later converted and used in training, and is now based at Duxford airfield in Cambridgeshire. Nobody was more surprised than I to find myself back at the controls of an aircraft I'd last flown in 1942. It's just like riding a bike, though – you never forget and, after ten minutes, it all came back to me. That really was something special and a memory I'll treasure for the rest of my days. I feel really lucky to have had that opportunity.

Which is where the story of 151 Wing, and its little-known expedition to Russia, ends. It's been a privilege being allowed to share it.

Appendix

Tim Elkington kept a copy of the take-off brief that was handed out to all twenty-four pilots on the *Argus*, and it is worth reproducing in full:

HURRICANE PILOTS – INSTRUCTIONS FOR FLYING OFF HMS ARGUS INTO RUSSIA

Information

1. Aircraft will be flown off in flights of 6. The first 6 aircraft will be erected on the flight deck & it is anticipated that the succeeding 3 flights will be ranged from the hangar & flown off at 40 minute intervals after the first flight has left the deck.

Take-off

2. All spectators are to be in the starboard netting. Pilots are to run up their own aircraft when ranged & are to indicate that their aircraft is in all respects ready to take off by raising the left thumb.
3. All movements of aircraft on the flight deck are controlled by the flight deck officer who will stand on the port side of the aircraft he is controlling. The executive signal for take-off is the lowering of a green flag.
4. On receipt of the executive signal pilots are to release the brakes & carry out a normal runway take-off under high wind conditions but sitting up as high as possible to obtain a good view of the deck immediately on opening the throttle & thereby ensure a take-off run with wheels either side of the centre line.

5. For best take-off from a carrier deck the following settings are required:
   a. Flap setting 25 degrees
   b. Engine RPM 3000
   c. Mixture RICH
   d. Engine boost +12
6. Air Ministry figures for deck take-off with Hurricane II are:

Distance to Unstick	Wind over Deck
287 feet	30 knots
356 feet	25 knots
396 feet	22 knots

All aircraft in the range will be given a take-off run of at least 400 feet before reaching the accelerator ramp. Should for any reason an aircraft not be sufficiently airborne to clear the ramp, the pilot is to ease back the stick until over the ramp & then level off until the remaining 32 feet of the deck run has been completed. On no account is a turn to be commenced until the aircraft is 50 feet above flight deck level & past the bows of the ship.

Flight Ashore

7. On taking off, aircraft are to turn to port, proceed to the waiting position, one mile astern of the ship at 2000 feet or below cloud, & carry out a left-hand circuit. Departure is to be taken from over Argus as soon as all aircraft are in formation on their leader.
8. If weather conditions are not at all favourable, flights are to take departure over Argus & set course to pass over a destroyer which will have been previously stationed inshore of the carrier & on the correct bearing.
9. Aircraft should normally be flown at economical cruising speed, namely:
   a. Engine RPM 2000
   b. Mixture WEAK
   c. Blower Medium Gear

Appendix

W/T Communication

10. With reference to Air Ministry Signal War Order No. 50 and Appendices A and B, 'Argus' will maintain W/T silence but will keep listening watch on No.151 Wing frequency.

    It is essential that the ship's position should not be jeopardised by unnecessary aircraft R/T transmission and R/T silence is to be maintained as far as possible.

    Any R/T messages made by aircraft should be addressed to No. 151 Wing, and NOT repetition NOT addressed to 'Argus'.

11. Pilots may press Button B on flying off, but are not to transmit to a shore station until they are over land and have altered course to fly along parallel to the coast. This should only be relaxed if they do not reach the coast after an interval of time which it should reasonably have taken them to reach the coast.

12. In the event of an aircraft forced landing in the sea when the flight is out of visual touch with 'Argus' a brief R/T message should be made giving time of origin in order that the position to which a destroyer should be sent to search can be calculated in 'Argus'.

13. The gist of these instructions has been passed to No. 151 Wing Signal Officer, Flight Lieutenant Fisher.

Aerodrome

14. There are only a few buildings and tents in the vicinity of the aerodrome. There is a damaged wooden hangar on the aerodrome boundary. Offices & other accommodation are in caves in the hills in the vicinity. There are a number of aircraft pens partially underground & camouflaged around the boundary of the aerodrome. Care should be exercised near the aerodrome boundaries to avoid soft patches.

15. A landing 'T' will be exhibited. Aircraft should land as close as possible to the 'T'. A WHITE flag will be waved near the 'T' to give permission to land. A RED flag will be waved if for any reason a landing should not be made.

Appendix

Topography

16. The country north & west of Murmansk is low hills, dark green in colour with many scattered lakes. The River Tulmola & all lakes are brown in colour. The approach to the aerodrome should be made down the river. A single line railway runs from Murmansk north to the east of the aerodrome.

HMS 'Argus'   T.O. Bulteel
4 Sept 1941   Captain

Acknowledgements

M y eternal thanks are due to my son Andy, and his wife Mary, for their help with all parts of the book, and for Andy's many trips from the USA to the UK.

To Paul Wiseman and his wife Mandy for sheltering me on many occasions.

To Steve Brooks and all at Boultbee Academy of Flying for giving me the chance to fly a Spitfire at the age of ninety-three and the desire to tell my story in this book, and to Richard Tavor for the super photos he took of the Spitfire while I was flying, and while in formation with me.

To Adam Aspinall and Rosalyn Golds for their help in every possible way in making this book possible.

Paul and Hazel Read for their unstinting help at all times.

Although the events that I describe in this book are as they appeared to me, and as I recall them, they also represent the words and memories of countless others. To all of you, both named and anonymous, who gave up your time and your memories, thank you.

Eric Carter

This book wouldn't have been possible without the help, assistance and encouragement of so many people who worked tirelessly behind the scenes. One of those is Air Commodore Phil Wilkinson, who has shown great generosity and patience in working so tirelessly with me on this book. Phil, your support, encouragement and commitment have been way beyond what I could have expected – thank you.

Acknowledgements

Following his retirement, Phil maintained and kept up to date the work done by Peter Fearn, the remarkable man who had made it his mission to track down every surviving member of 151 Wing and bring them together.

He managed to trace some fifty veterans globally, of whom some thirty turned up to the original gathering that Peter had organised for them at the RAF Museum in London. It took place on 11 September 1991, fifty years to the day since 151 Wing's first combat sortie in Russia, and saw widespread coverage in the media.

What Peter achieved with his energy and initiative was a logistic and energetic masterpiece, and laid the groundwork for the RAF Russia Association which Peter established. Throughout his life, he championed the ever-dwindling number of survivors. He made it his job to bring them together each year, arranged their first, and many subsequent, return visits to Russia, and he was one of the first people to begin fund-raising for the Soviet Memorial which sits in Geraldine Mary Harmsworth Park, adjacent to the Imperial War Museum.

At one of the London reunions, Peter was introduced to Percy Durham, a former soldier who had held an affection for the Hurricane since seeing his first one in 1936. Percy's invisible hand has guided me and helped me immeasurably in writing this book and his role can't be overstated; quite simply, the archive work that Percy has done over more than fifteen years is nothing short of extraordinary. It was Percy who encouraged all the survivors to commit their memories to paper; it was Percy who chased up, recorded, typed and bound all of those memories, added in the contemporaneous writing of certain individuals, collated and archived their photos and looked after it all, leaving behind a massive collection of unpublished diaries recording so much of what happened while the wing was in Russia. Percy's painstaking efforts in recording their thoughts stands as both his and their legacy.

Acknowledgements

Given his close involvement throughout, it was to Phil Wilkinson that the archives were entrusted when Peter died. Phil's continuous involvement with the veterans, and their next of kin when they have passed on, has made him something of an expert on the wing and its mission. I couldn't have written this book without him, but I have felt the ghost of Peter Fearn guiding my hand. I also owe a considerable debt to and must express my admiration for Percy Durham, the honorary and entirely honourable wing archivist.

I feel as if I've come to know the pilots and aircraftmen that made up 151 Wing and have become very fond of them. Through the colourful writing of Hubert Griffith and Ray 'Artie' Holmes, both trained journalists before and after the war, I've acquired an insight that has been both informative and enjoyable. Ray's extensive diary has been of immense help to me in the story that you've just read, and I've quoted from it extensively and wherever possible. It was written while he was there and accurately and colourfully records what it was like.

Others have told part of this story before. John Golley's 1987 book *Hurricanes over Murmansk* is a thorough review of the deployment, and this story owes a great deal to the work John did in researching it. The wing adjutant, Flight Lieutenant Hubert Griffith, was given surprisingly free rein to produce his detailed and well-illustrated story of the deployment in his 1942 book *RAF in Russia*, kindly lent to me by Tim Elkington, which is effectively a compilation of events from his personal diary and the Wing Operations Record Book.

A documentary film was made about 151 Wing's mission to Russia by Atoll Productions, with some financial support from the RAF Historical Society. It too has been an invaluable resource. It premiered at the Imperial War Museum in 2011, on 9 May – the day that each year marks for Russia the anniversary of the end of the war in Europe, their 'Victory Day'. The showing followed the remembrance ceremony and wreath-laying outside the museum, at the Soviet Memorial, which has been an annual event since the memorial was unveiled in 1999. It has always been well supported and attended by veterans of the wing, and their families.

I'd like to thank Eric, Tim, Peter, Nat and Vic, those five of the surviving members of 151 Wing, who gave up their time to share their thoughts and recollections with me; and Percy Durham, whose tireless work in the early nineties saw a great many of the veterans commit their memories to paper. Quite simply, without Percy's devotion and energy in collating, recording and archiving those memories and pictures, this book wouldn't exist.

I'd like to thank Dermot O'Leary, for seeing the potential in this book from the very beginning after that chance meeting with Eric Carter, and for his support in telling the story. Thanks are due too to James Wills at Watson, Little. And I must pay tribute to the calm professionalism of my publisher Rupert Lancaster and his belief that this story deserved to reach a wider audience, and for the support he's shown through the twists and turns in bringing it to life. Also to Kate Miles, Maddy Price and all at Hodder who have worked for so long to make this book what it is – thank you for your support, enthusiasm and sheer hard work.

Special thanks as ever to Carol; for your patience, belief in me, putting up with the inconvenience and for the endless support and countless long nights poring over the text. I couldn't have done it without you.

Group Captain Paul 'Godders' Godfrey was brilliant in bringing the Hurricane to life for me and for turning things around at short notice – thanks, mate. Also, Ralph Gibson at RIA Novosti for your generosity and help with images from those long-ago days in Murmansk, and Simon Pearson for your help and advice in navigating my way through the archives to find what I needed.

I must also thank Michael Naxton, curator of the Lord Ashcroft Collection, and James Morton of Morton and Eden Auctioneers

Acknowledgements

for their help in unravelling, and making sense of, the complex story behind the awards made to several members of 151 Wing.

Finally, special thanks to my friends and family, who have supported me throughout.

Antony Loveless

Bibliography

Personal Testimonies

Author Interviews
- Eric Carter, 81 Squadron
- Peter Knapton, 134 Squadron
- Tim Elkington, 134 Squadron
- Air Commodore Phil Wilkinson (Ret'd)
- Vic Bashford, 134 Squadron
- Nat Gould, 134 Squadron
- Michael Naxton
- James Morton
- Stuart and Susan Haw

Imperial War Museum, London
Sound Archive: George Cormac, Ministry of Economic War, Personal Diary, 1942
Sound Archive: Wag Haw, Tape 12028

Public Record Office
151 Wing, operations record book
81 Squadron, operations record book 1941–1942
134 Squadron, operations record book, 1941–1942
Air 8/840: Chief of the Air Staff Sir Charles Portal, Murmansk File, 1941
Air 8/938: Papers relating to formation of 153 Wing, 1942

Privately Supplied Memoirs and Papers

Flt Lt Raymond Towers Holmes, Diary for 1941

Flt Sgt Eric Carter, Diary for 1941

Group Capt. Peter Knapton, OBE, DFC, Diary for 1941–43

Wing Commander John Francis Durham 'Tim' Elkington, Logbook, Private Papers

Nikolay Gerasimovich Golodnikov, report on being trained by 151 Wing

Flt Lt Jack Ross, DFC, Diary for 1941

Flt Sgt J. B. Rigby, Diary for 1941

Flt Sgt Freddie Crewe, Narrative of time spent in Murmansk 1941 (unpublished)

Reg Osborne, Memories of serving with 151 Wing during 1941 (unpublished)

Sqn Ldr Alan Forbes, *Russian Interlude* (unpublished)

Portal, 1st Viscount, Christ Church College, Oxford (unpublished papers)

Air Commodore Phil Wilkinson, papers and documents.

FCO, Churchill & Stalin: Documents from the British Archives, Unpublished Volume, March 2002

Sources

Titles on which I have drawn extensively for my own narrative, or which I have quoted from directly, are shown below:

Hubert Griffith, *RAF in Russia*, Hammond, Hammond & Co., London, 1942

John Golley, *Hurricanes over Murmansk*, Patrick Stephens Ltd, Shrewsbury, 1987

Ray Holmes, *Sky Spy: From Six Miles High to Hitler's Bunker*, AirLife Ltd, Shrewsbury, 1989

Max Hastings, *All Hell Let Loose – the World at War 1939–1945*, HarperCollins, London, 2012

284

Other books that I have referred to are as follows:

James Holland, *The Battle of Britain*, Bantam, London, 2010
Michael Ashcroft, *Heroes of the Skies*, Headline, London, 2012
Geoffrey Wellum, *First Light*, Penguin, London, 2002
Lord Cameron of Balhousie, Marshal of the RAF, *In the Midst of Things*, Hodder & Stoughton, London, 1986
Leo McKinstry, *Hurricane: Victor of the Battle of Britain*, John Murray, London, 2010
Feliks Topolski, *Fourteen Letters*, Faber & Faber, London, 1988
Charlotte Haldane, *Russian Newsreel*, Penguin, London, 1942

Magazines
Philip Wilkinson, 'Sons of the brave 65 years on', *RAF Spirit of the Air*, Volume 1, Number 4, 2006
Philip Wilkinson, '1941: The Royal Air Force in North Russia', *RAF Spirit of the Air*, Volume 1, Number 5, 2006

The story of RAF 151 Wing's 1941 mission to North Russia is told in a DVD documentary, *Hurricanes to Mulmansk*, available from Atoll productions www.atollproductions.co.uk or email atollprod@aol.com

Notes

Chapter One: The Gathering Storm

1 Holland, *The Battle of Britain*, p. 325
2 Robert Murphy, *Realism and Tinsel: Cinema and Society in Britain 1939–48*, Routledge, 1992
3 Holland, *The Battle of Britain*, p. 325
4 Stephen Bungay, *The Most Dangerous Enemy – a History of the Battle of Britain*, Aurum Press, 2009, pp. 203–5

Chapter Two: The Battle of Britain

1 Hastings, *All Hell Let Loose,*
2 Ernie Pyle, *Brave Men*, War Time Printing, 1944
3 Lord Cameron of Balhousie, *In the Midst of Things*, p. 27
4 Hastings, *All Hell Let Loose*
5 Pete Brothers, quoted in James Holland's *Battle over Britain*, HarperPress, 2010, p. 548
6 Golley, *Hurricanes over Murmansk*, p. 42
7 Holmes, *Sky Spy*, p. 45
8 Ibid., p. 46
9 Ibid., p. 63
10 Ralph Barker, 'Scramble to glory', *Sunday Express*, 7 September 1980. Reproduced with permission
11 Tim Clayton and Phil Craig, *Finest Hour*, Hodder & Stoughton, 1999, p. 317
12 Holmes, *Sky Spy*, p. 105

Chapter Three: Ad Astra

1 Joe Shute, writing in the *Daily Telegraph*, 28 August 2013
2 The Churchill Society, London
3 Hastings, *All Hell Let Loose*

Chapter Five: Force Benedict

1 Hastings, 'Barbarossa', *All Hell Let Loose*
2 Hastings, *All Hell Let Loose*
3 *World War II Chronicle*, Legacy/Publications International Ltd, 2007, p. 146
4 Hastings, *All Hell Let Loose*
5 A. Boyd, *The Soviet Air Force since 1918*, Macdonald and Jane's, London, 1977
6 FCO Historians, *Churchill and Stalin: Documents from the Archives*, March 2002, No. 7 PREM 3/401
7 Ibid
8 Ibid
9 Ibid
10 Hastings, *All Hell Let Loose*
11 Constantine Pleshakov, *Stalin's Folly: The Tragic First Ten Days of WWII on the Eastern Front*, Houghton Mifflin Harcourt, p. 248
12 'Seventy Years Ago', *RAF Spirit of the Air*, MoD Publications, vol. 1, no. 5, 2006
13 Daniel Goldhagen, *Hitler's Willing Executioners*, p. 290
14 Ibid
15 Ibid
16 Air Commodore Philip Wilkinson, RAF, personal papers
17 Golley, *Hurricanes over Murmansk*, p. 61
18 Personal papers of Charles Portal, 1st Viscount Portal of Hungerford and Chief of the Air Staff, 1940–46, National Archives
19 Ibid

Notes

Chapter Six: An Assembly

1 Personal papers of Charles Portal, 1st Viscount Portal of Hungerford and Chief of the Air Staff, 1940–46, National Archives
2 Griffith, *RAF in Russia*
3 Ray Holmes, personal papers and diary
4 Griffith, *RAF in Russia*
5 Ibid
6 Lord Cameron of Balhousie, *In the Midst of Things*

Chapter Seven: Convoy

1 Topolski, *Fourteen Letters*
2 Feliks Topolski, *Russia in War*, Methuen, London, 1942
3 Ibid
4 Peter Knapton, *It Was All Teddy's Fault or How I Got to Moscow*, unpublished memoir
5 Topolski, *Fourteen Letters*
6 In a conversation with Air Commodore Phil Wilkinson
7 Griffith, *RAF in Russia*, p. 23
8 Ibid
9 Secret Cypher Message, ACHS(I), Air Ministry to BRITLISTAFF Moscow, CAS Personal Papers 1941, National Archives
10 Air 378/13/8, National Archives
11 Air Commodore Phil Wilkinson, 'The RAF in North Russia', *RAF Spirit of the Air*, vol. 5, 2006
12 Haldane, *Russian Newsreel*
13 Group Captain Peter Knapton, OBE, DFC, 151 Wing Royal Air Force, northern Russia, 1941, unpublished memoirs

Chapter Nine: The Erection Party

1 Lord Cameron of Balhousie, *In the Midst of Things*, p. 43

Chapter Ten: Acclimatisation

1 Lord Cameron of Balhousie, *In the Midst of Things*, p. 38

2 Operations Record Book, Air/26/216, 151 Wing Form 540, National Archives, p. 1

3 Griffith, *RAF in Russia*, p. 52

4 Geoffrey Raebel, *The RAAF in Russia – Eastern Front 1942*, 455 RAAF Squadron, p. 79

5 Flight Sergeant Frederick John Crewe, 81 Squadron, unpublished private papers, 1941

6 Lord Cameron of Balhousie, *In the Midst of Things*, p. 41

7 Ibid

8 Air/26/216, 151 Wing Form 540, Operations Record Book, National Archives, p. 4

9 Lord Cameron of Balhousie, *In the Midst of Things*, p. 40

Chapter Eleven: First Blood

1 Wellum, *First Light*, p. 148

2 Combat Report by Pilot Officer James Walker, 12 September 1941, 151 Wing Operations Record Book 540, Air 26/216, National Archives,

3 Text from an interview with Ibby Waud by Golley in *Hurricanes over Murmansk*, pp. 102–29

Chapter Twelve: An Arrival and an Aftermath

1 Golley, *Hurricanes over Murmansk*

2 Ibid., p. 133

3 Ibid

4 27/678, 81 Squadron Operations Record Book 540, National Archives online, pp. 1–2

5 Griffith, *RAF in Russia*, pp. 45–6

6 During the coding of the signal, the 'probable' victory had been confirmed as 'certain'

7 Griffith, *RAF in Russia*, pp. 44–5

Chapter Thirteen: Reunited

1 Air 26/216, 151 Wing Operations Record Book, National Archives, p. 5

2 Griffith, *RAF in Russia,* p. 50

3 Air 26/216, 151 Wing Operations Record Book Form 540, Combat Report Form 'F', P/O B. Bush, 17 September 1941, National Archives

4 Air 27/678, 81 Squadron Operations Record Book Form 540, National Archives, p. 2

5 Griffith, *RAF in Russia,* p. 46

6 Churchill and Stalin, Documents from the Archives, FCO Historians March 2002, No. 14, PREM 3/403, T543A, 4/9/41

7 Churchill and Stalin, Documents from the Archives, FCO Historians March 2002, No. 15, PREM 3/403, T583, 15/9/41

8 Air 8/840, CAS Papers Relating to 151 Wing Operations in Murmansk 1941, National Archives

9 Ibid

10 Ibid

11 Ibid

12 Griffith, *RAF in Russia,* p. 59

Chapter Fourteen: Killing Time

1 Ray Holmes, unpublished diaries, 1941

2 Griffith, *RAF in Russia,* p. 59

3 Interview with Wag Haw, IWM sound archive tape 12028

4 Holmes, *Sky Spy,* pp. 199–200

5 Air 26/216, 151 Wing Operations Record Book Form 540, Combat Report, P/O S. Edmiston, 16 September 1941, National Archives

6 Air 27/678, 81 (F) Squadron Operations Record Book Form 540, National Archives, p. 2

7 RAF Russia Association, *Memories from Russia,* vol. III: 'The Wing's Air Gunner', unpublished personal accounts

8 Griffith, *RAF in Russia,* pp. 62–3

9 Group Captain Peter Knapton, OBE, DFC, 151 Wing Royal Air Force, northern Russia, 1941, unpublished diary
10 Griffith, *RAF in Russia*, p. 64

Chapter Fifteen: Whiteout

1 Ibid
2 Ibid
3 Ibid
4 Chris Bellamy, *Absolute War: Soviet Russia in the Second World War*, Macmillan, London, 2007, p. 316
5 US Army Center for Military History, *Effects of Climate on Combat in European Russia*, University Press of the Pacific, 2005
6 Bob Carruthers, *Hitler's Forgotten Armies: Combat in Norway and Finland*, Pen & Sword Military
7 Chris M. Mann and Christer Jörgensen, *Hitler's Arctic War*, Ian Allan Publishing Ltd, 2002, pp. 83–4

Chapter Sixteen: A Rude Awakening

1 Artie Holmes, unpublished diaries, 1941
2 Ibid
3 Air 27/678, 81 Squadron Operations Record Book Form 540, October 1941, National Archives, p. 1
4 Ibid
5 Air 27/946, 134 Squadron Operations Record Book, Form 541, October 1941, National Archives, p. 1
6 Holmes, unpublished diaries, 1941

Chapter Seventeen: Russian Conversion

1 Golley, *Hurricanes over Murmansk*, p. 185
2 *Correspondence between the Chairman of the Council of Ministers of the USSR and the Presidents of the USA and the Prime Ministers of Great Britain during the Great Patriotic War of 1941–1945*, Progress Publishers, Moscow, 1957

3 Winston S. Churchill, *The Grand Alliance*, Second World War Book Series, Houghton Mifflin, 1948, p. 745

4 Golley, *Hurricanes over Murmansk*, p. 188

5 Ray Holmes, unpublished diaries, 1941

6 Ibid.

Chapter Eighteen: Endgame

1 Griffith, *RAF in Russia*, pp. 72–3

2 Air 8/840, CAS File, Secret Cypher Telegram, WX 1182, National Archives

3 Churchill to Portal, 24 October 1941, Portal papers, Folder 2/4/12

4 Air 8/840, CAS File, Secret, 6352, Memo to WSC, National Archives

5 Air 8/840, CAS File, RAF Form 96A, X186, 28/10/41, National Archives

6 Artie Holmes, unpublished diaries, northern Russia, 1941

7 *Recollections of Russian Pilots in Hawker Hurricanes during the Great Patriotic War 1941–1945*, RAF Russia Association, unpublished diaries. This story is also mentioned by Griffith in *RAF in Russia*, his book from 1942, in which he says, 'Many of the medical details of this extraordinary achievement were substantiated by our own M.O. who visited the pilot in hospital.'

8 Air 27/678, Operations Record Book RAF Form 540, 81(F) Squadron, November, National Archives, p. 1

9 Holmes, *Sky Spy*, p. 216

Chapter Twenty: Band of Brothers

1 Air 8/840, CAS File, Secret, CAS 1008, 11 February 1942, National Archives

2 DFM – Distinguished Flying Medal, a second-level decoration issued to those below commissioned rank for gallantry in the air against the enemy; DFC – Distinguished Flying Cross, the same award for officers

3 Ashcroft, *Heroes of the Skies*

4 Ibid

5 Holmes, *Sky Spy*, pp. 313–14

6 Lord Cameron of Balhousie, *In the Midst of Things*, p. 49

Chapter Twenty One: Epilogue

1 Hastings, *All Hell Let Loose*

2 Ibid

3 Sound and Vision Archive, George E. Cormack, personal diary (unpublished), Imperial War Museum

4 Air 8/938, FC/S.29176, memo to CAS from Sholto Douglas, 22 June 1942, National Archives

5 Air 8/938, extract from C.O.S (42) 212th Meeting, Monday, 20 July 1942, National Archives

6 *Recollections of Russian Pilots in Hawker Hurricanes in the Great Patriotic War 1941–1945*, unpublished accounts

Index

Index

Index

Index

Index

Vaenga aerodrome 95, 98, 104, 120–27,
    141, 152–5, 156–8, 170–71, 174–7
  German raids on 199–204, 218
  modern Severomorsk 215
  winter conditions 190–91, 192
Vaenga cemetery 155, 184, 269
Vaenga village 161, 171, 172, 265
Valley, RAF 40–41, 52–3, 54–5, 70
Varangeren Fjord 58
Victorious, HMS 89
Vyle (radio officer) 84
Vyshinsky, Andrey Januarevich 64

Waffen SS 66, 147, 193–4
Walker, Jimmy 73, 133, 135, 136–7,
    143–4, 202

Waud, Ibby 71, 86, 99, 120, 122, 123,
    124–5, 133, 135, 137–9, 144,
    145–6, 155, 157, 225, 234
Wehrmacht 60, 66, 147
Wellum, Geoffrey 2
Wick, Helmut 14
Wilkinson, Angie 6
Wilkinson, Phil 6, 268
Winkle Barge 106–7, 109–10
Wollaston, Dicky 73, 91, 98, 115, 118,
    182, 258

Yacobenko, Russian flying
    instructor 212
Yeltsin, Boris 268
Yugoslavia 60

Picture Acknowledgements

© AKG-images: 2 above/Ullstein Bild, 2 below, 14 above right/ Russian Picture Service, 14 above left/RIA Novosti. Author's collection: 1, 5 below. © Getty Images: 2 below, 5 above left/IWM via Getty Images. © Imperial War Museums: 4 above/IWM A12882, 4 below/IWM 18888, 7 centre/IWM CR 63, 9 below left/ IWM CR183, 9 below right/IWM CR36, 10 above/IWM CR60, 12 above/IWM CR 142. The National Archives UK (AIR 8/840): text pages 149 and 169. © Richard Paver: 16 centre. Private collections: 3 above, 5 below right, 6, 7 above, 8, 9 above, 10 below, 11 above, 13 above left and right, 14 below, 15 below, 16 above and below. © RIA/Novosti/photos@novosti.co.uk: 5 above right, 7 below, 11 below, 12 below, 13 below, 15 above.

Every reasonable effort has been made to trace the copyright holders, but if there are any errors or omissions, Hodder & Stoughton will be pleased to insert the appropriate acknowledgement in any subsequent printings or editions.

Text Acknowledgements

Ralph Barker: 'Scramble to glory' from *Sunday Express* (7 September, 1980), reproduced by permission of Express Newspapers/Express Syndication.

Quotes/transcriptions from documents held at The National Archives are reproduced by permission of The National Archives, Kew, Richmond, Surrey TW9 4DU.

An invitation from the publisher

Join us at www.hodder.co.uk, or follow us
on Twitter @hodderbooks to be a part of
our community of people who love the very
best in books and reading.

Whether you want to discover more about a book
or an author, watch trailers and interviews, have the
chance to win early limited editions, or simply browse
our expert readers' selection of the very best books,
we think you'll find what you're looking for.

And if you don't, that's the place to tell us what's missing.

We love what we do, and we'd love you to be a part of it.

www.hodder.co.uk